RETHINKING HUMAN RIGHTS

Palestinians have used the language of human rights to articulate their struggle against the Israeli occupation and internationalise the injustices they face. Palestinian young people learning about human rights at school experience a dissonance between the aspirational and internationalised framework of those norms and the layers of injustice of their own lived experience. Drawing on research in the occupied West Bank, this book explores the three layers of marginalisation faced by Palestinian young people – the Israeli occupation that denies them their humanity; the Palestinian pseudo-state that denies them a voice; and patriarchal structures that deny them agency – to show how these barriers influence their understanding of, and scepticism towards, human rights. Influenced by decolonial theories, this book illuminates how space needs to be created for the counter-narratives of the oppressed in human rights discourse, which may not align with more conventional representations of human rights. It contends that human rights and, by extension, human rights education in the Palestinian context (and beyond) needs to be critiqued, decolonised and ultimately transformed.

Volume 30: Human Rights Law in Perspective

Human Rights Law in Perspective

General Editor: Colin Harvey
Professor of Human Rights Law
School of Law

Queen's University Belfast

The language of human rights figures prominently in legal and political debates at the national, regional and international levels. In the UK the Human Rights Act 1998 has generated considerable interest in the law of human rights. It will continue to provoke much debate in the legal community and the search for original insights and new materials will intensify.

The aim of this series is to provide a forum for scholarly reflection on all aspects of the law of human rights. The series will encourage work which engages with the theoretical, comparative and international dimensions of human rights law. The primary aim is to publish over time books which offer an insight into human rights law in its contextual setting. The objective is to promote an understanding of the nature and impact of human rights law. The series is inclusive, in the sense that all perspectives in legal scholarship are welcome. It will incorporate the work of new and established scholars.

Human Rights Law in Perspective is not confined to consideration of the UK. It will strive to reflect comparative, regional and international perspectives. Work which focuses on human rights law in other states will therefore be included in this series. The intention is to offer an inclusive intellectual home for significant scholarly contributions to human rights law.

Recent titles in this series

Protecting Human Rights and Building Peace in Post-Violence Societies
Nasia Hadjigeorgiou

Collective Trauma and the Armenian Genocide: Armenian, Turkish, and Azerbaijani Relations since 1839
Pamela Steiner

The Times and Temporalities of International Human Rights Law
Edited by Kathryn McNeilly and Ben Warwick

Social Rights and the Constitutional Moment: Learning from Chile and International Experiences
Edited by Koldo Casla, Magdalena Sepúlveda, Vicente Silva, and Valentina Contreras

Article 8 ECHR, Family Reunification and the UK's Supreme Court: Family Matters?
Helena Wray

Rethinking Human Rights: Critical Insights from Palestinian Youth
Erika Jiménez

For the complete list of titles in this series, see 'Human Rights Law in Perspective' link at www.bloomsbury.com/uk/series/human-rights-law-in-perspective/

Rethinking Human Rights

Critical Insights from Palestinian Youth

Erika Jiménez

• HART •
OXFORD • LONDON • NEW YORK • NEW DELHI • SYDNEY

HART PUBLISHING

Bloomsbury Publishing Plc

Kemp House, Chawley Park, Cumnor Hill, Oxford, OX2 9PH, UK

1385 Broadway, New York, NY 10018, USA

29 Earlsfort Terrace, Dublin 2, Ireland

First published in Great Britain 2024

A catalogue record for this book is available from the British Library.

A catalogue record for this book is available from the Library of Congress.

Library of Congress Control Number: 2024940166

ISBN: HB: 978-1-50995-482-7
ePDF: 978-1-50995-484-1
ePub: 978-1-50995-483-4

Typeset by Compuscript Ltd, Shannon

To the children of Gaza.

Acknowledgements

THE JOURNEY TOWARDS the completion of this book has been a long one interrupted by critical illness, surgery, maternity leave and a global pandemic. And so, I am grateful for many people who helped me to persevere. In particular, I want to thank my PhD supervisors, Lesley Emerson and James Nelson at Queen's University Belfast, who supported me when I carried out the work for this book, and for their commitment to academic rigour, their hearts for conducting research through a social justice lens, and for reading drafts that were much longer than they needed to be! Thanks to Marwan Darweish and Caitlin Donnelly for examining my doctoral thesis with such care. Your expert feedback has greatly improved this work.

I have been fortunate to cross paths with academics from Queen's University Belfast and the University of Nottingham, and have gleaned much from their expertise and friendship. I would like to thank Rebecca Loader, Alison Gardner and Alice Panepinto for their wisdom, approachability and ongoing support when it comes to navigating academia, as someone from a working class background and as a mum of young children. A special thanks goes to my writing community and colleagues at the School of Law, especially Nisan Alici, Gift Sotonye-Frank, Chulani Kodikara, John Taggart and Stefano Angeleri, who encouraged me to send off draft chapters when I wanted to keep editing. I am grateful to Billy Frank, Chulani Kodikara, Alison MacKenzie, Conall Mallory, Daniel Soule and my Leverhulme Early Career Fellowship mentor, Colin Harvey, who read draft chapters and offered detailed comments and feedback. This book is much better thanks to you.

Research for this book was supported by the (then) School of Education at Queen's University Belfast, which awarded me a postgraduate studentship funded by the Department of Employment and Learning. Thanks to the Leverhulme Trust for awarding me a fellowship that allows me to build on this work and continue to conduct research that amplifies voices that are marginalised in research and society.

I want to thank my family, especially my husband, Francisco, for his love and support, good questions and practical help; and my son Job and daughter Leila for showing me why it's good to listen to children and helping me to not take myself too seriously. A special thanks to my inspiring and supportive big brother, Billy, for reminding me that, the last time he checked, commas were a good thing. It would be impossible not to mention my late parents, who had to leave school before they were 15 and because of this taught me about the value of education from a young age. Whilst they never got to see me finish this book, I know that I would never have even dreamed it was possible had they not encouraged me to pursue this path in the first place.

And finally, special thanks go to Jumana Kaplanian for engaging in this research wholeheartedly from start to finish and completing such thorough translation work for this book. I would also like to thank 'O' for enabling me to access the important stories of some of my participants. Crucially, I want to thank the adult and youth participants and YPAG members, and the schools that facilitated their involvement. I will remain grateful for the time, insight and enthusiasm you dedicated to this work. I have learned and unlearned so much from you all.

Contents

Abbreviations

ACHR	Arab Charter of Human Rights 2004
BGS	Boys' government school
BPRM	Bureau of Population, Refugees, and Migration
CDHRI	Cairo Declaration on Human Rights in Islam 1990
CEDAW	Convention on the Elimination of All Forms of Discrimination against Women 1979
CRPD	Convention on the Rights of Persons with Disabilities 2007
DCI	Defense for Children International
DOP	Declaration of Principles
GGS	Girls' government school
HRCRT	Human Rights, Conflict Resolution and Tolerance
HRE	Human rights education
HRO	Human rights organisation
ICCPR	International Covenant on Civil and Political Rights 1966
ICESCR	International Covenant on Economic, Social and Cultural Rights 1966
IGO	Inter-governmental organisation
MoEHE	Ministry of Education and Higher Education
NGO	Non-governmental organisation
NIS	New Israeli shekel
OPT	Occupied Palestinian Territories
PA	Palestinian Authority
PBUH	Peace Be Upon Him
PLO	Palestinian Liberation Organization
PS	Private school
TWAIL	Third World approaches to international law

UDHR	Universal Declaration of Human Rights 1948
UN	United Nations
UN OCHA	United Nations Office for the Coordination of Humanitarian Affairs for the occupied Palestinian territories
UNCRC	United Nations Convention on the Rights of the Child 1989
UIDHR	The Universal Islamic Declaration of Human Rights 1981
UNDHRET	United Nations Declaration on Human Rights Education and Training 2011
UNESCO	United Nations Educational, Scientific and Cultural Organization
UNGA	United Nations General Assembly
UNGS	United Nations girls' school
UNRWA	United Nations Relief and Works Agency for Palestine Refugees in the Near East
YPAG	Young person's advisory group

Figures and Tables

FIGURES

TABLES

1

Introduction

I. INTRODUCTORY REMARKS

IT WAS AROUND 10:00pm on a chilly February school night when Israeli soldiers forced their way into Lina's refugee camp in the occupied West Bank. They broke into family home after family home in search of someone they wanted to detain. As they forced entry into one house, they shoved a woman who was pregnant out of their way. Children like Lina who were asleep woke up to the sounds of live ammunition being indiscriminately fired across the camp. Lina's cousin climbed onto the roof to get a better view of what was happening. Moments later, a bullet struck him hard in the leg. The electricity was turned off. It went pitch black.

In the morning, Lina woke up early and put on her school uniform – a green and white striped long-sleeved pinafore – like it was any other day. These incursions, while terrifying, were relatively common for Lina and her refugee community. Before leaving her house, Lina was told that her cousin was in hospital recovering from surgery on his wounded leg. As she arrived at school, talk of the camp invasion filled the school corridors as teachers and pupils tried to piece together all that had happened the night before. Halfway through their school day, Lina along with seven of her classmates withdrew from their lesson and made their way down the corridor to their run-down yet peaceful library to join a focus group that I had invited them to participate in. The aim of the discussion was to learn more about how Palestinian youths construct their own understandings of human rights. These girls were eager to take part and to ensure their voices were heard. But on this occasion, they also were keen to share their accounts of the night-time raid they had experienced less than 24 hours ago. After they recounted what had happened and how scared they had felt, Lina looked me in the eye and bluntly asked: 'Yeah, so what do you expect from us? We learn about rights because of what is happening to us daily'.

Her words struck me, and have stayed with me ever since. What did I expect from these girls? Did I anticipate that they would speak in platitudes about human rights and their potential to bring about a peaceful resolution to Israel–Palestine relations? Lina's question is still worth reflecting on: What do we expect from oppressed groups like these refugee girls when it comes to their attitudes towards human rights? The way human rights are conceived and mobilised is often shaped by people's own concrete experiences of human rights, or lack of them, particular to their own contexts (Perugini and Gordon 2015).

The occupied Palestinian territories (OPT) is a unique context to explore ground-up constructions of human rights. Until late 2010, Arab societies were marked by political passivity; Palestinians however have always been an exception to this trend (Brichs and Lampridi-Kemou 2013). Since the Palestinian Authority (PA), established after the Oslo Accords, was never granted full autonomy over the lives of Palestinians in the West Bank, the people have remained relatively free from the control of authoritarian regimes in neighbouring countries (Kazziha 2010). Palestinians have been engaged in anticolonial resistance and a struggle for survival for decades; therefore, they are not a people who would be easily subjected to the political will of either Israel or the PA (Kazziha 2010). As the struggle against the Israeli occupation intensifies, so does the political mobilisation of the Palestinian people across the generations. Palestinians have adopted the language of human rights to articulate their struggle against the occupation and internationalise the oppression they face. Human rights culture has been propagated across Palestinian society from the PA's security forces right through to the refugee camps (Allen 2013). Cynicism towards the human rights scheme in the OPT increased following Oslo, the establishment of the PA and the influx of foreign aid. This lack of faith in the emancipatory potential of human rights is still present in the OPT and has likely skyrocketed since 7 October 2023. The decline in faith in human rights discourse can also be traced back to the failure of NGOs and groups monitoring human rights abuses caused by the occupation or the PA to end these violations along with the lack of intervention from the international community post-Oslo (Allen 2013). Palestinian children and young people learn about human rights at school through human rights education (HRE), whether they come from lower income, rural and elite middle-class backgrounds. Nevertheless, how do young people and their educators respond to the dissonance that can exist between the predominantly Eurocentric, depoliticised and decontextualised version of human rights that they learn about or teach through HRE inside school and their lived reality outside school?

This book is an attempt to explore these issues and learn more about the diverse and complex ways Palestinian youths interpret, talk about and deploy human rights. It offers an original contribution to the field from the ground-up to theoretical debates around human rights and in doing so dismantles and supplements Eurocentric narratives that are privileged. Over time, Palestinians have been denied 'permission to narrate' (Said 1984) and their voices have been silenced or delegitimised. In response, this book seeks to enable the knowledge, narratives and experiences of Palestinian young people to come forth. These stories are largely about struggles for human rights.

What this research unearthed was that Palestinian youths encountered at least three layers of marginalisation in relation to their human rights: the occupation that denies them their *humanity*; the authoritarian Palestinian pseudo-state that denies them a *voice*; and patriarchal structures that deny them *agency*. These layers of marginalisation influenced their understandings of human rights. But they also used human rights discourse as a vehicle to struggle against these very factors that sought to marginalise them. Throughout this book, I argue that human rights and HRE in the OPT (and more generally) needs to be expanded, critiqued and decolonised not only by academics and practitioners but by *learners* as well. Specifically, I contend that space needs to be created for the counter-narratives of the colonised, oppressed and minoritised, such as Palestinian youths, within human rights discourse. Consequently, some of the interpretations of human rights presented throughout this book will jar against the more sanitised and overly legalistic narratives that so often dominate human rights discourse and mainstream academic literature.

II. RESEARCH METHODS

In the year 2014, 546 Palestinian children living in the West Bank and Gaza were killed by live ammunition, airstrikes and tank-fired shells (Defense for Children International (DCI) Palestine 2024). It had been a particularly deadly year for children and young people in Gaza because of the 2014 Gaza War. During this violence, 3,436 children were injured, around a third of which were left with life-long disabilities (United Nations Relief and Works Agency for Palestine Refugees in the Near East (UNRWA) 2014). This war had been prompted by the Israeli military force's response to the disappearance of three Jewish-Israeli teenagers: Eyal Yifrah, aged 19; Gilad Shaar, aged 16; and Naftali Fraenkel, aged 16. They had been kidnapped in the West Bank whilst hitchhiking between Hebron and Bethlehem from a religious school located in an illegal settlement (Beaumont and Orlando 2014). Their abduction led to the revenge killing of a 16-year-old Palestinian boy from East Jerusalem called Mohammed Abu Khdeir weeks later, who was kidnapped and then burnt alive (Beaumont 2014).

I began the work for this book around six months after the start of these events. The young people I interviewed were very mindful of the recent suffering encountered by Palestinians in Gaza as a result of the 2014 war and referred to the rights-concerns of their peers in Gaza often during discussions. The tragic death of Mohammed Abu Khdeir was also raised by participants.

Further north, *Daesh*[1] was in a strong position in Iraq and Eastern parts of Syria during the time I was in Palestine, and so this also informed conversations. Those living in the West may have looked on at the Syrian civil war with horror, but it was an atrocity taking place some place 'out there'; for Palestinians, this was a conflict unfolding within driving distance. Even as a non-Palestinian,

[1] *Daesh* is an Arabic acronym for *al-Dawla al-Islamiya fi al-Iraq wa al-Sham*, also known as Islamic State. This is the preferred term used by many Muslims (as it was for my participants) as it distances them from the group and is a play on (Arabic) words that can mean 'to trample or crush' or 'a bigot who imposes his view on others' (Khan 2014, n.p).

the proximity of the Syrian conflict felt more palpable whilst living in the West Bank partly due to everyday conversations and in part because of how much geographically closer it all seemed. For instance, during a trip to the occupied Golan Heights, I saw plumes of smoke and heard artillery being fired by the government opposition group *Al-Nursa* Front across the border. Back in the West Bank, videos and newspaper articles of the beheading of a group of 21 Coptic Christians in Libya by *Daesh* were being circulated (Black 2015). This understandably provoked much fear among Palestinian Christians who worried that they too might soon become the targets of this group. One educator belonging to the Palestinian Christian community had a very frank conversation with me about what he and his family had planned to do were *Daesh's* movement to gain any kind of momentum in the OPT. Muslim adult and child participants often felt the need to differentiate themselves from *Daesh*. For instance, one of the research advisors referred to her uncle as 'very religious but not *Daesh*' during one session. These key events framed and informed certain discussions that took place with participants and will be traceable throughout chapters four to seven.

I carried out most of the field research for this book in 2015, conducting participatory focus groups with young people, interviews with school staff, observing human rights lessons, and drawing on analysis of extracts of textbooks that were being used in 2015.[2] This research followed on from shorter trips to the region where I had recruited and set up two local young person's advisory groups (YPAGs) and made networks with local academics, educators and schools. I lived in an apartment owned by a Palestinian family who lived in the apartment below. I was based in Bethlehem and lived a 20-minute walk away from Checkpoint 300 and the separation barrier. When not interviewing participants, I taught English as an additional language on a voluntary basis and began my Arabic language learning journey with a teacher from a refugee camp. Choosing to live in the West Bank, learn Arabic and teach English facilitated access, as did conducting research at a Northern Irish university because of the history of Irish–Palestinian solidarity.[3] Interviewees, Ministry and UNRWA officials were very open to my study, often commenting how they wanted their voices to be heard by those in Ireland, the UK and further afield. A taxi driver who often took me to nearby schools to conduct interviews would ask me about the research and was keen to assist me with it so much so that he even arranged for me to meet his former school principal, which enabled access to one of the schools in this research.

[2] The curricula used in government schools was revised after I completed the work for this research. Revised textbooks were implemented across government schools in the OPT at the start of the 2018/19 academic year (Alayan and Riley 2023: 25).

[3] It is important to point out that as a White researcher with UK citizenship, I was able to travel freely to different research sites in the West Bank in a way that Palestinians are unable to due to the occupation. For a discussion on how my raced, gendered and class positionalities shaped the research process and interactions with participants see Jiménez (2023, 2021).

Since I was interested in ascertaining the perspectives and experiences of Palestinian youths in relation to human rights, a qualitative methodological approach was adopted to best suit the aims of this investigation. The research was conducted according to a broadly transformative approach. This paradigm was developed in response to a paucity of representation of minoritised groups in existing research paradigms (Mertens 2007). Through engaging qualitatively with these underrepresented groups, this approach aims to expose versions of reality that get privileged in society and research, address power inequalities, and foreground indigenous knowledge. Palestinian young people are often disenfranchised on the basis of their age or gender due to the patriarchal aspects of their culture (Nguyen-Gillham et al 2008) or because they do not belong to the political ruling class (Høigilt 2016), or simply because they are unequally affected by the asymmetrical violence (Habashi 2011). Thus, it seemed fitting that this research operationalised the transformative paradigm so as to generate grassroot insights that could dismantle the narratives of the powerful which so often dominate in research and Palestinian society.

Whilst transformative research has been conducted with a range of marginalised groups such as those affected by HIV (see Chilisa 2005), the deaf (see Gerner de Garcia 2004), and minority groups (see Clarke and McCreanor 2006), there is a scarcity of studies that conduct this type of research with young people affected by political violence. It is often this population who are disproportionately affected by the impact of war (McEvoy and Lundy 2007) and yet, whilst a plethora of research done *for* and *on* children exists, they are rarely consulted on these matters which concern their lives (for notable exceptions see Wessells 2018; Hart 2012; Boyden and de Berry 2004). Consequently, this research is based on the premise that in a society affected by settler colonial violence, it is even more crucial that children's rights are upheld in research when everywhere else poses a threat of right violations.

Additionally, transformative research aims to be rights-respecting. Given that the main participants in this study were young people, I also adopted a children's rights-based approach and worked alongside youth research advisors in the form of two YPAGs – often a central aspect of this approach (Lundy and McEvoy 2009). These research advisors closely represented the young participants and informed my understanding of what questions to ask and how best to ask their peers about the topics under investigation. When the data had been collected, they then helped me to make sense of it from the eyes of a young person and from the eyes of a Palestinian. And so, the YPAGs were involved in the research design, co-creation of questions, selection of methods and analysis of data. Members of YPAG 1 included six youths (four male and two female) aged 14–15 enrolled in a private school and YPAG 2 was made up of six refugee girls aged 12–13 who were enrolled in an UNRWA-run school. Two members of YPAG 1 had been born in Gaza and had completed part of their education there. Working with young people in advisory groups was invaluable since YPAG members were able to advise me (a non-Palestinian) on what was culturally appropriate, and ways to handle particularly sensitive issues that arose due to the context in which the research took place and the respective vulnerability of the research participants.

Working with a YPAG can be used as part of a decolonising research strategy since the researched community (in this case Palestinian young people) are able to theorise their own experiences. In the process, hegemonic relationships that would give primacy to academic rather than indigenous knowledge are contested (Zavala 2013). Involving the YPAGs at the analysis phase of the research was part of my effort to hinder my colonialist impulse to project my own interpretations onto the young people's narratives as the YPAGs could provide indigenous understandings of their peers' voices.[4] Moreover, their participation throughout this research enhanced the rigour of the study in terms of the research design, methodological choices and the analysis of data. YPAG 2 also drafted a child-friendly summary[5] of the findings. This, alongside both YPAGs' analysis, guided my own thematic analysis journey and will be drawn upon at various points throughout chapters four to seven.

I was not only interested in learning about human rights discourse in the Palestinian context, but also how human rights are embodied within the educational real-life settings which both teacher and pupils inhabit. Therefore, I decided that schools would provide the best location in which to access the voices of young people and their educators. There are three school sectors which provide education for Palestinians in the West Bank and Gaza: government (PA), UNRWA and private schools. UNRWA is the main provider of education for Palestinian refugees in Lebanon, Syria and Jordan as well as the West Bank and Gaza Strip (Ministry of Education and Higher Education (MoEHE) 2014). Interviews were carried out at an all-girls' UNRWA school (UNGS) where the principal and teachers were also registered refugees. The girls lived in a refugee camp located in a place where violence erupts frequently between the Israeli military and PA security forces, and Palestinian demonstrators. The camp community was often subjected to military raids, power-cuts, arbitrary arrests and shootings. Some of the educators came from the same refugee camp as the students (such as Amina, the principal), but some lived in different nearby refugee camps (such as Hala, the civics teacher). In this school, it was apparent that efforts had been made to minimise stress for the students such as the use of a piano playing in between classes instead of a bell that might be misheard as a siren. Students and educators were all from a Muslim background.

In the West Bank, UNRWA provide free education for refugees (both boys and girls) for six years of primary education and four years at preparatory level (UNRWA 2012). Many of these students continue their education in government-run secondary schools. The Boys' Government School (BGS) in this study

[4] For a more in-depth discussion on the process of working alongside YPAGs and its potential to be a decolonising approach to childhood research, see Jiménez (2021).

[5] The full version of this can be found in ch 5.

provided education for grades 10 upwards and so it emerged that some of the students attending this school were residents of refugee camps and had previously obtained part of their education in an all-boys UNRWA school. Students who attended the BGS were predominantly from a Muslim background but a minority were Christians. Naseer, the school principal, also informed me that some of the pupils had been detained in Israeli prisons. Whilst MoEHE advises against the use of corporal punishment in government schools, it is still legal (End Corporal Punishment 2021). During one of my visits to the school I saw a teacher holding a black and white baton, which the boys later informed me was used to discipline students.

Whilst classroom sizes and the school layout seemed similar in the BGS and Girls' Government School (GGS), the ambience seemed notably different in the GGS: teachers and students seemed to enjoy closer relationships, and corporal punishment did not occur. All the students and teachers in this school were from a Muslim background apart from two Christian teachers. Sally, the civics teacher, indicated that in the past there had been a minority of Christian students but that increasingly parents were securing places for their children in private schools that had been founded by Christian churches.

Government schools offer secondary education, which after it had been subsidised, costs families an annual fee of 70 New Israeli Shekel (NIS) (approximately £15) in 2015. Many private schools rely on external funds as well as fee-paying students. The private school (PS) fees in this study were approximately 19,000 NIS annually (around £4,000) in 2015. The PS was founded by Western missionaries during the late Ottoman Empire, was attended by those from elite echelons of society and is noted for its political activism. Whilst supervised by a church,[6] the majority of students and educators at this school were from Muslim backgrounds with a smaller percentage coming from the Christian community. It was apparent from my time in the school that students did not adhere to social norms when it came to segregation of the sexes outside school. Many of the students from this school had travelled to Europe and North America and hoped to pursue higher education abroad. Many of the young people spoke English with North American accents and used US terminology.

Although these three school sectors fall under the auspices of the MoEHE, they follow the Ministry's National Curriculum to different degrees. This means that the aims, content and delivery of HRE may also vary across these schools. In government schools, young people may learn about human rights in civics education every week (Qazzaz et al 2010) whereas in private schools, who enjoy more autonomy, HRE may be included in ethics or religious education lessons – as was the case in the PS. And whilst UNRWA schools follow the MoEHE's curriculum, when it comes to HRE, they supplement this with enrichment resources (UNRWA 2013). Additionally, the development and delivery of

[6] Naming the specific denomination could compromise ethical protocol.

the MoEHE's curriculum is monitored by three parties: the PA, Israel and the United States (Velloso de Santisteban 2002). The Palestinian education system to this day functions with limited autonomy because the MoEHE is accountable to Western sites of power as well as their occupier and, secondly, because many schools depend on international aid. Therefore, interviewing youths and educators across these school contexts was intentional so as to explore the different ways their HRE was being influenced by a Eurocentric rights discourse and to capture diverse perspectives from youths who learn about human rights via these various HRE provisions.

I conducted 12 participatory focus groups[7] consisting of eight Palestinian young people aged 13–15 (96 in total) who attended four different schools in Area A of the West Bank (although some young people and educators lived in towns and villages located outside Area A). This meant that the youths came from various religious (Christian, Muslim and secular) backgrounds and socio-economic circumstances (from refugee camps, villages and cities), thereby adding a comparative dimension to the research.

Interviews were held with 11 educators who worked at these respective schools, including three principals, one vice-principal (who was more akin to an acting principal), and six teachers who taught HRE. Additionally, one senior educator at UNRWA who had helped develop the HRE toolkit used in these schools and one school counsellor who had worked in all three school contexts during the course of his career were interviewed.

Whilst extracts of textbooks relating to human rights were analysed, I was also interested in how participants interacted with these documents. For instance, during one teacher interview, an educator enthusiastically jumped out of her seat out to show me the Human Rights, Conflict Resolution and Tolerance (HRCRT) toolkit (used in UNRWA schools). In contrast, another educator slammed down a pile of MoEHE documents in frustration during his interview. Observations of lessons discussing human rights were also undertaken. These were useful in providing a snapshot of how rights were being embodied across the schools.

It is primarily the thematic analysis of focus group discussions and interviews that are examined in greater depth in chapters four to seven, with textbook extracts and classroom observations also drawn upon. Where focus groups and interviews were conducted in Arabic, these have been translated into English.[8] The terminology in this book has been largely influenced by the

[7] Focus groups included pair-work, creative methods and a walking debate.

[8] Of the 12 focus groups, nine were conducted with a local interpreter: the PS students were comfortable and willing to participate in English. Many of the educators were keen to conduct the interviews in English, thus only three interviews required live translation. However, in the UNGS and government schools, the translator sat in the room with me and the interviewees knew they could avail of additional support if needed (a couple of whom did). The classroom observations were also translated, and sessions conducted with YPAG 2 also required translation. The translator provided written translation of consent forms and she also translated extracts relating to human rights from textbooks.

terms the participants chose to use. Pseudonyms have been used throughout and I have been purposefully vague about the locations in which this research was conducted so as to protect the anonymity of the participants and schools.

III. DECOLONIAL APPROACHES TO HUMAN RIGHTS, HUMAN RIGHTS EDUCATION AND CHILDHOOD RESEARCH

Anyone wishing to learn more about human rights is likely to first encounter the narrative that interprets human rights from a particular vantage point – a Eurocentric one. As someone who was relatively new to the field, this was the first reading of human rights that I came across. After spending time in the West Bank and listening to Palestinian teenagers talk about human rights, I began a journey of unlearning the little I knew. After returning from the field, I revisited the literature on human rights, this time starting at the peripheries of the discipline. There, I began to engage with decolonial theories and Third World approaches to human rights. Section II of chapter two reflects this journey.

A decolonial critique of human rights is influenced by Latin American thought (scholars such as Dussel, Maldonado-Torres, Mignolo and Quijano), Subaltern Studies (including academics such as Bhadra, Chakrabarty, Chatterjee and Spivak) and Third World approaches to international law (TWAIL) – a scholarly network that includes authors such as Anghie, Barreto, Baxi, Chimni, Gathii, Mutua and Rajagopal. Decolonisation (more broadly) refers to 'a way of knowing that resists Eurocentrism of the West and makes an effort to correct the wrongs of colonial domination' and is achieved by undoing the structures of imperialism that continue to enable the oppression of the colonised (Zembylas 2017a: 397). Decolonisation also requires the creation of an epistemic space in which knowledge is generated, transformed and circulated. This is done in a way that is not reliant upon or a response to the problems of the Global North, but rather to the needs of the 'colonial differences' (Mignolo 2002: 80).

When it concerns human rights discourse, decolonial approaches maintain that it is not only knowledge production but also human rights discourse itself that has been colonised since the West often determines what constitutes a true vision of human rights. The global human rights scheme is often depicted as the 'depoliticised original' detached from any culture, history or civilisation (Perugini and Gordon 2015: 15). However, decolonial scholars underscore the ways it is entrenched in Eurocentric thought and arose from a community steeped in a history of colonisation – though this is rarely acknowledged (Zembylas 2017a). Furthermore, TWAIL scholars such as Anghie (2005) interrogate the colonial origins of international law and how manifestations of the 'civilising mission' are reproduced throughout history and in legal theory such as in doctrines of natural law, positivism, and pragmatism. And so, decolonial human rights theorists seek to dismantle, reframe and supplement the conventional Eurocentric histories and theoretical development of international law and human rights. This is achieved by including alternative lineages that stem from a range of Third World perspectives. In doing so, they unhinge the West's exclusive ownership of human rights doctrine. Decolonial human rights scholars engage with the 'what', 'who for', 'where from' and 'what for' dimensions of human rights (Barreto 2013a). They propose that Eurocentric conceptualisations of human rights are privileged because of European imperialism and colonialism. Therefore, what has been portrayed as universal is not an impartial rights regime but rather a narrow Western liberal conceptualisation of human rights. As Zembylas (2017a: 398) contends: 'The hegemonic Eurocentric framing of human rights is the outcome of particular historical and political processes – namely, modernity and coloniality – that have been depended on the military, economic and political dominance of European cultures.'

When it comes to conceptualising human rights, it is the inclusion of epistemic diversity that exists within these entangled spaces, such as alternative histories, interpretations and resistance enacted by the colonised and those subjected to international law, which is of importance (Barreto 2013a; Gathii 2011; Baxi 2007; Anghie 2005). Interpreting human rights from a Third World vantage point entails interrogating and re-articulating the conventional history and its original authors. It involves questioning Eurocentric legal thought and the doctrine of the generations of rights. It requires asking who are included or excluded as the beneficiaries of human rights and examining the individual and collective features of rights (Barreto 2013a).

The Eurocentric vision of human rights is defined, managed and promoted by powerful elites (in the form of the UN, HROs or government officials) and portrayed as the only possible version of human rights. This neutral and depoliticised interpretation of human rights is often deployed by those in power to evaluate and regulate the law, policies and practices of nation-states across the geopolitical order (Sharma and Gupta 2006). It is translated or 'vernacularised' at local level not only by state actors but also their populations (Merry 2006). However, this global discourse is interpreted by state actors as well as individuals and groups within these nation-states. Even before this discourse is interpreted, the unique lived experience of a particular people at a particular moment in time can mould how human rights are understood and invoked (Baxi 2000). I suggest that it is not only how human rights are understood by so-called specialists that is relevant, but also how everyday people define and grapple with human rights concepts in their own particular contexts. This book is concerned with how young people themselves seek to unhinge the West's hegemony over the rights discourse, interrogate the *human* and *rights* of 'human rights', and expose the prevalence of Orientalist attitudes within the international rights discourse.

Whilst the international human rights scheme is often portrayed as the 'depoliticized original' and uncritically accepted and legitimised by the international community (Perugini and Gordon 2015: 15), there is no fixed way of conceptualising human rights. Goodale's continuum helps to illuminate this, as does Dembour's (2010) framework. Goodale (2007: 7) proposes, that a 'restricted' orientation towards human rights centralises the law and upholds the belief that human rights are defined neatly by international legal instruments. At the other end of this continuum is the 'expansive' approach to human rights in which the role of the law ceases to be the sole focus, but rather human rights discourse itself (Goodale 2007: 7). Dembour's (2010) model identifies four specific schools which lie along this spectrum: the natural, deliberative, protest, and discourse (see Figure 2.1 in chapter two). These four schools take different approaches towards: the claim that rights are universal; the foundation for rights; how they are realised, if at all; the significance of human rights law; and the degree of faith held in the concept of human rights. At various junctures of this book, I draw upon Dembour's (2010) taxonomy to analyse how certain schools of thought may appeal to, or conflict with, notions of human rights within the Palestinian rights discourse. In the final chapter (eight), I question whether a Palestinian school of thought might need to emerge: one which is guided by human rights praxis which allows for epistemic diversity.

When I began this research, I was aware that in Western academe, the relationship between religion and human rights – a secular initiative – is often considered incompatible (Johnston 2015). When it comes to Islam and Arab and Muslim-majority contexts, since the War on Terror era and following the Arab revolutions, there has been a preoccupation in public debates and Western scholarship with questions of whether there is potential for ideological harmony between Islam and human rights (Allen 2013). And yet, neither Islam nor human rights have fixed meanings (An-Na'im 2011a). This was evident during my time spent with Palestinians in PA-controlled areas of the West Bank (a majority of whom are Sunni Muslims). Therefore, this book dispels some of these commonly held assumptions about the relationship between religion and human rights by exploring Islamic constructions of human rights and Islamic critiques of the Eurocentric human rights system. I pose the question: is it the case that Islamic critiques are predominantly decolonial challenges to the universality of a Western secular vision of human rights as found in the international human rights system?

HRE remains largely undertheorised by practitioners and scholars (Coysh 2017; Osler 2015) and the discourse aspect of HRE has gained little attention. The main and oft-cited models include those proposed by Tibbitts (2002), Flowers (2003) and Bajaj (2011a). These models tend to prioritise the *purposes* and *processes* of HRE with more recent models attending to how HRE is *conceptualised* such as that proposed by Coysh (2017). I wanted to broaden this scope by exploring how *human rights* (which underpin these approaches to HRE) are conceptualised using Dembour's (2010) schema as a critical lens to achieve this.

In terms of empirical research, scholars have concentrated on the augmentation of HRE initiatives at institutional, curricula and grassroots levels internationally since the 1990s, such as the work of Surarez and Ramirez (2004). Studies have also focused on the role of culture in facilitating education about human rights such as research done in India by Bajaj (2012) and Wahl (2013).

However, this book offers an original empirical contribution to the field since it explores how young people *themselves* make sense of HRE initiatives – an area which has received less attention (for notable exceptions see Bajaj 2017; Hantzopoulos 2012, 2016). Thus, there is a need to understand more fully how young people's experiences inside and outside school influence how they understand, articulate and appropriate education about human rights.

Analysis of UNRWA's HRE curriculum (HRCRT) has been carried out in Gaza (Albhaisi 2022) and the West Bank (Pinto 2014). Abu Moghli (2017) explores influences guiding HRE in government schools in the West Bank and how HRE helps shape learners' engagement in the Palestinian struggle. My work extends this important research adding a comparative lens since it explores a range of voices from within Palestinian society such as refugees, and those from lower income, rural and elite middle-class backgrounds, since research was conducted in all three educational settings rather than just one. This is significant because it illuminates how Palestinian young people may have different ideas and concerns from their peers, family, teachers, politicians as well as academics and practitioners when they discuss and engage with human rights. Overall, this book builds on an emerging body of literature that seeks to appraise and decolonise HRE (Ahmed 2021; Ahmed et al 2020; Zembylas and Keet 2018; Coysh 2017; Zembylas 2017a, 2017b; Keet 2012, 2015).

Critical scholar Coysh (2017) analyses the production, distribution and consumption of HRE by the UN, governments and NGOs. Drawing on her research in Tanzania, she criticises the way that HRE initiatives are often directed at groups vulnerable to rights violations and how this is often accompanied by the assumption that powerless groups such as victims of conflict, refugees and children do not know about human rights and have little to offer epistemologically. This book responds to this call for the reassertion of local forms of knowledge because it positions the Palestinian young people as equal knowledge-holders rather than merely beneficiaries of HRE programmes, and presents the reader with an opportunity to engage with grassroots insights into how young people (and at various points their educators) in the OPT wrestle with the inconsistencies between the declarationalist narratives promoted through the curriculum compared with their experiences of rights violations outside school.

The theorisations and voices of children and young people are often missing in scholarly debates. Assumptions are made that children can only ever offer deficient views, or that they will automatically reproduce the attitudes of the adults around them. And it is often assumed that childhood(s) in contexts of war is marked only by hardship (Twum-Danso Imoh 2016; Hart 2004). But there is a plurality of childhoods among Palestinians as there is in Ireland, for example. When I began the work for this book, a Palestinian educator said that my research would produce more interesting findings if conducted with university students rather than 13–15-year-olds, since the latter do not know much about human rights. I believe that the narratives contained within this book dispute this.

But there are multiple reasons why the views and experiences of Palestinian children and youths should be included in human rights discourse. First, the median age in the West Bank and Gaza is 19.6 years, making the OPT a particularly young demographic. Furthermore, Palestinian youths are often the targets of settler colonial violence (Shalhoub-Kevorkian 2015a), as has been witnessed in Israel's latest military campaign in not only Gaza but the West Bank. Second, the struggle against the occupation is often articulated in terms of different generations[9] (Schiocchet 2013). Youths have played, and continue to play, a key role within the collective struggle (Darweish and Rigby 2015). Additionally, in research involving children from the Third World, assumptions are often made that these children have little, if anything, to contribute epistemologically (Jiménez 2021, 2023) and often they only ever remain empirical examples (Balagopalan 2019). Throughout this book, I aim to redress this and have done so by purposefully foregrounding the diverse voices of the young people in chapters four to seven. If I had only consulted adults about what youths think then insights into two layers of marginalisation would have been lacking (patriarchy) or absent (Palestinian pseudo-state).

IV. ORGANISATION OF THE BOOK

This book explores how Palestinian young people understand, articulate and appropriate human rights and the factors that influence how they do this. Concepts and context are interwoven in chapters two and three so that the scene is set not only historically and politically, but also in light of the broader conceptual debates in human rights discourse. Chapter two outlines the mainstream Eurocentric account of human rights whilst interrupting and dismantling this narrow representation with decolonial critiques, interpretations from a Third World perspective and Islamic contributions. In section IV, a historical background of the human rights movement in the OPT is then detailed, providing not only insight into how Palestinians have employed the language of human rights as part of their grassroots struggle against the occupation, but also how human rights became institutionalised after Oslo, explaining the current cynicism towards the discourse. In chapter three, definitions and models of HRE are critiqued using Dembour's (2010) schema to examine whether HRE also privileges certain interpretations of human rights. Section VII of this chapter considers whether Palestinian youths are more likely to encounter a predominantly depoliticised, universalist and declarationalist HRE at school and begins

[9] Those who experienced the *Nakba* of 1948 are referred to as *Jeel al-nakba* ('the *Nakba* generation'). This was followed by those belonging to the *Jeel al thawra* ('generation of the Revolution') in the 1950s who connected the Palestinian struggle to other anti-colonial struggles taking place in the Arab world and other Third World contexts, and, youths who participated in the *First Intifada* were named *Jeel al-Intifada* ('the *Intifada* generation') (Schiocchet 2013).

to unpack some of the reasons behind this. It is argued within these first two chapters that human rights and HRE need to be interrogated not only by theorists and practitioners but by learners as well.

Chapters four to seven are the empirical chapters, of which chapters four to six explore the three layers of marginalisation experienced by young people in relation to their rights. In chapter four the first barrier is addressed: the occupation that denies Palestinian youths their humanity. It examines how Palestinian youths deploy decolonial strategies to interrogate and reclaim the human of human rights all the while exposing Orientalist notions that exist in human rights discourse. Analysis of the second layer of marginalisation is addressed in chapter five: the authoritarian pseudo-state that denies youths a voice. It explores how those who represent the state hinder the civil and political rights of non-elites (in politics and in school) by various means (both violent and bureaucratic). Chapter six provides an analysis of the third barrier facing youths in relation to their rights: the patriarchal aspects of Palestinian culture that deny agency to young people. The diverse views of the youths and their educators on the intersection of religion and human rights is explored. Two additional themes are addressed: how the patriarchal system endorses the discrimination of girls; and how it denies children and young people agency. Across chapters four to six, the youths use the language of human rights to make sense of and to challenge the factors that seek to oppress them as Palestinians, non-elites, youth and girls.

In light of these themes, chapter seven explores how the youths and their educators respond to the dissonance that can exist between what is taught through HRE inside school and their lived experiences outside school. It examines the ways that young people reproduce, resist and refashion definitions of human rights. It considers how learning *about*, *through* and *for* aspects of HRE influence how the youths engage with and their overall faith in human rights. Chapter eight is the concluding chapter, summarising the research and its implications, and offering recommendations for future research and practice.

***

Since this research was undertaken, Palestinians in Gaza experienced another war in 2021 and at the time of writing are currently living through another one. On 7 October 2023, Hamas launched its largest armed attack against Israel in years. Israel responded by launching airstrikes and a *complete* siege on Gaza, where Hamas are in power. At the time of writing, 30,035 Palestinians in Gaza are estimated to have been killed, of which 10,000 are children, with scores missing under the rubble (Save the Children 2024; UN Office for the Coordination of Humanitarian Affairs for the occupied Palestinian territories (OCHA oPt) 2024). Those who survive may be left with life-changing disabilities, without parental care and with long-term adverse effects on their mental health and well-being. As the complete siege continues, others will die of hunger, lack of access to life-saving medical care or water. Meanwhile in the West Bank (while eyes are on Gaza) there has been an escalation of forced evictions, house demolitions and camp incursions as well as the indiscriminate killings of Palestinian young people. Therefore, I believe this book and the narratives of the young people from 2015 are still relevant, possibly now more than ever, as Palestinians face an ongoing *Nakba* – continual dehumanisation – and as ever, a relentless struggle for human rights.

2

Human Rights: The Dominant Global Discourse

I. INTRODUCTION

THE ONGOING WAR on Gaza (at the time of writing), has once more undermined the West as the legitimate guardians of human rights. This war has exposed the fragility of international law and the hollow claims around the universality of human rights. Although this is not the first time that the hypocrisy of Western political leaders has been put on full display, these atrocities are being played out in real time over social media. Even so, the West will continue to boast that human rights are one of its most significant contributions to world politics (Maldonaldo-Torres 2021). Anyone interested in learning about the historical and theoretical development of human rights is bound to first of all encounter a mainstream account that privileges a Eurocentric reading of the discipline. Human rights may be a relatively modern concept, but the authorship of human rights theory and expressions of human rights activism predate the formation of the United Nations (UN) and existed before they were formally enshrined in international law.

In section II of this chapter, I trace this conventional Eurocentric representation of the development of human rights, but do so by interrupting this narrative with decolonial critiques. I intentionally include these more conventional accounts of human rights because doing so helps demonstrate how the international human rights system is not untouched by culture, history or a particular civilisation, as is often portrayed. But rather, this narrow representation of human rights has been privileged due to imperialism and has managed to exclude Third World theories, histories and struggles for human rights. In order to dismantle the West's hegemony of human rights discourse, I discuss some of the alternative genealogies, theorisations and histories that exist on the periphery of the discipline.

This leads to the discussion in section III of some of the Islamic contributions to human rights discourse and critiques of the human rights scheme. I consider the different religious, cultural and political aspects that have influenced Islamic engagements with the rights discourse. I argue that where caution towards the international human rights system has been articulated, this is often wrongly attributed to Islamic religion when it largely stems from the fear that it is a form of Western 'soft' colonialism.

The majority of Palestinians living in Palestinian Authority (PA)-controlled areas of the occupied West Bank are Muslim religiously and Arab culturally, and live under an authoritarian pseudo-state. Palestinians have chosen to deploy the discourse of human rights to articulate their struggle against the occupation and to internationalise the injustices they face. Therefore, section IV of this chapter provides a historical overview of the human rights movement in the occupied Palestinian territories (OPT), including how it gained momentum in the form of a grassroots struggle during the First *Intifada* in 1987. Subsequently, I consider how this movement was harnessed, hijacked and demonised following the Oslo Accords 1993–1994 as a result of the influx of foreign aid, and the establishment of the PA. Whilst many Palestinians have become largely disillusioned with the human rights regime – since it has failed to bring an end to the occupation and its ensuing rights violations – human rights discourse continues to be appropriated in order to articulate the oppression they face to international actors. Section IV concludes by unpacking how these developments have contributed to the current state of cynicism in the occupied Palestinian territories (OPT) with regard to the human rights regime.

II. DECOLONIAL CRITIQUES: DISMANTLING AND SUPPLEMENTING THE MAINSTREAM HUMAN RIGHTS NARRATIVE

The international human rights scheme is embedded within Eurocentrism and is underpinned by theories of liberalism, individualism, rationalism, secularism and universalism. According to mainstream analyses, the origins of human rights are often dated back to ancient Greek, Roman and Medieval civilisations; others argue that the Torah – through the Ten Commandments – provide an even more archaic example of the construction of rights (Vincent 2010). More specifically, the theoretical birth of human rights is usually traced back to the context of the Age of Enlightenment and European thinkers such as Grotius, Hegel, Hobbes, Kant, Locke, Paine and Rousseau, who discussed the individual within the restrictive feudal system. Theories of natural law were a core theme of the seventeenth- and eighteenth-century discussions about rights. This theory, originally steeped in Christian tradition, became secularised by replacing God with reason (Freeman 2017). Whilst a list of human rights was not compiled, Thomas Paine wrote 31 articles (Paine 1792) justifying revolution if the natural rights of people were to come under threat. The rights that were codified in the French Declaration of the Rights of Man and Citizen (1789) and the Bill of Rights in America (1776) were predominantly protective ones that promoted notions of liberty, popular sovereignty and individualism (Vincent 2010). These philosophical debates relating to the equality, autonomy and the rights of all men under natural law did not remain within the confines of the coffee houses of Europe, but led to political unrest and revolutions. Within the mainstream Eurocentric account, the human rights of today are often described as the descendants of 'the traditional rights of man' (Wellman 1999: 13–14).

In contrast, Third World approaches seek to dismantle, reframe and supplement this conventional account of human rights. Third World genealogies include voices and struggles from the Global South. Rather than focusing on the relationship between the individual and the state, a decolonial reading centralises the relationship between the colonised and the empires. It explores how international law – a product of states and associated global power dynamics – was developed to justify colonial projects. A decolonial approach also examines how human rights have been deployed by the colonised in their struggles for self-determination. A central argument of this approach to human rights is that human rights theory and praxis was *not* first operationalised by European thinkers and during bourgeois revolutions (as is often conveyed), but can be traced much earlier to sixteenth-century theorists. This includes figures such as Bartolomé de Las Casas and Francisco de Vitoria, both of whom were preoccupied with the relationship between the indigenous people and the Spanish invaders during the conquest of America.

Francisco de Vitoria, a sixteenth-century Spanish theologian and legal jurist, used natural law to legitimise the Spanish Empire's colonial endeavours. He is considered to be one of the founding fathers of international law and his work *De Indis Noviter Inventis* the first international law text (Barreto 2013c). Vitoria applied natural law to the indigenous (unlike many of his contemporaries) but less as a recognition of their humanity and more as a means to bring them under the Spanish Empire's sovereignty (Anghie 2005). Drawing on the words of Aristotle, Vitoria argues that the Indians are 'insufficiently rational to govern themselves, but are rational enough to take orders' (De Vitoria 1991: 239). To put it another way, the Indians possessed enough reason to be subjects of the law of nations but were not quite human enough to exercise full sovereignty. For Vitoria, the 'civilised' (Christian Europeans) and their ways of life were the universal standard against which he measured the cultural practices of the 'uncivilised' (non-Christian non-Europeans). Vitoria's comparison formed the basis of what Anghie (2005) terms 'the dynamic of difference', which Vitoria and others engaged in the 'civilising mission' since have sought to address through various means. For Vitoria, war became a legitimate mode by which this gap could be bridged. He proposed a system that allowed the Spanish to enter indigenous lands as part of their right to 'travel' and 'sojourn'. If, when exercising these rights, the colonisers were met with resistance from the native population then they were justified in acting in self-defence. In other words, he devised a legal framework that the indigenous were bound to violate and which in turn, enabled the Spanish Empire's relentless accumulation of Indian territory since only the Spanish (as Christians and those with sovereignty) could wage 'just' war.

In the sixteenth century, natural law was also operationalised by Bartolomé de Las Casas, an Andalusian bishop who lived in Mexico. Las Casas, informed by his philosophical, theological education alongside Romana and canonical law, extended natural law and international law but, unlike Vitoria, with the aim of protecting the indigenous population and confronting the atrocities committed against them by the colonial powers (Dussel 2013). He emphasised the humanity and dignity of the Indians, arguing that that they too, like their oppressors, were made in the image of God, possessed reason and could exercise sovereignty (Tierney 2004). Challenging the brutality of the colonisers, Las Casas (1992: xxi) wrote: 'By what authority have you made such detestable wars against these people who lived peacefully … on their own lands? Are these not men? Do they not have rational souls?'

In contrast to Vitoria, he viewed the Indians as the *subjects* of international law rather than the *objects* of it. Importantly, it was his theory of natural law that provided a basis for the right to self-determination for the colonised. When participating in the Valladolid debate[1] he defended the Indians, arguing that even if they were barbarians as the Spanish colonisers maintained, this did not mean they were 'incapable of government' and in need of being 'ruled by others' (Las Casas 1999: 42). He went on to argue that 'they are not ignorant, inhuman, or bestial. Rather, long before they heard the word Spaniard they had properly organized states, wisely ordered by excellent laws, religion and custom' (Las Casas 1999: 42).

According to the conventional Eurocentric account, the right to self-determination is a principle that can be traced in the French and American Revolutions. It is seen as that which then took root in the twentieth-century following Wilson's Fourteen Points speech in 1918 and a year earlier by Lenin in his book *The Right of Nations to Self-Determination* (1914). The right to self-determination became a priority of the UN following the Second World War, becoming enshrined in Articles 1 and 2 of the UN Charter. However, notions of self-determination were articulated by Las Casas 400 years previously and were operationalised in Caribbean and South American anti-colonial struggles in the seventeenth and eighteenth centuries (Barreto 2013c).

Decolonial scholars highlight that whilst France ratified the Declaration of the Rights of Man and Citizen (1789), within which the equality of mankind was emphasised as in the Declaration of Independence (1776), they then revoked them to people and slaves in the colonies (Bogues 2013). Nonetheless, the doctrines of rights promoted in the revolutionary documents once translated and placed in the hands of the colonised in the Caribbean and South America was used as a vehicle for their struggles for independence and appropriated into

[1] The Valladolid debate took place between Las Casas and humanist scholar Juan Ginés de Sepúlveda between 1550 and 1551. The moral and theological debate, the first of its kind, sought to discuss issues relating to the rights of the indigenous, the relationship between the colonisers and the indigenous, and the conversion of the Indians to Catholicism (Brunstetter and Zartner 2011).

their ensuing national constitutions (Barreto 2013c). For instance, the preamble to the Haitian Constitution (1805) offered the most inclusive articulation on the equality of mankind of its era since it addressed issues of racial oppression such as slavery – an aspect that was not addressed in the French and American revolutionary documents (Bogues 2013).

The Haitian Revolution has been described as having two impulses: 'the abolition of racial slavery'; and 'the establishment of an independent republic' (Bogues 2013: 218). The concept of citizen as rights-holder and how this was different from being a subject was a key feature of the French and American declarations; however, in the Haitian Revolution and Constitution of 1805, citizenship was associated with both the ability to own property and a positive identification with Blackness. Thus, issues of slavery, identity and the struggle against domination have been central to Caribbean notions of freedom and offer an alternative understanding to the conventional Eurocentric normative political understandings of freedom that centralise the individual in relation to the state.

Anghie (2005) describes the interwar period (1919–1930) as a pivotal moment in the development of international law, outlining how once more it sought to obscure its complicity in colonialism. The mandate system was established by the League of Nations and oversaw territories that had previously made up parts of the Ottoman Empire (such as Palestine) or that had been annexed by Germany. Unlike previous colonial enterprises, the mandate system aimed to turn these territories into independent states to be self-governed by the indigenous people. Anghie (2005) maintains that this new international system built on some of Vitoria's ideas such as the view that the indigenous were like 'infants' who required a form of guardianship. He notes that the mandate regime was significant because unlike nineteenth-century positivist international law, the aim of this new guardian was to *civilise* rather than *exploit* the native. Although attempts to address the 'dynamic of difference' were undertaken during this period, international law adopted more neutral discourses. The First World would resolve Third World problems through economic and scientific development, signalling a departure from explicit racist rhetoric. This new system sought to usher these former colonised people towards self-government and independence on the one hand, and to integrate them into this international system on the other. This marked the beginning of a new era of decolonisation, an initiative that the UN would later oversee, and a new 'set of technologies for the management of colonial problems' (Anghie 2005: 195). Palestine came under British occupation during this interwar period but it was unlike the other post-war mandates.

In the Balfour Declaration of 1917, Britain publicly promised their support of the establishment of a 'Jewish national home' in Palestine (Balfour Declaration 1917). The British military administration then paved the way for the realisation of this promise when it formally announced on 27 February 1920 that it would implement the Declaration (Darweish and Rigby 2015). And so, what made the British Mandate for Palestine unique was that the British government chose to support the self-determination of one group (the Jews) that made up only nine per cent of the population. By default, they denied the Palestinian Arabs who made up around 91 per cent of the population that same right to self-determination. Whilst the Declaration included a clause that 'nothing shall be done which may prejudice the civic and religious rights of non-Jewish communities in Palestine', it did not pledge support for their political rights (Shlaim 2005). Instead, the British Mandate facilitated the inward migration of Jewish people from Europe who were experiencing an intensification of antisemitism. Then one of these new technologies – the UN – went on to recommend the partition of this territory into an Arab and Jewish state, which led to the *Nakba* and the realisation of the state of Israel. Comparing jurisprudence of this interwar period to that of the nineteenth century, Anghie (2005: 194) concludes that international law went from: 'Positivism to pragmatism; from law to institutions; from sovereignty to government; from race to economics; from conquest to decolonization; from colonialism to neo-colonialism; from exploitation to development; and from England and France to the United States'.

Returning to the conventional lineage of human rights, the year 1948 is often considered a defining moment in Western human rights history, one that is often underscored in not only academic literature but also the contents of human rights education (HRE) (for a more in-depth discussion of this in relation to HRE see chapter three). Typically, emphasis is placed upon how leading up to the Universal Declaration of Human Rights (UDHR) (1948), a large portion of Europe abandoned human rights values altogether as seen by the rise of totalitarianism, the devastation of two World Wars and the Holocaust (see Fields 2003). This was a time in Europe in which the rights of the individual were quashed ideologically and in practice by oppressive regimes, the eugenics movement, and war. The fall of the Third Reich and the end of the Second World War prompted the formation of the UN and the drafting of human rights standards in international law through the UDHR in the 1940s. During this decade the focus on the rights of the individual in relation to the state re-emerged with the purpose of empowering individuals with the 'civic courage to stand up when the state ordered them to do wrong' (Ignatieff 2001: 5). Paradoxically, this meant the state was also legitimised to become the primary protector of human rights in this post-war human rights system (Perugini and Gordon 2015).

In his analysis of the so-called return to human rights in this era, Césaire (2000) concludes that it was a reaction to antisemitism and Nazism specifically rather than colonialism and racism. Instead, people living in the colonies were excluded as the humans of human rights not only in the UDHR, but also in the following decade when a clause was added by colonial powers to keep it this way (Roberts 2014). Therefore, according to some decolonial critiques, the UDHR did not adequately address the 'whom for' dimension of human rights (Maldonado-Torres 2021). Furthermore, according to Eleanor Roosevelt, the statements contained within the UDHR were issued in the hope that that a 'curious grapevine' would spread concepts of human rights to every individual, throughout every land (Goodale 2007: 3). However, underlying her grapevine allegory was the assumption that concepts of human rights had not already being operationalised in other lands and that the source of rights emanated from the West or that they had suddenly been meaningfully born in 1948.

In quick succession of the Declaration and subsequent conventions, some authors acknowledge that an activist movement gained momentum in which non-governmental organisations (NGOs) held states that had ratified conventions to account. They point out that had it not been for this drive at grassroots level to ensure practice emulated rhetoric, these human rights instruments would have been simply 'a revolution on paper' (Ignatieff 2001: 10). Moyn (2010) goes a step further by proposing that it was not until after 1977 following US President Jimmy Carter's endorsement of human rights that a modern human rights system was truly established. He contests the recent histories of human rights arguing that the UDHR was unenforceable and that human rights garnered little interest among civil society actors and international lawyers before the late 1970s.

However, critics of Moyn's (2010, 2018) revisionism point out that his account of the history of human rights is selective, unconvincing, and reductionist (Alston 2013). His account is arguably not Eurocentric but US-centric, and even then only partially since it does not acknowledge even key declarations and struggles that arose from the US context such as the Declaration of Independence, nineteenth-century anti-slavery struggles and the Civil Rights Movement of the 1950s and 1960s (Barreto 2015).

Anghie (2013) scrutinises Moyn's discussion of the relationship between self-determination and human rights and his portrayal of decolonial struggles in the Third World as nationalist projects against colonialism rather than significant moments in the evolution of human rights jurisprudence. He also underscores that when Moyn argues that human rights were the 'last utopia' more universally, he is actually speaking for a particular group of people mostly those situated in non-Third World contexts. Those engaged in indigenous struggles were and are engaged in the quest for an 'old utopia', one that includes 'self-determination, recognition of nationhood, and sovereignty' (Anghie 2013: 74). Therefore, Moyn's (2010: 9) 'true history of human rights' is even narrower than that of those who consider the 1940s as the dawn of the modern human rights scheme, placing Europe's events and thinkers at its epicentre.

According to conventional narratives, the lineage of rights is often traced back to the Enlightenment, therefore it is also closely associated with *rationalism*. Decolonial human rights theorists (Mignolo 2013; Barreto 2013a; Baxi 2007) challenge this notion of rationalism that pervades the dominant rights discourse. They make a connection between human rights, colonialism and suffering. This approach to human rights consequently facilitates the voices of the violated and allows suffering to emerge and jar against the more sanitised, abstract and legal discourse that dominates Western rights discourse (Baxi 2007). According to Baxi (2002: 14), the Eurocentric theory of human rights 'disembodies human suffering' and instead theorists, by concentrating on philosophical or legal considerations, have positioned themselves at a distance from the victims of rights violations. However, for victims of rights abuses, as Barreto (2013b: 110) states, 'the violation of their rights does not mean first of all the breaching of constitutions or international treaties, nor the negation of political ideals or ethical principles', but rather an encounter with *suffering*.

Therefore, the discourse of suffering may be the only language by which victims may express themselves in a meaningful way (Barreto 2013b). Although it is possible to argue (as it often is) that the drafters sought to prevent the repetition of horrific acts such as the Holocaust elsewhere, it was done so from a particular vantage point – a Eurocentric one. Moreover, this version of the history of human rights centralises European suffering and excludes suffering that had been endured by colonised people before 1948 at the hands of these same European empires (Barreto 2013b). Or as Maldonado-Torres (2021: 78) puts it: 'the politics of Europe as the place with a maximum civilization join the politics of Europe as the place where the maximum suffering occurred'. He goes on to explain that because of these set of circumstances, opposition to antisemitism and racist rhetoric (even if rhetorically) became paramount for Europeans as well as the inclusion of Jewish people into the category of whiteness (Maldonado-Torres 2021). White European suffering to this day is often considered more lamentable than that of Black or indigenous suffering. The European and North American public's statements of solidarity and governments' willingness to receive Ukrainian refugees compared to those fleeing Afghanistan after the withdrawal of US, UK and other forces followed by the Taliban's return to power in May 2021 provides a clear example of this (see De Coninck 2022).

As has been explored, the development of human rights found in Western legal instruments has to be understood in the historical context and political struggles in which they arose (Stammers 2009). To this end, the term 'generation' has been used in Eurocentric rights discourse to describe the evolution of human rights law (Vašák 1977). The first generation includes civil and political rights which were incorporated into the eighteenth-century French and American documents (Fields 2003) and later codified in the International Covenant on Civil and Political Rights (ICCPR) (1966). Following 1918, an interest in economic and social rights arose along with ideas of the Welfare State, and as a result, in 1966 a comprehensive list of economic, cultural and social rights emerged (Vincent 2010). These rights are referred to as 'second generation rights' and are defined in the International Covenant on Economic, Social and Cultural Rights (ICESCR) (1966).

These generations of rights became politicised during the Cold War in which the US gave priority to first generation rights whereas the Soviet Union placed a greater emphasis on social and economic rights. In other words, there emerged two human rights cultures: the communist one and the capitalist one. After the fall of the Soviet Union, capitalist culture largely flourished whilst communist culture languished (Ignatieff 2001). Decolonisation movements, which gained momentum in the 1960s, prompted the emergence of what has been termed 'third generation rights'.

Third generation rights have also been coined 'solidarity rights' by Vašák (1977). This generation of rights has a collective focus and includes the rights to development, peace and self-determination. According to the traditional human rights narrative, this generation of rights also arose arguably because of the individual's desire for *fraternity*, not just liberty and equality (Wellman 2000). Some activists and decolonial scholars have rejected these so-called generations of rights because of how they have come to be positioned hierarchically, often with third generation rights remaining on the periphery of international law and thus deemed less important (Barreto 2013c). According to a Third World historical reading of the development of human rights, the right to self-determination would be situated as a first generation of rights instead of civil and political rights since they concur that the foundation for this collective right had already been laid by Las Casas in the sixteenth century. Nevertheless, decolonial scholars call for the removal of such a hierarchy and emphasise the interdependence of rights. When encountering the Eurocentric dominant narratives on human rights, it is important to consider how the unique political struggles of one specific age and region of the world led to the subsequent codification of certain rights (Goodale 2007) and that 'our truth is not the whole truth' (Dembour 2001: 71). And whilst dominant human rights discourse is presented as neutral and void of a particular context, it is entrenched in Eurocentric thought (Barreto 2013a).

Moving to the twenty-first century, Anghie (2005) underscores the War on Terror as a form of neo-colonialism and a recent example of how international law has sought to shroud its complicity in colonialism. He draws a parallel between how the administrations that launched the War on Terror made the case for pre-emptive defence before invading Iraq and Afghanistan, and Vitoria, who made the case for the Conquistadors' colonial expansion by framing it as a mode of self-defence against a hostile native population. Alongside the concepts of pre-emptive self-defence and 'rogue states', the military campaign against terrorism was also underpinned by the promotion of democracy as a means to 'liberate' these populations and 'civilise' them so that they would become societies that no longer posed a threat to the US and its allies.

Anghie (2005) argues that terrorism is closely associated with Muslim and Arab societies, combining the discourses of race (as seen in the nineteenth century), economics (evidenced under the mandate system) and also war as self-defence (traceable in the sixteenth century). What this more recent campaign reveals, yet again, is the West's hegemony over the human rights discourse and how European and North American powers have come to position themselves as the champions and guardians of human rights with the authority to manage the human rights project globally, all the while determining who qualifies as the 'humans' of 'human rights'. This has been exemplified more recently in the inconsistency of North American and European powers when it comes to invoking international law in relation to Russia's occupation of parts of Ukraine and disregarding it when it concerns Palestinians living under a complete siege and military bombardment in Gaza. Ultimately, human rights can have a dubious relationship with power and can be used as a tool to dominate other groups and individuals (Perugini and Gordon 2015; Stammers 2009).

Another theory underpinning the Eurocentric rights discourse is *universalism*. A core debate within rights discourse is the tension between universalism and cultural relativism. Central to some relativist debates is the question of whether human rights are solely a by-product of Western philosophy, values and traditions and, if so, what relevance do they have in other non-Western contexts. And what right does the West have to impose international human rights standards upon the rest of the world? A critique of universalism was articulated during the Enlightenment period by contemporaries such as Burke, Hume and Bentham, and in the following century by Marx. Marx (1975: 162) claimed that universalism was a method of protecting the rights of the bourgeois man, referring to the 'rights of man' as 'nothing but … the rights of egotistic man, of man separated from other men and from community'. However, Rajagopal (2003) maintains that the universalism and cultural relativism debate, contrary to popular wisdom, emerged much later, in the early 1980s, in the context of debates regarding the development agenda and the tension between tradition and modernity.

According to Donnelly (1989), there is a corresponding continuum along which universalism and cultural relativism are positioned, ranging from strong to weak expressions of both. Although often presented in binary terms, weak relativism is often the predominant view underpinning relativist critiques and those who express a relativist critique do not reject all aspects of universality (Rajagopal 2003). It is also misleading to categorise any cultural relativist challenge into a 'non-Western' group, as there is no generic non-Western challenge to universality. In fact, there are various critiques including those that have arisen in the West (Bricmont 2006; Pollis and Schwab 1979).

Decolonial scholars consider universalism part of Western imperialism. This has provoked a range of responses. Some view the human rights scheme as that which has been irreversibly manipulated by the Global North into a tool by which to punish the rest of world (Brown 2004; Mutua 2001). Southern jurists such as Abdullah An-Naim, Francis Deng and Yash Ghai rely on the international human rights framework as a basis for some of their arguments and are not fully opposed to the universality of rights (Twining 2013). For instance, An-Naim (2021: 14–15) calls for what he terms 'self-determined universality' where the implementation of human rights is achieved via the 'free choice and dignity' of rights-holders across different cultural contexts. When analysing An-Na'im's philosophy of cross-cultural universality, Baderin

(2022: 613) disputes arguments that suggest that this approach is another form of cultural relativism:

> [A]dvocates for 'cultural pluralism,' which is both inward and outward looking, in the universality of human rights. This stands in contrast with the concept of 'cultural relativism,' which is only inward looking. This philosophy would involve a cultural dialogue of human rights values, in which all cultures would have a right to participate, contribute, and convince *rationally* on any cultural value brought into the dialogue.

Moreover, An-Naim (2021) suggests that technically every person is a cultural relativist – even ardent universalists – since human rights do not stand above culture or politics.

Ghai (2018) and Baxi (2002) adopt a more pragmatic approach towards the UDHR and the human rights scheme, with Baxi offering a more critical commentary on its limitations, contradictions and fragility. As Perugini and Gordon (2015: 16) contend, underpinning both fervent universalist and ardent cultural relativist arguments is the belief that human rights 'have some kind of stable core that is either inherently good and therefore needs to be uncovered and deployed or inherently bad and consequently, cannot be used under any circumstances'. However, scholars such as Mignolo (2011), rather than rejecting the rights discourse altogether, contest universalism offering an alternative to a cultural relativist argument by suggesting the discourse needs to be 'pluriversalised'. According to Mignolo (2011), pluriversality is a way of viewing the world as entangled through and by 'the colonial matrix of power' rather than neatly compartmentalised into separate units as cultural relativism would propose. Therefore, when it comes to conceptualising human rights, these scholars are concerned with the inclusion of epistemic diversity that exists within these entangled spaces, such as the narratives of the indigenous, colonised and oppressed.

Shaped by public discourses following the War on Terror, essentialist arguments are often made about the incompatibility between Islam and human rights. So how do some of these critiques of the Eurocentric rights regime and its underlying theories such as secularism or individualism play out in relation to the broader Islamic and Arab contexts within which Palestinians are situated? Discussion in the next section aims to dispel assumptions that Islam and human rights are ideologically opposed by providing the range of views that exist in the Islamic human rights discourse. Consideration of the different religious, cultural and political aspects that have influenced Islamic engagements with the rights discourse will be taken.

III. ISLAM AND HUMAN RIGHTS: CONTRIBUTIONS AND CRITIQUES

Broadly speaking, two main attitudes emerge concerning the relationship between religion and human rights (Banchoff and Wuthnow 2011). First, that religion is irreconcilable with human rights especially when rights are closely associated with the UDHR – a secular initiative; secondly, that religion can contribute to, and has historically been, a motivation behind struggles for justice, often with a focus on human dignity. In the West, the secularist narrative predominates discussions around the relationship between religion and human rights (Johnston 2015). From this position, many Western scholars consider the role of Islam as largely irrelevant regarding constructions of human rights (Meyer 1999). This assumption and disinterest in other philosophical and religious ideas (such as Islam) along with the secular foundation of the UDHR is, in part, what makes some Muslims critical of the human rights regime (Sachedina 2007). In contrast, Muslim human rights scholars, who underscore the possible synergies between Islam and (secular) human rights, often do so with an esteem for the international standards (An-Naim 2022; Meyer 1999).

Nonetheless, in both public and academic discussions there remains a preoccupation with the question of whether there is potential for ideological harmony between Islam and human rights (Allen 2013). Some have taken a more radical stance arguing that *Shari'ah* law, Islamic culture and civilisation are the factors driving rights abuses in Muslim-majority countries (Hirsch 2008). The European Court of Human Rights has also indicated that Europe's concepts of democracy and the *Shari'ah* are awkward bedfellows (see Rehman 2011). However, this preoccupation with the compatibility of Islam and human rights ignores the fact that Islam is not a monolithic religion and, thus, the diversity within Islam as a religion and culture is not taken into consideration (An-Na'im 2011a). In fact, neither Islam nor human rights have fixed meanings.

A. Diverse Religious Voices

Abou El Fadl (2003), a leading Muslim scholar on Islam and human rights, argues that Western scholars often present a two-fold argument that Islam and human rights are incompatible entities based upon, firstly, the generalisation that Islamic teachings do not harmonise with ideas of individualism and, secondly, that duties are given primacy above rights (Hille 2006; Ignatieff 2001; Meyer 1999; Donnelly 1989). For instance, Donnelly (1989) makes this case when he argues that *Qur'anic* texts tend to emphasise the individual as one who solely has a set of obligations to carry out rather than one who is a possessor of rights. He also claims that whilst in Islam the notion of human dignity is apparent, caution must be taken not to equate this with human rights. He argues that in Islam, duty towards God and fellow men is placed above the rights of the individual, and if one possesses rights this is not as a result of merely being human, but as a direct reward for the individual's actions (Donnelly 1989). The importance of duties towards God, the state and the community are articulated in Islamic human rights instruments such as the Universal Islamic Declaration of Human Rights (UIDHR), in the work of Brohi (1978) and Nasr (1981) as well as in areas of Islamic law.[2] However, duties can also be found in international human rights standards, such as in the preamble of the ICCPR and the ICESCR and Article 29 of the UDHR. Rights and responsibilities often appear in tandem in the context of educating children about human rights in Global North contexts such as Australia (George et al 2016) and the UK (Amnesty International 2010). Therefore, in response to claims that primacy is given to responsibilities over rights in Islamic human rights discourse, Muslim scholars argue that these claims are overemphasised, essentialist and wrongly attributed to religion (Saeed 2018; Abou El Fadl 2003). However, from a theological viewpoint, they highlight the ways Islam supports the notion of the rights of the individual much more readily than collective rights. They point to *Qur'anic* verses that demonstrate that man was created as an individual image-bearer of God and as an individual who will give an account for his own actions in the Hereafter (Saaed 2018). Similarly, within Islamic law, the individual is prioritised such as in contract law and property law in relation to inheritance provisions (Saaed 2018; Schacht 1967). In his rebuttal, Abou El Fadl (2003) argues that any conceptualisations which are collectivist or duty-driven stem not from Islamic teachings as presumed, but rather from the predominance of more socialist-leaning politics that were adopted by many Muslim and Arab states during the 1950s and 1960s. These ideologies of Pan-Arabism prioritised a more duty-driven and communitarian approaches towards human rights.

Space does not allow a discussion of the full range of views that exist on Islam and human rights among Muslim thinkers. Therefore, I will provide an overview of some perspectives and approaches taken by those who are considered traditionalist and reformist. My aim is to demonstrate how there is no generic Islamic position. And what is often presumed to be a challenge based on religious grounds is often a reaction to fears of Western moral imperialism.

Among those who maintain more traditionalist interpretations of Islamic law, two main responses have emerged: the 'puritan' (or 'exceptionalist') and 'apologist' (Abou El Fal 2003). These two positions remain a principal trend in modern Islam. The puritans, a term used by Abou El Fadl (2003), are Islamic jurists who are concerned with the letter of the law rather than the spirit behind it, and give preference to positive law rather than natural law (Johnston 2015). Abou El Fadl (2003: 120) explains that the exceptionalist discourse emerged in response to the Islamic renewal in the 1970s in which those part of this puritan movement (many of whom belonged to the Wahabi and Salafi theological movements) called for the return to an 'authentic' form of Islam through reintroducing *Shari'ah* law (Abou El Fadl 2003: 120). This was a response to how *Shari'ah* had been replaced by colonial legal systems and Eurocentric laws (apart from family laws) during the colonial period and remained after Muslim-majority

[2] For example, Islamic law emphasises that children have not only rights but also responsibilities, in particular to support their parents in old age (Saeed 2018).

populations had gained independence from these regimes (An-Na'im 2011a: 63). A culture of anti-Westernism gained momentum in tandem with a religious revival spurred on by the Iranian Revolution of 1979. The universality of human rights in international law also underwent greater scrutiny by Islamists in the wake of the Islamic resurgence (Ignatieff 2001) whose movement was 'far more anti-Western than it was pro-Islamic', according to Abou El Fadl (2003: 122).

To this day, puritans continue to see no need to reconcile Islam and human rights, since the only legitimate universals are those derived from Islamic thought. This orientation does not adopt a cultural relativist stance as such, but rather believes that 'whatever rights human beings are entitled to enjoy, they are entirely within the purview of *Shari'a* law' (Abou El Fadl 2003: 310). Underlying this position are concerns that the embrace of international human rights law will place Muslims at risk of subjugating themselves to the cultural domination of the West. Furthermore, according to the puritan orientation, those who seek to reconcile Islamic and secular rights schemes are often accused of 'suffering from Westoxification' and can be viewed as traitors of Islamic tradition (Abou El Fadl 2003: 311). Meanwhile, apologists emphasise both the 'compatibility and supremacy of Islam' (Abou El Fadl 2003: 118). They hark back to the pre-modern Islamic era in which the arrival of Islam brought along with it human rights not already established in Western institutions; for example, the rights of women (Elboubekri 2015). Critics of this orientation claim that apologists selectively reference extracts of religious texts, fail to engage critically or historically with the Islamic message, and (similar to the exceptionalists) neglect the areas of dissonance that can arise between the ideology of human rights and Islamic religious beliefs (An-Na'im 2011a; Abou El Fadl 2003).

Islamists such as Maududi, an influential thinker and key figure in the mid-twentieth century, preferred to discuss *Islamic* human rights. He was critical of Western constructs of human rights, arguing that they were theoretically weak and hypocritical in practice. He claimed that human rights being demanded by individuals in the West could already be found within the *Shari'ah* (Nasr 2014). According to Maududi (1976), rights given by the state or legislative assemblies can be just as readily revoked, whereas, in Islam, rights cannot be withdrawn or altered because they have been sanctioned by God. An-Na'im (2011: 64), who described Maududi's vision of human rights as an example of 'romantic naïveté', argues that one of the flaws of his argument is that governments cannot be forced to respect rights 'simply because some scholars say God has decreed those rights'. Islamists maintain that God as the source of these entitlements is a more convincing foundation than justifications found within secular discourses (Arat 2020).

There are Muslim scholars who also explore how through *ijtihad* (independent legal reasoning) and the reinterpretation of the *Qur'an* and the Sunna/Hadith (a collection of sayings about the Prophet Muhammad), Islam can uphold international human rights. This approach has been adopted by certain Muslim feminist thinkers in relation to women's rights who claim that it is the male-dominated interpretation of the *Qur'an* that has resulted in the oppression of Muslim women as opposed to the actual content of the religious texts (Golley 2004; Majid 1998; Ahmed 1992). I will come back to Islamic feminism later but for now, An-Nai'm (2011a) underscores the limitations of this eclectic approach, arguing that *Qur'anic* verses can be utilised to both uphold and deny certain rights, such as the rights of women. Instead, he argues that a 'consistent framework of interpretation' is required (An-Na'im 2011a: 65; Moosa 2000). An-Na'im (2011a) goes on to suggest the doctrine of reverse *Naskh*[3] (abrogation) that was proposed by his mentor Taha (1987). He contends that this methodology provides a consistent framework and has the potential to further the internal reformation of Islamic law (Baderin 2022). This concept involves making a distinction between that which was revealed in the earlier Mecca era (context of peace) from the later Medinan period (context of conflict) and enabling the messages from the Mecca period that were abrogated to be revived so as to provide moral guidance and to serve as the foundation of law. Thus, another position taken by reformist scholars such as An-Na'im (2011a; 2011b) is that Islam is 'evolutionary', possessing conceptualisations of rights that also evolve throughout history (Hunter and Hunter 2008: 279). In line with this, Moosa (2000: 209) contends that 'it is the location of the interpreter, the reading of the text and the social conditions that generate different responses to issues such as human rights'. However, the concept of reverse *Naskh* has garnered a range of responses among scholars and criticism among Muslim authors such as Kamali (2003), Safi (2001) and Sachedina (1993) who question its viability. They argue that adhering to certain parts of the *Qur'an* and discarding other parts is non-sustainable and counterproductive, arguing that the *Qur'an* in its entirety should be followed (Baderin 2022). Sachedina (1993), another reformist, contends that there are Medinan verses that also complement human rights such as those relating to freedom of choice in religion. This demonstrates that there are differing views among those who seek to explore the synergies between human rights and Islam when it comes to methodologies of re-interpretation.

Overall, reformist scholars seek to engage with points of tension that arise between Islamic and secular notions of rights within Islamic human rights discourse. For instance, Moosa (2000) explicitly lists the key areas of dissonance – forbidding conversion out of Islam; the equal treatment of non-Muslims living in Muslim-majority contexts; and the rights of women – since these can all be justified or condemned by using the same scriptural sources. Sachedina (2009) advances debates on gender equality and the treatment of non-Muslims in Muslim-majority states, drawing on Shia and Mutazilite methodologies. However, it is worth pointing out that many of these more liberal-minded reformists have been educated or are educators in the West, and as Johnston

[3] When inconsistencies arise in the *Qur'an*, the process of abrogation is practised in which earlier verses override later ones (Arat 2020).

(2015) points out, are less conservative than the majority of Muslim societies in other parts of the world. Nonetheless, their arguments confront the generalisations made by many in Western academe who claim that questioning religious texts is not permitted in Islam (Freeman 2002) or who start from the assumption that there are no synergies between these systems.

Underlying these approaches from across the spectrum (traditionalists and reformists) is a deep awareness of how Western policies have brought about harm to Muslims not only during the colonial period and the War on Terror era, but even at the time of writing when Western ruling elites are aiding and abetting Israel's war against the Palestinians of Gaza. Attitudes towards the international human rights system may vary among different Muslim scholars, but it is important to stress that colonialism and its accomplice, Orientalism, have shaped how human rights are understood in the 'Muslim social imagination' and that for some, the human rights arena remains 'thoroughly political' and 'plagued by widespread Western hypocrisy' (Abou El Fadl 2003: 117–118). Rather than shutting down dialogue with Muslim thinkers who adopt an anti-Declaration position or who criticise the hegemony and hypocrisy of proponents of secular human rights systems and discourses, there needs to be meaningful engagement with these voices. I agree with Sachedina (2007) who states that, if not, this may run the risk of 'marginalizing human rights in the Muslim world'.

B. Muslims, the UDHR and Islamic Human Rights Instruments

Not only has secularism, which pervades the international human rights regime, been scrutinised by Muslim thinkers, but also universalism. This was apparent during the drafting of the UDHR. Whilst different countries were represented in this process, it is important to acknowledge that it was chaired by North Americans and the agenda was driven by the Western Allied Forces – Britain, France and the United States. Crucially, most Muslim-majority states were under colonial rule at the time when the UDHR was being drafted (Saeed 2018). This context is important to bear in mind when it comes to cynicism towards the UDHR and the universality of rights (Koraytem 2001). Nonetheless, it is often wrongfully presumed that representatives from Muslim-majority countries were either not present at the drafting, or that their contribution was insignificant, or that they were unanimously opposed to the drafting of the UDHR (Waltz 2004).

The Saudi Arabian UN delegation's decision to abstain from voting on the UDHR has diverted attention away from the involvement of other Muslim-majority states such as their commitment to socioeconomic rights (Waltz 2004). Saudi Arabia's objection to Articles 16 (relating to marriage) and 18 (relating to religious freedom) are often cited by Western scholars as examples of a generic Islamic challenge to human rights (Ignatieff 2001; Donnelly 1989). Firstly, this is debatable since other Muslim voices were not only present at the drafting but were not necessarily in agreement with the Saudi Arabian proposals for amendments. Secondly, the amendments put forth by Saudi Arabia were not explicitly based upon an Islamic theological argument but more of a cultural one (for instance the practice of arranged marriages). It is helpful to consider that the Islamic resurgence did not take place until the 1970s, which was much later than the drafting of the UDHR (Abou El Fadl 2003); therefore, it is mistaken to associate the Saudi Arabian objections as affiliated with Wahhabism[4] since this movement emerged much later (Johnston 2015). Furthermore, Jamil Baroody who represented Saudi Arabia was a Christian originally from Lebanon who was not qualified to offer any Islamic theological contributions (Sachedina 2007).

Thirdly, it is possible that these representatives of Muslim-majority states as well other non-Western representatives were not necessarily 'in touch' with the populations they were representing since many of them were secular and had lived outside of these states and had been educated at Western institutions (An-Na'im 2011b). Fourthly, and importantly, much of the Muslim-majority states did not first experience Western conceptualisations of human rights as enshrined in the UDHR, but rather prior to 1948 as victims of the colonial enterprise in which European natural law was manipulated in order to justify the exploitation of these territories and populations (Abou El Fadl 2003). This has influenced the way in which the human rights discourse has come to be perceived – oftentimes with suspicion.

Therefore, it is useful to also bear these factors in mind when examining the objections put forth by the Saudi Arabian delegation at the drafting of the Declaration, such as their objection to Article 18, which states that the individual has the freedom to choose his or her religion (UNGA 1948). The assumption is often made that the objection to Article 18 was made from a classical Islamic theological perspective – that it is forbidden for a Muslim to turn away from Islam (Moosa 2000). On the contrary, the Pakistani delegate argued that religious freedom is upheld in the *Qur'an*, and when it came to voting on the article no Muslim-majority state objected (Meyer 1999). Moreover, at the heart of the Saudi Arabian disagreement with the inclusion of this phrase was the concern that it endorsed Christian missionaries to convert Muslims (Waltz 2004). This was informed by the historical backdrop of the Crusades and colonial practices in which Muslims were forcefully subjected to the proselytising efforts of missionaries. Baroody expressed his concerns that:

> Throughout history missionaries had often abused their rights by becoming the forerunners of a political intervention, and there were many instances where people had been drawn into murderous conflict by the missionaries' efforts to convert them (cited in Waltz 2004: 815).

[4] An ultraorthodox sect of Islam that adheres to literal interpretations of religious texts. Whilst this movement was founded in the 18th century in Saudi Arabia, it gained momentum in the late 1970s.

Hence, his argument was not informed by Islamic religious nor Arab cultural beliefs, but rather by the historical frame of colonialism. The Saudi Arabian representative, Baroody argued that aspects of the Declaration imposed Western standards globally whilst failing to respect and incorporate other cultural values present in other non-Western civilisations. This debate also emerged when discussing the initial version of Article 16 in terms of gender equality in marriage.

Article 16 of the Declaration was a source of contention for the Saudi Arabians as it directly undermined the practice of arranged marriages. A universalist would simply contest this objection, on the grounds that just because a custom may have been part of a culture for a long period of time, does not mean that it is a justifiable practice if it is harmful to the dignity of the individual (Donnelly 1989). Baroody sought to amend the phrasing with regard to two issues: first, the age of eligibility for marriage; and second, he proposed that the legal requirements of the host countries should provide the framework for marriage rather than the Declaration (Waltz 2004). In 1947, Saudi Arabia's opposition to the imposition of Western standards over the practices of other cultures was recorded (cited in Johnson and Symonides 1998: 52–53):

> The authors of the draft declaration had, for the most part, taken into consideration only the standards recognized by western civilization and had ignored more ancient civilizations which were past the experimental stage, and the institutions of which, for example, marriage, had proved their wisdom down through the centuries. It was not for the Committee to proclaim the superiority of one civilization over all others or to establish uniform standards for all countries of the world.

The main thrust of this argument was not religious but informed by concerns around moral imperialism. For Baroody, the Committee were endorsing one world view (a Western one) over others when it came to the practice of marriage. This also exposes how even at the drafting stage, the UDHR was not untouched by culture. However, not all Muslim-majority state delegates expressed discomfort with initial versions of this article and some non-Muslim state representatives contested this article on marriage, based on other arguments. For instance, the Mexican delegate wished to amend the article in order to prevent restrictions based on race, nationality or religion (Waltz 2004). Although according to the five schools of Islamic thought, it is not acceptable for women to marry non-Muslim men, it is also worth remembering that the United States also opposed the phrasing of this article with regard to the right to marry members of a different ethnicity (Johnston 2015). It is important to note that the Saudi Arabian objection was not representational of all Muslim-majority state delegations. At a later stage in 1950, during the Third Committee, discussions emerged around gender equality. Once more, a cultural relativist argument emerged from the Yemeni delegate surrounding the disregard of the legal provisions in different countries regarding marriage, divorce and inheritance; however, the Iraqi (Muslim) representative rebutted this argument stating:

> If all nations loved in accordance with the spirit and the letter of their religion there would be no need for a covenant on human rights. No covenant could, in any case, demand so much in respect of human rights as Islam did. The Commission on Human Rights should concentrate its attention on the similarities rather than the differences among conflicting views on human rights and thereby draft a covenant to protect the common interests of humanity (cited in Waltz 2004: 822).

Despite the involvement of delegates representing Muslim-majority populations, Western colonial powers were in the driving seat, ensuring that the human rights system aligned their 'own *liberal relativism*' in a way that would enable their ongoing dominance over their former colonies (An-Naim 2021: 31). This, along with the absence of what Sachedina (2007: 54) describes as a 'serious Muslim participation' during the drafting of the UDHR, continues to cause an uneasiness among some Muslim thinkers and societies who are unable to unsee its secular and Eurocentric bias.

Scrutiny of the universal applicability of international human rights standards to those in Muslim communities has prompted the formation of Islamic human rights instruments. In response to the 1967 Arab–Israeli war which resulted in Israel's occupation of the West Bank, Gaza, Golan Heights, East Jerusalem and the Sinai Peninsula, The League of Arab States established the Permanent Arab Commission on Human Rights in 1968 (Donnelly 2013). Attempts to reconcile Arab cultural and Western conceptualisations of human rights through Islamic human rights instruments continued from the 1970s. These efforts were influenced by Islamic culture especially with regard to the importance of the family unit and religious devotion (Rehman 2010). Different Arab states made contributions to human rights instruments; for example, The Tunisian Charter of Human Rights was adopted by The Tunisian League of Human Rights in 1985, the Green Charter of Human Rights was formulated in 1988 by Libya, and a human rights charter was drafted in Morocco in 1990 (Saeed 2018).

The development of an Arab vision of human rights for Arab peoples can be seen in the Arab Charter of Human Rights (ACHR). Versions of this Charter were drafted and then revisited in the early 1990s. Saeed (2018) describes the Charter as 'a defensive response to international pressure', which was compared to 'a regional shield against international pressures on Arab states' in the domain of human rights by a spokesperson from the Egyptian delegation (An-Na'im 2001: 714). In 2008, The Arab Charter for Human Rights, after having been revised, was signed by more than three-quarters of Arab League members (Saeed 2018). However, the effectiveness of the committee can be questioned since some members are in government roles in the states that they monitor (Donnelly 2013). In Rishmawi's (2005) analysis of the Charter, he notes that restrictions apply regarding rights to assembly and association as well as children's rights especially their civil and political rights. Therefore, whilst described as a positive step towards advancing human rights, the Charter has been criticised for the restrictions found therein.

In 1981, the UIDHR was adopted at the International Islamic Conference in Paris (Saeed 2018). This Declaration upholds an Islamic vision of human rights where God is viewed as the source of rights and it is guided by the *Shari'ah* (Saeed 2018). Although it is influenced by the UDHR, it deviates from secular notions of human rights in that it (in common with other Islamic human rights schemes) gives certain duties primacy over rights (Moosa 2000). Also drawing on the *Shari'ah* is the Cairo Declaration on Human Rights in Islam (CDHRI), which was formulated and adopted in 1990 in Cairo by the Organisation of Islamic Cooperation. The emphasis placed on the role of the *Shari'ah* as a lens to interpret human rights provisions found within this Declaration has been criticised since it undermines the universality of rights and can be used by governments to protect their powers rather than the rights of individuals living within their states (Kayaoğlu 2012). Despite certain shortcomings to these various human rights instruments, what they indicate is that an indigenous expression of human rights is deemed important among Muslims (Saeed 2018).

Moosa (2000) contends that despite the development of these Islamic human rights declarations, there are limitations when it comes to the status of women. With the exceptions of Somalia and Sudan, most Arab states have ratified the Convention on the Elimination of All forms of Discrimination against Women (CEDAW) (Monforte 2018). Despite their engagement with the Convention, many of these states have entered reservations against certain articles, most notably, provisions found in Article 16 in areas addressing women's equality in marriage and family life (Jaffal et al 2022; Freeman 2009). Criticism of the CEDAW is mainly instigated by traditional Islamic scholars, political parties and tribal leaders who both warn and persuade the public that implementation of the Convention will lead to the substitution of Islamic laws with Western ones (Hattab and Abualrob 2023; Spierings 2014). Resistance to fully embracing the CEDAW, as with the UDHR, stems from concerns that a set of standards, which reflect Western cultural values, will be imposed onto the lives of Muslim women. The right to freedom of religion has also been used as a justification for denying women other rights that would achieve women's equality and prevent discrimination against them (Ali 2006). Instead, issues relating to family life such as inheritance laws, marriage, divorce, guardianship, and the custody of children are often addressed by Arab states in their respective family law or domestic personal status law that align with *Shari'ah* (Hattab and Abualrob 2023). However, Hattab and Abualrob (2023) suggest that this has less to do with states wanting to uphold the *Shari'ah* and more to do with their desire to appease clerics and tribal leaders and to prevent social and political unrest among the people they govern. However, HROs and women's organisations in Arab and Muslim contexts campaign for reforms to family law and personal status law that would advance gender equality (Hattab and Abualrob 2023).

This has included campaigning against polygamy, and for women to file for divorce and exercise freedom of choice in marriage, drawing on Islamic feminist arguments in their advocacy work.

C. Islam and Feminism

The relationship between Islam and patriarchy, and what this means for women's rights, is a debate that many Muslim scholars are engaged in (see Barlas 2009; Ali 2006; Mir-Hosseini 2003, 1999; Wadud 1999, 2006; Yamani 1996; Ahmed 1992). There are two main streams of struggle for women's rights and calls for reform being made in majority-Muslim and minority contexts. The first is being led by Muslim feminists and the second by Islamic feminists. Muslim feminists draw on secular international human rights norms in their campaign for gender equality. There may be fewer engaged in this mode of struggle, but their contributions are significant (see, for instance, the work of Women Living under Muslim Laws international solidarity network) and is sometimes being done purposefully under the radar. In brief, according to this approach, *Qur'anic* provisions in other areas of life (for example, taxation) have undergone reform in Muslim-majority contexts and so this is also possible in issues relating to women's rights. For Muslim feminists, reluctance to do so is down to continuing patriarchy and a lack of political will (Lucas 2019; Shaheed and Shaheed 2011).

As for the second strategy, Islamic feminism is a global movement that first gained momentum in the early 1990s. It is a term used to differentiate itself from other forms of feminism and to describe Muslim women's campaigns to reform legal provisions and practices upheld by Muslim societies to improve the lives of women in public and private spheres (Moghissi 2011). According to Islamic feminism,[5] Islam is viewed as an ally of Muslim women and a source of their liberation. Consequently, Islamic feminists endeavour to disentangle Islam from patriarchal attitudes and customs. Islamic feminists largely adopt three main strategies: they reinterpret religious texts; underscore acts of resistance by Muslim women from within Islam and its institutions; and redirect their critique away from Islam and towards the West (Bouachrine 2014).

Al-Hibri (1982: 207) contends that there are two dominant perspectives: 'those who believe that Islam as it is today is fair and just to women, and those who believe that Islam *as it is practised today* is utterly patriarchal, but that *true* Islam is not'. Islamic feminists adopt the latter perspective, often contending that women's rights were apparent in the teaching of the *Qur'an* but were lost after the death of the Prophet Muhammad, and that the fusion of existing local cultures and Islam has led to the discrimination Muslim women can currently face in certain contexts (Ahmed-Ghosh 2008; Sidani 2005). With regard to the

[5] Not all Muslim feminists identify as Islamic feminists.

status of women following the arrival of Islam, the *Qur'an* challenged discriminatory practices towards women such as banning female infanticide, restricting polygamy and improving the rights of girls (Saaed 2018; Rehman 2011). The *Qur'an* also enabled women to own property, their dowries and improved their inheritance rights. It granted agency to women in their marriage contracts, to initiate divorce and protected them from being required to return their dowry to their husbands in their wills. Whilst polygamy was allowed, restrictions to this practice were applied in order to protect orphans and widows from exploitation.

Therefore, within this pre-modern historical context, Islam ushered in new protections and rights for women. Although this period enabled women's participation in political, military and public life, following the death of the Prophet Muhammad, their role not only in the public and political spheres diminished, but also their involvement in the interpretation and discussion of the scriptures and Islamic law (Warren 2008; Al-Hibri 1997). As Panepinto (2022) expounds, women played a key role in transmitting the *hadith* with over 2,000 sayings being attributed to the Prophet Muhammad's widow, Aishia, according to Ahmed (1992). This, as Panepinto (2022: 181) maintains, serves as a 'strong argument for gender equality in the study and promotion of Islamic law'.

And so, women's legal status as an agentic decision-maker is present in Islamic law theoretically; however, in practice, restrictions exist when it comes to their legal capacity and ability to make decisions independently because of the way men and women's lives have been segregated along with how women's movement between private and public spheres has been curtailed (Saaed 2018; An-Na'im 1987–1988). Consequently, some Islamic feminists contend that Islamic jurisprudence needs to undergo regeneration to align with human rights standards and to offer relevance to contemporary issues. This, they argue, would lead to women's liberation, economic empowerment and gender equality in Muslim and Arab societies (Wadud 1999). Islamic feminism is therefore a religiously grounded argument for women's rights, which at times draws upon religious texts or calls for a renewed interpretation of these texts. It can contest knowledge production where male interpretations of religious sources have dominated and where Western interpretations of 'third world' women have prevailed.

Colonial feminism also re-emerged as part of neo-Orientalist rhetoric in the West following the War on Terror. This need to (selectively) save and liberate Muslim women has not only been used to justify military intervention by governments (such as the Bush and Blair administrations) but also NGOs and HROs (Perugini and Gordon 2015). Invoking the rights of Muslim women in this way can become a mechanism for 'white men ... saving brown women from brown men' (Spivak 1988: 50). Thus, human rights discourse has become so entangled with negative constructions of veiled Muslim women who need salvation from elsewhere; this has furthered the dichotomy between the West and Islam and 'fundamentalism and feminism' (Abu Lughod 2002: 789). Even since the intensification of hostilities between Israel and Hamas (at the time of writing), White women are commenting on how best women's rights in Gaza should be realised. For instance, Sisters Uncut was criticised in a piece in the *Jewish Chronicle* for its participation in a demonstration at Liverpool Street Station in London on 31 October 2023 where it called for a ceasefire and an end to the arms trade with Israel. The author (a White woman) implied that it was preferable for women in Gaza to be bombed and killed given Hamas's record on women's rights, and that Sisters Uncut should be protesting against Hamas instead (Freeman 2023). In other words, a White woman was proposing that Israel's war on Gaza may liberate these women from Hamas.

Alternatively, Islamic feminism can provide individuals with an appealing alternative to Western feminism which is often associated with Orientalist attitudes, secularism and imperialism (Elboubekri 2015). Bouachrine (2014), whilst acknowledging the important contributions of Islamic feminists such as Mernissi and Wadud, questions whether these arguments further entrench discrimination towards Muslim women. For instance, she takes issue with Wadud's analysis of a passage from the *Qur'an* that instructs husbands to strike women who are disobedient. Wadud proposes that verse 4:34 can be interpreted as 'setting an example', instead arguing that this does little to protect women against violence in other contexts (Bouachrine 2014: 57). She maintains that 'Islamic feminists give the false impression that all that needs to be done to achieve justice is to reinterpret scriptures' (Bouachrine 2014: 58). Overall, one of the main criticisms of the Islamic feminist argument is that it often fails to fully address the discrepancies that exist between the ideals about women's rights they point to in religious texts, and the unique forms of oppression that Muslim women face in their local settings, which are often also justified using a different interpretation of those same texts (Ahmed-Ghosh 2008).

This debate concerning Islam and the rights of women is often centred on whether or not Islam is an expression of patriarchy. Patriarchy can take on a different meaning in the Arab cultural context compared to the West. Pateman (1988) denotes patriarchy in the West as that which became 'fraternal' and it is concerned with the way men 'as men' as opposed to men 'as fathers' exercise power over women (Joseph 1996: 14). In contrast, in the Arab cultural context, the root of patriarchy is in the family where hierarchies of *age* as well as *gender* are often at play; therefore, it is concerned with the way men have power over women 'as fathers'. Patriarchy facilitates kinship structures and values, which in turn endorse these aged and gendered hierarchies (Rubenberg 2001).

The 'shame and honour' discourse upholds patriarchy. In brief, the honour code and culture of shame demands that men conduct themselves in a certain manner and that women behave according to another set of rules. Fulfilling these roles perpetuates the patriarchal system. Women are responsible for the maintenance of their family's honour. However, since family is a patriarchal unit, it is the honour of the men (who are the woman's patrilineal kin) that women are duty-bound to uphold (Hasan 2002). Different expectations are placed upon men and women when it comes to honour. For instance, men can earn honour through certain behaviours such as hospitality, generosity and providing for the family (Rubenberg 2001). Meanwhile, as Goddard (1987) highlights, female honour is passive since women can only damage or lose it, and it is largely centred on a woman's sexual conduct (Hasan 2002). Mernissi (1975: 19) contends that different underlying assumptions regarding gender inequality exist in Islamic culture compared to that of the West:

> In the Western culture, sexual inequality is based on the belief in the biological inferiority of women. In Islam, it is the contrary: the whole system is based on the assumption that woman is a powerful dangerous being. All sexual institutions (polygamy, repudiation, sexual segregation, etc.) can be perceived as a strategy for constraining her power.

Thus, one of the expectations placed upon men is that they maintain dominance over their dependants, including women and children. And, if the honour code is undermined, so are the power structures within this system (Hasan 2002: 3).

Hierarchies of age are often excluded in Western feminist definitions of patriarchy, however, in the Arab context, as aforementioned, it is men as 'fathers' who seek to control women (Joseph 1996). The pyramidal orientation of the traditional Arab family means that these vertical relationships are often based on *unilateral* respect as opposed to *mutual* respect (Barakat 2005; Sharabi 1992). Therefore, not only are the voices of men privileged over those of women, but the voices of those who are older over those who are younger. This also hinders the participation of young people and women in politics where they live in an authoritarian state. For instance, in the OPT, Arab patriarchy can be experienced by female and young activists across Palestinian political parties (Høigilt 2016). According to Barakat (2005: 163) these stratified relations are often manifest in school settings between educators and their students, and are part of an ideology of '*at-tarhib* (scaring) and/or *at-targhib* (enticement)'. However, these patriarchal relations are not necessarily unique to Arab political regimes, schools and families and equally, not all Arab political systems, schools or families are structured in this manner. Joseph (1996: 15) explains that 'kinship transports patriarchy into all spheres of social life'. The Arab family can be seen as a microcosm of society, and similarly, society a reflection of the pyramidal structure of the family (Barakat 2005). Therefore, it is possible to observe how patriarchal power relations are reproduced in both the private and public spheres.

D. Human Rights in Muslim-majority Contexts

Individual (and collective) voices of dissent are not merely discouraged in certain political ruling regimes within Muslim-majority countries, but when voiced can have life-threatening consequences, as has been witnessed during the Arab Revolutions (see Amnesty International 2015) and the wave of protests led by women in Iran (see BBC News 2022). Whilst these states' poor human rights records have been attributed to religion at times (Hirsch 2008), the majority of these countries' modes of governance do not adhere to Islamic values (Saeed 2018). According to a study by Cole (2013: 374), which analysed the relationship between a state's human rights record and religion, 'religious composition is only weakly associated with human rights outcomes'. This study also noted that Catholic, Orthodox and Jewish-majority states with cultural ties to the West had some of the worst human rights records. With this in mind, it is vital to examine the role of the state within various political contexts across Muslim-majority states when debates around human rights are concerned.

Throughout Arab and Muslim-majority countries, Hajjar (2006) argues that there are three traditional models that can be drawn upon in order to categorise the role of the state and its relationship with religion. She argues that the state either communalises religion, nationalises it or the state fully embraces it and becomes a theocracy (Hajjar 2006). The first model is apparent in more religiously diverse contexts, such as Israel, where a degree of autonomy is given to religious bodies apart from the mainstream national legal system (Hajjar 2006). The second model of nationalising religion is commonly found in contexts where the majority faith is Islam. Here, the state integrates aspects of the *Shari'ah* into its national administration. Prior to the Arab Revolutions, many countries, such as Libya and Egypt, would have followed this model, and countries that have a monarchy such as Morocco continue to do so (Hajjar 2006). Finally, the third model is theocratisation – this refers to a state which is fully Islamic. Iran is an example of a theocracy in which its laws and governance completely mirror the *Shari'ah* (Hajjar 2006).

In the two latter models, efforts have been made to preserve the patriarchal family structures. This ideology may not be about the promotion of Islam so much as it is about maintaining an authoritarian unrivalled leadership and perpetuating loyal subjects. For instance, the protection of the rights of the individual when it concerns the state is an important aspect of Islamic law (Saeed 2018). These hierarchical structures, which are promoted throughout the politics of Muslim-majority contexts, sit in direct conflict with notions of universalism and individualism inherent in secular human rights discourse.

However, arguably, whilst authoritarianism is deeply rooted across the political systems of Muslim-majority states, it also is promoted through other world religions, perhaps to a greater degree. For instance, there are no central Islamic religious institutions containing a powerful religious hierarchy of popes or bishops (Zakaria 2003). Islam also has an anti-authoritarian dimension to it which permits a Muslim to disobey the dictations of a leader if it contradicts Islamic law (Zakaria 2003). According to Ibn Khaldun, a Muslim historian and sociologist, there are three political models: the Natural system in which the most powerful oppress the rest of society; the Dynastic system, which is similar to the first but ruled by a monarch; and thirdly, the Caliphate in which both the state and populace are accountable to the *Shari'ah* (Abou El Fadl 2003). The latter model can be interpreted in its ideal form as a way in which the power of the state is curtailed; however, as has been shown through the campaign of *Daesh*, this system in practice can also manifest itself as vehemently anti-human rights. Moreover, prior to the Arab Revolutions, there was little in the way of free press or political opposition; therefore, the mosque became an important arena in which politics was discussed, as Zakaria (2003: 142) points out 'the language of opposition, in these lands, became the language of religion'.

A major current obstacle regarding the relevance of human rights in Arab and Muslim-majority contexts is the West's lack of credibility and consequently, its human rights rhetoric. Human rights discourse has been amalgamated into Western foreign policy across Muslim-majority contexts since the launch of the War on Terror. In the weeks prior to the US-led invasion of Iraq and Afghanistan, the oppression of Muslim women within these contexts suddenly came to the fore across Western media. There were strong implications that the aim of the Western powers was not only to end terrorism in these lands, but also to release Afghani women from the oppressive regime of the Taliban (Karam 2010). Incidentally, the Western powers had failed to acknowledge women's rights violations for over 15 years prior to the 2001 terrorist attacks in New York and have been largely disinterested since the withdrawal of US and NATO (German, Italian, Australian, and British) troops from the region in the summer of 2021. The foreign policies of Western liberal democracies have led to the portrayal of human rights as 'mechanism[s] of domination' as opposed to 'instrument[s] of emancipation' (Beitz 2009: 6). The inconsistency of the West in terms of its intervention in the name of human rights has led other cultures, particularly in Muslim-majority states, to perceive human rights as a rhetoric utilised to exert power over them.

The Israeli–Palestinian conflict is an integral part of Arab disillusionment with the integrity of the international human rights system. Palestinians took part in the most democratically held elections in the Middle Eastern region in 2006, in which 75 per cent of the people participated and Hamas was fairly elected in Gaza. Despite the democratic process which took place, there has been a refusal by the West to cooperate with Hamas and instead the human rights of the people of Gaza have been denied (Kazziha 2010). And as I write, the US and UK Governments also continue to prioritise the security of Israel over and above the human rights of the Palestinian people, as has been witnessed in the war on Gaza following 7 October 2023. As Johnston (2015) argues, it is misleading to claim that Muslim-majority states are overly averse any more than the West is overzealous when it comes to furthering human rights. Consequently, it is possible to question whether it is not the values of human rights which are rejected but what they have come to represent at the hands of those who endorse them rhetorically as Kazziha (2010: 58) explains:

> The credibility of the West has reached its lowest ebb in the region with its deadly silence on Israeli atrocities, the violation of human rights in Iraq and Afghanistan, the illegitimacy of Guantanamo, the humiliation of Arab leaders, and the deliberate disrespect for the symbols and values of Islam.

From this perspective the West has attacked on three fronts, which have been discussed throughout this section: the Islamic faith; Arab culture; and the politics of the region. Once more, it is apparent that human rights, whilst often associated with emancipation, can be tools of domination (Perugini and Gordon 2015).

Nonetheless, essentialist commentaries predominate when it comes to the so-called dissonance between Islam (the religion) and human rights. Similarly, assumptions are made regarding the compatibility of human rights in the political sphere of Muslim-majority contexts. As previously mentioned, the Orientalist discourse often dichotomises the Orient from the Occident by depicting the former as homogenous, passive and anti-modern, and the latter as active, modern and constantly evolving (Said 1978). This characterisation of the East can be traced back to discussions during the Enlightenment period in which there was a preoccupation with the power of the state. Monstesquieu, an eighteenth-century political philosopher solidified the term 'oriental despot' (Rubiés 2005). Ventura (2017) explains that distinctions were made between rulers who exercised arbitrary power as opposed to rulers who exercised absolute power. Unlike the European monarch, the oriental despot was depicted as one who had no regard for the natural rights of the individual since the 'sultan' ruled in a capricious manner over a population of slaves (Ventura 2017: 287).

These stereotypes depicting rulers in Muslim-majority states have re-emerged in Western analyses of the Arab Revolutions, and debates centre on whether democracy (and by association human rights) is compatible in these contexts. Whenever aspects of human rights or democracy are displayed within these contexts it is often viewed as having been 'borrowed' from the West (Arat 2020). Also, within this preoccupation is the underlying assumption that Western democracy is the ideal end goal for which the entire world is striving to reach (Ventura 2017). Conversely, Arab regimes can be more liberal than the vast majority of people they rule – many of whom would prefer to be ruled by Islamic parties (Zakaria 2003). These parties and their supporters may view democracy as a means to overthrowing autocrats rather than an end itself (Brichs and Lampridi-Kemou 2013).

Democracy is often portrayed as a necessary pre-requisite in order for human rights to flourish; however, as Freeman (2017: 78) argues, they have 'different and potentially competing theoretical foundations'. Human rights empower individuals to limit the power of the state and also demand positive action by the state to respect, protect and fulfil human rights whereas democracy is based upon a collective notion that the people (or a majority of them) should rule. Arguably, human rights can be enjoyed in non-democratic jurisdictions and human rights can be abused in democratic contexts (Milton-Edwards 2011); therefore, they are not necessarily mutually supportive (Freeman 2017). This argument highlights how amid discussions about the compatibility of the Muslim-majority states with democracy, debates around the compatibility of human rights with political regimes these contexts often become confused or intertwined. Resistance to democracy among autocratic leaders and monarchies in Muslim-majority states may be packaged as part of the anticolonial struggle and may involve the deployment of religious rhetoric and motifs. However, it is the threat that democratic processes pose to the power of these rulers and elites that lies behind rejections of democracy and, as Saaed (2018: 89) argues, 'there is probably little in Islam that can be used to wholly reject democracy'. Yet again, in Western commentaries, resistance to democracy in certain Muslim-majority states is wrongly attributed to Islam the religion.

This discussion highlights that what is often represented as a generic Islamic cultural relativist challenge to universalism inherent in the international human rights scheme is actually largely a challenge to Western moral imperialism along with caution towards the privileging of secularist foundations of this discourse. This cynicism towards human rights, apparent at the drafting of the UDHR, following the Islamic revival of the 1970s and currently as neo-Orientalist attitudes have emerged, stem from a fear that human rights standards are a 'Trojan Horse of secular fundamentalism come to silence the voice of Islam in the public sphere' (Johnston 2015: 140). Therefore, arguably, the Islamic challenge to human rights is predominantly a *decolonial* challenge to the universality of a Western secular conceptualisation of human rights as articulated in the international human rights system.

So far, this chapter has demonstrated that human rights are contested concepts that take on different forms at different times, places and through different languages. Therefore, the next section provides a brief historical overview of the human rights movement in the OPT, drawing largely upon Hajjar's (2001) work and Allen's (2013) more recent work.

IV. HUMAN RIGHTS DISCOURSE IN THE PALESTINIAN CONTEXT: EMBRACED, HARNESSED, HIJACKED AND DEMONISED

There is a correlation between social movements in different geographical contexts and the struggle for certain human rights. When exploring human rights discourse in the Palestinian context, it is important to trace the social engagement of the Palestinian people and their own use of the rights discourse. The Palestinian human rights movement gained momentum during the 1980s and early 1990s but then languished as the 'paradox of institutionalisation' (Stammers 2009) set-in following the Oslo Accords. I will trace how some of the socio-political developments of the past five decades have shaped current attitudes towards human rights in the Palestinian context.

A. Establishment of Israel and the Dispossession of Palestine Embedded within the Human Rights Regime

Around the time the United Nations General Assembly (UNGA) met in the hope of constructing a more peaceful future, Palestinians experienced an episode of conflict that forced around 750,000 of the population to flee their homes (Nicolai 2007) – a refugee crisis which remains unresolved to this day (BADIL 2015). Therefore, whilst for much of the world, 1948 marked the year of progress in human rights following the drafting of the UDHR, for Palestinians it signified the establishment of the state of Israel and the subsequent trauma of dispossession and displacement. It is generally acknowledged that the UDHR and the international human rights regime was, and continues to be, largely associated with the Holocaust. In addition, as a humanitarian response to the atrocities suffered by the Jewish people at the hands of a totalitarian state, the international community facilitated and legitimised the establishment of the settler colonial state of Israel (Perugini and Gordon 2015).

The UN played a controversial role in the lead-up to the creation of the Jewish homeland by recommending the partition of the British Mandate of Palestine into two states (UNGA 1947). The UN's proposal, whilst rejected by Palestinians, provided an impetus for the Zionist movement (Khalidi 1997) and, following the swift withdrawal of the British administration in May 1948, they declared the independence of the state of Israel (Milton-Edwards 2011), resulting in the *Nakba* (the catastrophe). It is within this context that not only the state of Israel was formed but also intricately associated with and legitimised by the international human rights regime (Perugini and Gordon 2015). Furthermore, Palestinians have not been included or involved in drafting or influencing international human rights instruments and ensuring their enforcement since they are people without a state and consequently unable to engage in these processes (Hajjar 2001). Nevertheless, Palestinians have adopted the language of human rights to articulate their struggle for rights to the international community and a human rights culture has been propagated across Palestinian society from the security forces to the refugee camps (Allen 2013). What follows is a discussion of how Palestinians have appropriated the rights discourse into their struggle against the occupation.

B. Human Rights Movement Gains Momentum: First *Intifada*

Although 1948 is often viewed as a significant moment in the (Eurocentric) human rights field, the global human rights movement gained momentum much later in the 1970s (Hajjar 2001). Reflecting this international movement, the human rights scene also established a presence in the Palestinian context. In 1979, one of the first Palestinian HROs, Al-Haq, was established. Initially, this HRO did not rely on external aid; instead it was run by a team of local volunteers who monitored and reported human rights violations caused by the Israeli occupation (Allen 2013). Al-Haq had two main target audiences: the global and the local. Al-Haq adopted a legal and objective tone in their reports in which they contested the practices of the occupying powers; these reports were intended for the eyes of the international community and were intentionally apolitical

(Hajjar 2001). Their professional approach captured the overseas attention they sought after. On a more local scale, Al-Haq compiled and distributed informative literature concerning Palestinian rights (Hajjar 2001); therefore, it played a key role in generating human rights activism locally (Allen 2013). The organisation stressed the collective interests of the Palestinian people rather than solely the rights of the individual within society through mobilising the participation of all within the community (Allen 2013). These principles of solidarity and mutual responsibility through societal participation that were evident in the early ethos of Al-Haq were also reflective of the political nationalist values which drove the First *Intifada*.

Events which unfold in the local sphere, such as changes in government, and new policies which subject people to new forms of violence and oppression, often act as '*triggers* that propel the 'importation' of a human rights discourse, which already exists in the international sphere' (Gordon and Berkovitch 2007: 247). Following the 1967 war or the *Naksa* (the setback), around 240,000 Palestinians were forcibly displaced for the first time, and around 193,500 for the second time (BADIL 2015). Additionally, Israel occupied East Jerusalem, the West Bank and Gaza and began to rule an additional one million Palestinians in what became known as the OPT. Consequently, whilst the human rights discourse began to gain popularity globally during the 1970s, it was arguably the tumultuous events on the ground at this time which acted as the main 'trigger' for the appropriation of the language of rights in the Palestinian struggle. Palestinians began to adopt the discourse of rights as a tool for challenging oppressive forces – namely the Israeli occupying forces in the territories, especially during the 1980s and early 1990s.

The First *Intifada*, which commenced in December 1987, was largely a non-violent civilian-based movement instigated by young people who had only known life under occupation (Darweish and Rigby 2015). It erupted in Gaza and spread to the West Bank in response to the harsh conditions experienced by Palestinians such as the expropriation of land, house demolitions, restrictions on freedom of movement, and economic hardships (Gelvin 2014). As previously mentioned, the uprising coincided with the explosion of the human rights scene in the OPT. HROs and NGOs were recognised by the populace as having a crucial part to play in the Palestinian cause both locally and internationally.

The period between 1990 and 1995 witnessed the establishment of over a third of the total Palestinian NGOs (Challand 2009). Similarly, human rights language became incorporated into political exchanges as an effective means of voicing political demands domestically and consequently, and the rights discourse became intertwined with state-building aims (Allen 2013). This was exemplified a year after the outbreak of the First *Intifada* when the Palestine National Council declared itself a 'peace-loving State' committed to the values enshrined in the UDHR (cited in Velloso de Santisteban 2002). According to Schultz (1999: 122), 'If Zionism was an ideology of the "chosen people", Palestinianism was an ideology of the "rightful people"'. Thus, the language of rights became embedded within the Palestinian nationalist struggle at this time. Rights discourse was also invoked as a way of gaining attention on a global level through the media (Allen 2009). As Hajjar (2001: 26) states, 'efforts to frame the struggle for Palestinians' rights in human rights terms were serving to internationalize the conflict'. Notably, the First *Intifada* also caused the importation of the rights discourse into Israel (Gordon and Berkovitch 2007).

It was also during this uprising that Palestinians began to disengage with the law as it was increasingly being perceived as a tool of the oppressor, which served to legitimise the abuses of the occupation, and functioned to further disempower the people (Hajjar 2001). It is worth repeating that the mass uprising was instigated by the younger generations rather than any formal Palestinian leadership, and they are known to this day as *Jeel al-intifada* (the *intifada* generation) (Schiocchet 2013). Therefore, rights discourse was not imposed in a top-down manner but rather intertwined in the grassroots struggle against the occupation. Thus, the human rights discourse during this period was not a legally driven one fought successfully in the court rooms, but rather a language of protest on the streets led by a social movement within the occupied territories (Hajjar 2001). Furthermore, rights were first and foremost for those who were suffering and in order to 'allow the status quo to be contested in favour of the oppressed' (Dembour 2010: 3).

Once more, political developments impacted the course of the Palestinian human rights scene, although this time they resulted in a decline in the movement and a growth in disillusionment. Although the First *Intifada* led to the peace talks between the Israeli and Palestinian leaders in Madrid and Oslo, these peace initiatives marked the beginning of the decline of the human rights movement in the OPT.

Whilst rights can be struggled for as a means of challenging oppressive powers, if successful, these demands once realised by governing authorities can lead to the institutionalisation of human rights. Ironically, the 'official' recognition of human rights does not necessarily guarantee respect for them. In fact, once institutionalised, human rights can be utilised as instruments of exerting 'power over' rather than as a vehicle by which one can contest power (Sharma and Gupta 2006). This process is what Stammers (2009: 115) terms the 'paradox of institutionalisation'. This refers to the process by which power relations become ambiguous as human rights act as tools for good and for the justification of the abuse of human rights. This can even occur simultaneously (Landy 2013). The human rights discourse became professionalised in the OPT following the peace process, and whilst techniques for monitoring violations became more advanced, this also led to the normalisation of human rights abuses and the structures perpetrating them (Perugini and Gordon 2015).

But why did the human rights movement become harnessed in the region and what were the underlying causes of the growth of cynicism within the Palestinian rights discourse which has largely remained to this day?

C. Human Rights Movement is Harnessed by Oslo

Firstly, during the Oslo era, international attention was steered away from human rights atrocities and instead towards the peace negotiations. Issues of 'security' and land partition domestically and abroad dominated the political narrative (Kimmerling and Migdal 2003). After the talks, the OPT witnessed a mass influx of financial investment mainly from Western powers. This contributed to one layer of institutionalisation in which NGOs and HROs who had previously been run by volunteers who had autonomy over the agenda of their activities, became economically dependent upon and driven by the political agenda of international donors (Allen 2013). Many of the Western funding applications offered to sponsor projects which promoted 'peace and coexistence' and withheld funds from projects which could be perceived as stirring incitement against Israel (Dana 2014; Pitner 2000: 35). Subsequently, competition for external funds not only intensified between NGOs and HROs, but they began to tailor their projects in such a manner as to fit the purposes outlined by the foreign donors (Allen 2013) and they assumed a tone of political neutrality (Hajjar 2001).

To this day, the pressure faced by HROs to ensure that the 'correct political conditions' are met is a strategy many Palestinians feel is aimed at divorcing Palestinians from politics (Jad 2007: 625). NGOs have also been pressured by Western donors to neglect social and economic rights (which appeal to nationalist goals) in pursuit of civil and political rights (Hajjar 2001). In fact, the principles which underpinned the First *Intifada* – solidarity and societal participation – are often utilised by Palestinians as a moral compass against which to measure the practices of the human rights industry,[6] the PA and subsequent uprisings (Allen 2013).

This reluctance from the West to fund projects which could be interpreted as too politically sensitive has also meant that human rights have been dislocated from the Palestinian historical narrative of loss. Zreik (2004), a Palestinian legal scholar, argues that in Palestine, the human rights discourse must be appropriated in such a manner that it 'reintroduces the totality of the Palestinian experience that was fragmented in 1948' since it is this historical backdrop which can enable Palestinians to claim their rights in a meaningful way. However, following the Oslo Accords, Palestinians have been reconstructed as 'intruders in their own land' as opposed to victims of a forced displacement (Roy 2012: 80) as well as passive victims of a humanitarian crisis (Landy 2013). Therefore, many Israelis and members of the international community deployed (and currently do) a depoliticised human rights narrative in their quest to, in turn, depoliticise Palestinians and deny them a voice. Palestinians fear that this political

[6] The term 'human rights industry' is distinct from 'human rights' and denotes the 'material and financial infrastructure' that props up the work done under the banner of human rights (Allen 2013: 5). The term also refers to those working for HROs and the activities these professionals do, such as writing funding applications and reports that will appeal to donors.

censorship is a form of soft colonialism which serves to subjugate Palestinian political agency as their financial dependence on the West increases.

This is exemplified in the following critique expressed by a man in Gaza:

> Western imperialism made us beggars in order to remain weak and stop fighting Israel. Was it really out of pity for the Palestinian people? No, there was an aim behind this. What was this aim? That the Palestinian forget his homeland since he takes the flour sack (cited in Feldman 2009: 28).

This account forms part of a larger critique of the role of human rights as a transnational regime in the global arena. That is, whilst human rights institutions operate to expose and challenge states' abuse of power, they can also function as a punitive tool for Northern states to justify (even military) intervention in the Global South (Grewal 1998).

This highlights another source of frustration in the Palestinian context with regards to the role of human rights – the West's 'selective' intervention. The Global North is content to pour aid into the OPT fully aware that it perpetuates the occupation and fosters a dependency culture. It is therefore unsurprising that within the Palestinian nationalist narrative it is possible to trace strong anti-Western sentiment, largely due to the ongoing silence primarily from the US and the EU with regard to Israel's continual contravention of international law of which Palestinians are victims. Yet again, the paradox of institutionalisation (Stammers 2009) emerges in the Palestinian context since the aforementioned Northern powers financially sustain the HROs who seek to challenge inequalities, whilst the reliance of the Palestinians upon these states serves simultaneously to reinforce these geo-political powers who condone Israeli policies and consequently, who refuse to prevent further human rights atrocities by their lack of intervention. The way that Israel and the international community have dislocated Palestinians from their historical and political experience has been perceived by Palestinians as a form of soft colonialism (Pitner 2000). This has been exemplified by the depoliticised rights narrative which has been endorsed by the donor community. Arguably, this highlights how the Palestinian state has been as Roy (2012: 82) claims, 'a U.S.-Israeli project not a Palestinian one'.

D. Human Rights Movement is Hijacked: Foreign Aid and the Human Rights Industry

A further hindrance to the human rights movement has been the widening gap between the human rights industry and the human rights principles first embraced by Palestinians. Stammers (2009) argues that it is not only the state which can enable the paradox of institutionalisation, but also NGOs. The ownership of the human rights agenda can become transferred from the people who began a particular struggle for rights into the hands of an elite group. This small group may even be driven by material gain off the back of human rights violations (Mutua 2009). This process of institutionalisation took place in the OPT following Oslo and the influx of foreign aid, during which the human rights industry began to prosper whilst violations continued (Allen 2013). Palestinians' distrust of the human rights regime increased as they experienced a greater alienation from HROs and their work. This phenomenon has been scrutinised by critics such as Petras and Veltmeyer (2001: 129), who accuse those who lead NGOs of 'trading in domestic poverty for individual perks'.

The human rights industry in the OPT has become an attractive career choice which promises overseas travel for a people whose freedom of movement is frequently curtailed, and company cars for individuals whose economy is crippled (Allen 2013). Those who choose to work for an NGO or HRO can expect to receive a higher income than that of a teacher or police officer (Allen 2013). The international community pours more money into organisations with a rights-based focus than they do into any other organisations, including educational ones; for instance, in 2008 the former received 30 per cent, while the latter were given 13.9 per cent (Allen 2013). Consequently, the lucrative human rights industry, whilst appealing to a few, has been rejected by many who conceive this dependency culture as a form of treason to former nationalist leftist ideals and simultaneously as another ploy of the international community and Israel to subjugate the Palestinian political voice (Allen 2013). Therefore, human rights are not always reflected by the human rights industry, but can instead be disfigured by it. In Palestine, this chasm between the human rights regime and human rights is felt by many members of society (Allen 2013). Following Oslo and the influx of aid, the human rights industry has prospered and yet many Palestinians feel that this has alienated them from the narrative they first adopted during the First *Intifada*. Another way in which the paradox of institutionalisation set in following Oslo was through the establishment of the PA, which has had a further detrimental effect on the human rights movement in the OPT.

E. Human Rights Movement is Hijacked: The PA

Despite the peace talks, which caught the attention of the media globally, the Declaration of Principles (DOP) and the formalisation of Palestinian politics in the form of the PA seriously marred the human rights scene (Hajjar 2001). Firstly, it led to the disengagement of the populace with politics. Initially, the PA represented a step towards the achievement of Palestinian independence, but it was fiercely opposed by others such as the Islamic party Hamas. Following the signing of the Oslo Accords, Hamas accused Fatah of committing 'a great historic act of treason and a dangerous one … which has sold the struggle, sold the blood and sold the rights of the Palestinian people' (cited in

Schulz 1999: 111). This speech not only provides an example of how the rhetoric of rights was entrenched in Palestinian political discourse of the Islamic opposition party during the height of the human rights movement, but it also alludes to the potential for the institutionalisation of power to work against the rights of the people. Admittedly, Hamas's ideological vision of a historic Palestinian state was at stake if there were to be a West Bank–Gaza trade-off with Israel. Nonetheless, in the years which followed Oslo, it became increasingly apparent that the Palestinians were not the intended beneficiaries of the DOP (Zreik 2004).

According to Abdelnour (2010), the economic inequalities were enshrined in the act of signing the Paris Protocol of 1994 which left Palestinians ensnared in the Israeli economy and unable to evolve theirs. In hindsight, Oslo left many issues unresolved such as the question of the refugees and the uneven distribution of land (Milton-Edwards 2011). To this day, the PA govern exclusively only 18 per cent of the West Bank (Area A) compared with the 60 per cent (Area C) under entirely Israeli military control (Allen 2013), and the construction of Israeli settlements is ongoing (B'Tselem 2017a).[7] Rather than steering the Palestinian people towards establishing an independent state, the PA are increasingly perceived as Israel's security agent. As a result of Oslo, Israel maintained authority but relinquished the burden of responsibility, and the PA assumed the responsibilities of a state without ever receiving the sovereignty required to fulfil the duties of a state (Zreik 2004). Nevertheless, the PA tried to assert their authority over the people through the introduction of the death penalty, the mimicry of Israeli torture techniques in prisons, and the highly centralised authoritarian style of governance commenced by former President Yasser Arafat (Hajjar 2001), which is continued by the current President, Mahmoud Abbas (Bryman 2011). The institutionalisation of political power in the form of the PA led to the increase in cynicism towards the human rights regime.

The PA's security forces are required to undergo human rights training in order to make their state-building efforts appear legitimate to the international community. Many of whom receiving the training are also cynical of the human rights regime, and as Allen (2013: 101) claims, the training 'reiterates the superficiality of the PA's commitment to human rights'. And so, the PA became quickly known for their 'track record for corruption and nepotism rather than respect for human rights and democratic processes' (Darweish and Rigby 2015: 67). Since the establishment of the PA, there has been an ongoing rivalry between the party and HROs which pre-existed the Accords. As international aid flooded into the territories following the peace agreement, previous donors began to

[7] The remaining Area B, which makes up 22% of the West Bank is under joint control of Palestinian civil administration and Israeli security control (see Singer 2021).

favour the PA over the NGO sector (Hajjar 2001). In addition, HROs extended their confrontation of human rights violations committed by the occupying powers to include the aforementioned human rights abuses committed by the PA. The PA in response have accused those who scrutinise them as hindering the state-building efforts (Hajjar 2001).

F. Human Rights Discourse is Demonised as a Western Import: The PA

Inherent within the Palestinian nationalist narrative there is strong anti-Western sentiment, largely due to Western governments' ongoing support of Israel's oppressive policies. This, along with the increase in funding from the West for HROs, has often been perceived as a mode of colonialism. The PA, who dismissed human rights as Western imports, optimised this sentiment (Hajjar 2001). The tension between the PA and HROs is not only apparent in the competition for funds, but is also exemplified in the debate over who best serves the common good of the Palestinian community (Hajjar 2001). Ingrained in the human rights narrative is the awareness of the rights of both the individual and the collective whole. Conversely, the PA's narrative emphasised the obedience of the people through the promotion of 'unity, loyalty, and order' (Hajjar 2001: 29). This attempt to maintain order has been more recently embodied through the PA's crackdown on protests during the Arab Revolutions and the censorship of state media (see Amnesty International 2017a, 2017b). This has been exonerated by Israel, but condemned the local people who perceive it as yet another attempt at curbing their freedom (Allen 2013). Simultaneously, the PA have engaged in the 'display' of human rights performances to assert their legitimacy as a state, as well as to secure their funding, which ironically flows from the West. Even though some Palestinians view human rights as a foreign import, the PA knows that the appearance of respecting the role of human rights standards is necessary (Allen 2013). This leads again to the paradox of institutionalisation in which the quasi-state of the PA goes through the motions of respecting human rights whilst continuing to abuse them to secure funding from the West.

In sum, it is possible to trace the current cynicism in Palestine back to: the influx of foreign aid post-Oslo and the establishment of the PA. The failure of human rights NGOs and monitoring groups to end abuses committed by either the Israeli occupation or the PA, in conjunction with the lack of intervention from the international community (after Oslo) in the OPT, has led to an increased sense of disillusionment amongst Palestinians when it comes to human rights (Allen 2013). Many Palestinians view human rights system and its discourse as a rhetoric that has not fulfilled the emancipatory promises first made.

G. Human Rights Discourse Appropriated Nonetheless

Despite the rise in cynicism towards the human rights system, Palestinians continue to use the rights discourse as a tool by which to challenge the PA, the occupation and to internationalise the oppression they face. Allen (2013) suggests that this is because Palestinians possess a unique legacy of struggle for the rights of the people, a history of political mobility and a moral ethic of solidarity, so human rights discourse remains a powerful tool, which enables the effective articulation of their struggle and a way of claiming their national rights. A key example of this is the Boycott Divestments and Sanctions (BDS) grassroots movement which began in 2005 and has gained international attention. Barghouti (2011: 6), a co-founder of BDS, describes the movement as that which is:

> Anchored in international law and universal principles of human rights, adopts a comprehensive rights-based approach, underling in the fact that for the Palestinian people to exercise its right to self-determination, Israel must end its three forms of injustice that infringe international law and Palestinian rights.

This movement is clearly situated within the struggle for rights and is guided by the human rights discourse. Another example of how the language of human rights has been deployed as a vehicle of struggle against injustice can be found in the Gazan Youth's Manifesto for Change; this group engages with the numerous oppressive forces apparent to them by challenging the rights discourse through social media:

> Fuck Israel. Fuck Fatah. Fuck UN. Fuck UNRWA. Fuck USA! We, the youths of Gaza are so fed up with Israel, Hamas, the occupation, the violations of human rights and the indifference of the international community! (Carbajosa 2011).

Similarly, when President Obama travelled to the OPT in 2013; the youths who met with him addressed him, making frequent reference to their rights (Qutteneh et al 2013). The following young person from Nablus city stated:

> This was the message I sent to the leader of the free world, a message to tell the world that we are humans who are being tortured and disgraced. A message to tell the world that we have rights like everyone else (Qutteneh et al. 2013: 81).

More recently, youths in Gaza and those in the diaspora addressed the international community calling for an immediate ceasefire in the days following Israel's ongoing (at the time of writing) war on Gaza (see Figure 2.1).

These examples show how the younger generations are also appropriating human rights language into their struggles to engage actively with the international community, challenge the occupation, and address their own political parties. This outline of the Palestinian human rights discourse resonates with Baxi's (2000) claim that human rights take on multiple meanings at different occasions by different subjects. In an age when human rights has 'lost some of its romantic appeal and moral purity' (Moyn 2012), can this cynicism be traced among youths living in the occupied West Bank?

Figure 2.1 Ceasefire now (Shwaikh 2023)

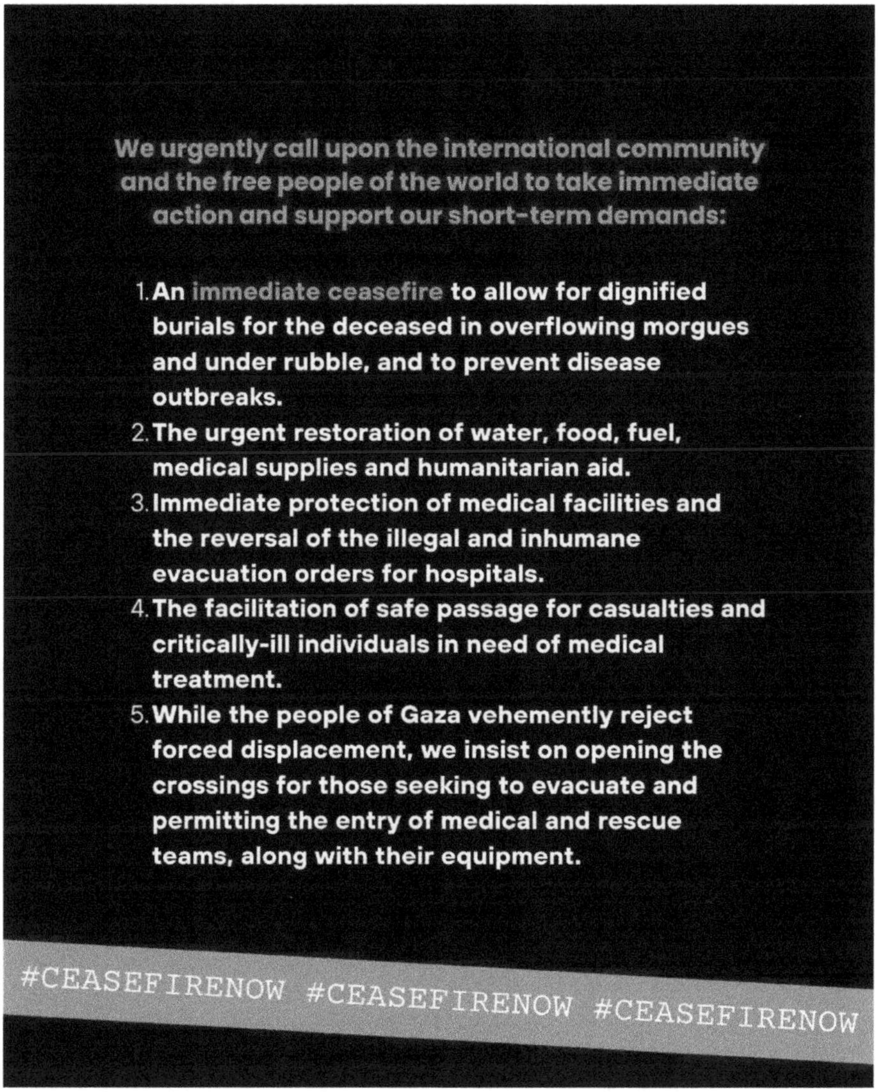

V. CONCLUSION

Tracing the lineage of human rights has revealed that a Eurocentric narrative has been privileged throughout the evolution of rights discourse, and more notably in the codification of human rights. It is a narrative that promotes universalism, individualism and rationalism, and one which continually seeks to obscure its complicity in colonialism. Caution towards the human rights system in non-Western contexts, such as Arab and Muslim-majority societies, is largely influenced by concerns around Western moral imperialism because of the legacy of European colonialism, Western hypocrisy in the human rights arena, and Western policies that have caused and continue to cause harm.

In the OPT, the ebb and flow of the Palestinian human rights movement alongside their experiences of human rights (more often denied) has led to the current state of cynicism towards the international human rights regime. Nonetheless, at the time the research for this book was conducted, it remained a discourse that had not been totally abandoned by Palestinians; this could have been because it was considered, 'the least bad available option' (Landy 2013: 424). However, during the ongoing war (at the time of writing) even this position has likely been deserted by many.

The next chapter considers whether HRE also privileges certain conceptualisations of human rights and whether it also gives primacy to Eurocentric theorisations and histories of human rights.

3

Human Rights Education: Narrow and Expansive Conceptualisations

I. INTRODUCTION

HUMAN RIGHTS EDUCATION (HRE) remains largely undertheorised and the discourse aspects of HRE has gained less attention in academic discussions (Zembylas and Keet 2018; Coysh 2017; Osler 2015). Throughout the literature on HRE there is a preoccupation with proposing definitions of HRE and models in order to categorise approaches to HRE. However, few scholars problematise the fact that the content privileged in HRE often reflects a narrow conceptualisation of human rights, marginalising other possibilities within the broader rights discourse. In this chapter, I explore how the UN's vision of HRE as a peace-building tool has led to the promotion of a Eurocentric, decontextualised and preventative narrative. This chapter examines how transformative approaches to HRE may help to expand conceptualisations of HRE and orient learners towards action but also how this may become hampered once institutionalised.

Whilst some authors argue that there is no global concept of HRE (Flowers 2003; Lohrenscheit 2002), this chapter illuminates how a global HRE, which is declarationalist and Eurocentric, has been institutionalised by the UN and uncritically adopted by governments, academics and non-government organisations (NGOs). I argue that human rights and by extension HRE needs to undergo a process of decolonisation and the supposed universality of human rights need to be contested through 'pluriversalising' (Zembylas 2017a; Mignolo 2006) the discourse to create space for the counter-narratives of the colonised to be not only included but foregrounded.

In section VII of this chapter, I briefly explore some of the reasons why Palestinian young people are more likely to encounter restricted and depoliticised rights narratives through HRE and one which focuses on learning *about* rather than *for* human rights. I argue that HRE needs to be critiqued and renewed not only by human rights theorists and practitioners but also by learners themselves, and that in order to achieve this, conceptualisations of human rights presented in HRE need to be expanded.

Prior to discussing these issues, I begin with an overview of Dembour's (2010) four schools of thought towards human rights. I then employ this taxonomy as a lens through which to critique the various models and definitions of HRE.

II. DEMBOUR'S FOUR SCHOOLS OF THOUGHT

Whilst the international human rights scheme is often portrayed as the 'depoliticized original', often uncritically accepted and legitimised by the international community (Perugini and Gordon 2015: 15), it is not the only construction of human rights possible. Goodale (2007: 7) proposes that a 'restricted' orientation towards human rights centralises the law and upholds the belief that human rights are defined neatly by international legal instruments. At the other end of this continuum is the 'expansive' approach to human rights in which the role of the law ceases to be the sole focus but rather human rights discourse itself (Goodale 2007: 7). The lens through which a person views human rights, consequently, will affect the manner in which they regard aspects such as the universality of or the role of the law in rights. The subject to whom rights belong, as well as their degree of faith in human rights altogether, can alter according to the expansive or restricted orientation one adopts in relation to rights (Goodale 2007). Dembour (2010) provides a useful framework for analysing rights discourse in more detail, identifying specific schools which lie along this spectrum. She proposes that there are four main schools of thought: *natural*, *deliberative*, *protest*, and *discourse*. This framework will be examined, revisited and adapted to analyse the particularities of the Palestinian context throughout the course of this book. For now, an outline of Dembour's (2010) taxonomy is presented.

Dembour (2010) describes four schools of thought in relation to how human rights are understood: by the claims that rights are universal; the foundation for rights; how they are realised, if at all; the role of human rights law; and degree of faith in human rights. Dembour (2010: 1) suggests that for *natural* scholars, human rights are understood as that which is *given*; for *deliberative* scholars human rights are *agreed upon*; *protest* scholars conceive of human rights as *fought for*; and for *discourse* scholars human rights are understood as *talked about*. Dembour (2010) also provides a visual model of the four schools which illustrates the human rights conceptual field (see Figure 3.1). She explains that the *natural* and *protest* schools, which sit at the top half of the schema, view human rights transcendentally whereas the *deliberative* and *discourse* schools consider human rights as a reality that is based on society or language. Subsequently, the *natural* and *deliberative* schools, situated on the left-hand side of the model, adopt a liberal and individualistic orientation towards human rights compared to the *protest* and *discourse* schools, which adopt a collective orientation of social justice (Dembour 2010).

Figure 3.1 What are human rights? (Based on Dembour 2010: 5)

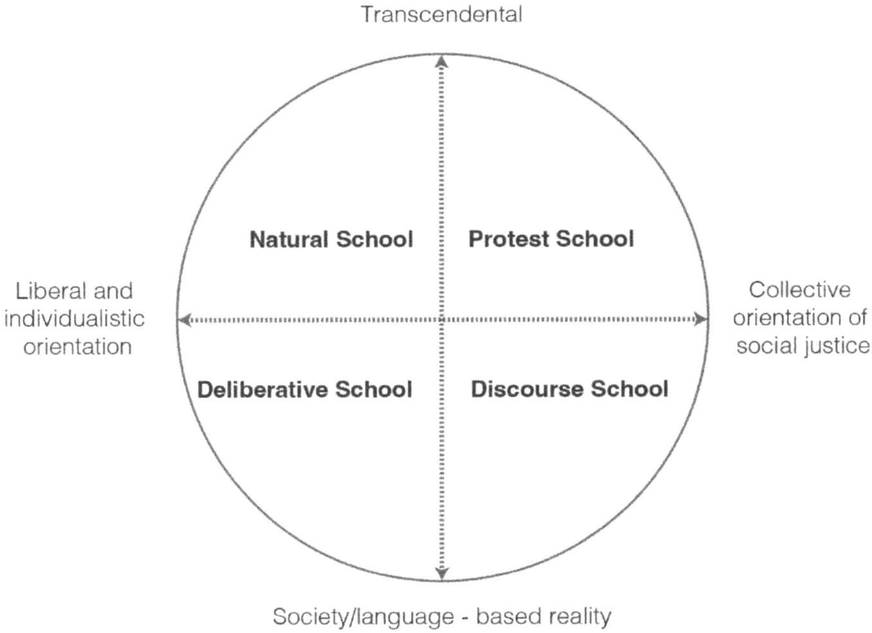

The *natural* school believes in the universality of human rights of which the individual is central. Its view that human rights are individual entitlements is encapsulated in Donelly's (1989: 49) oft-quoted claim that 'human rights are the rights one simply has because one is a human being'. For this school, human rights are built upon a moral or metaphysical foundation in which nature, God or reason are the source of these entitlements that are bestowed upon every human being (Dembour 2010). This school esteems human rights law and believes that human rights concepts are manifested therein. These scholars also mark the development of international law since 1948 as progress. Notably, this school holds the belief that there are societies that can and do exist where human rights are largely upheld and, where this is not the case, that they can be formed. *Natural* scholars have faith in human rights and according to Dembour's (2010: 3) religious analogy they represent human rights orthodoxy. This school and their conceptualisations of human rights have traditionally dominated academic discussions. However, the *deliberative* school has increasingly begun to assume this responsibility.

Deliberative scholars believe in the potential for the universality of human rights as consensus expands (Dembour 2010). However, this school rejects the natural foundation of the *natural* school and replaces this with the belief that human rights are birthed when they are seen as valuable and acknowledged through 'societal agreement' (Dembour 2010: 3). Ignatieff (2001), who is identified as a *deliberative* scholar by Dembour (2010), contends that universalism should not be based upon a metaphysical foundation as the *natural* school proposes, but rather upon a pragmatic one in response to human suffering. For *deliberative* scholars, human rights can be realised through fair political structures, processes and the law; therefore, the notion that human rights can be possessed does not align with this school's mode of thinking. This school views human rights as it is defined and articulated in human rights law. Thus, the use of the law and political participation will lead to the realisation of human rights. Although this school is committed to furthering human rights, they do not necessarily believe in them in the way that *natural* and *protest* scholars do. In her religious analogy, Dembour (2010) compares this school to secularism.

Unlike the *deliberative* school, human rights as seen within the *protest* school are not agreed upon, but *struggled for*, and the law is often viewed with suspicion. Human rights belong primarily to those who face oppression, injustice or poverty (Dembour 2010). The foundation upon which this school bases human rights can be metaphysical, as is found in the *natural* school. However, there are some within this school of thought who endorse the idea that rights are learned, hence this school's interest in human rights education (Dembour 2010). Although the suffering individual is the central subject of human rights, they fear that once an individual's rights are realised and enjoyed, that he or she may become apathetic concerning the rights of others – namely the oppressed. This is perceived as 'a betrayal of the human rights concept' (Dembour 2010: 8). Therefore, in contrast to the *natural* school, they do not view human rights as entitlements that individuals are 'selfishly at liberty to claim' for oneself, but instead are realised through a continual struggle for their realisation (Dembour 2010: 8). This school is wary of human rights law since it can be easily manipulated by elites and thus can fail to embody human rights ideals. This highlights a broader tendency amongst *protest* scholars who often distrust institutions including human rights organisations (HROs) to remain faithful to 'true' human rights ideals. Similar to the *natural* school, *protest* scholars have faith in human rights concepts; however, they are indignant about the way human rights are institutionalised and therefore deviate from their ideal. Dembour (2010) names them as the liberation theologians in her religious analogy.

According to the *discourse* school, human rights only exist when they are discussed; therefore, they are based upon language (Dembour 2010). Scholars from this tradition do not discuss the realisation of human rights since they lack faith in them. Instead, they are preoccupied with making the case that human rights are a promise-laden rhetoric which fails to fulfil its claims. They tend to view human rights law with an air of indifference in that it is no different than any other forms of law. This school is frustrated with those who make pretentious universal claims about human rights. They also regard the deliberative school's rhetoric of reaching agreement with caution because they believe that a focus on consensus can lead to concealing power relations (Dembour 2010).

Similar to the *protest* school, they believe human rights ought to belong to those who are oppressed; however, they are disillusioned with the inadequacy of human rights discourse to deliver its promise of achieving equality for all (Dembour 2010). This school is particularly preoccupied with the notion that human rights are a form of moral imperialism which the West seeks to impose elsewhere. In accordance with this, they are keen to point out the shortcoming of individualistic conceptualisations of human rights. *Discourse* scholars are compared with nihilists, in that whilst they do not believe in human rights, they are eager for the formation of a new model to replace the human rights regime since it has deviated from its original aims.

It is important to acknowledge that the aim of presenting these four schools is not to claim that it is possible to neatly compartmentalise scholars, but rather to provide a helpful framework which highlights the variety of viewpoints which exists within rights discourse. This discussion of the four schools highlights the fact that there is no singular agreed-upon definition of what human rights truly are amongst academics. It is also likely that there is no agreed upon conceptualisation amongst '"lay" people's accounts' (Stenner 2011: 1218). Similarly, just as Dembour (2010) stresses the fact scholars may shift their positioning, so may those who are not academics.

But what about HRE? Is a restrictive or expansive orientation towards human rights privileged?

III. A PREOCCUPATION WITH MODELS OF HRE

Whilst there is no shortage of definitions of HRE, there is an overall lack of a global consensus on what HRE is or ought to be, and consequently an array of approaches has been adopted (McEvoy and Lundy 2007; Flowers 2003). Ahmed (2021) suggests that three types of scholarship in HRE have emerged: diffusion, classification and critical scholars. Diffusion scholars (Russell et al 2019; Meyer et al 2010; Suárez 2007) are primarily interested in the diffusion of universal human rights values into national curricular and textbooks. This scholarship often measures this via quantitative methods that focus on and compare HRE across multi-country sites. Classification scholars (Tibbitts 2017a, 2002; Bajaj 2011a; Flowers 2004; Tarrow 1992) are concerned with categorising HRE pedagogical approaches. Classification and diffusion scholars tend to view HRE with optimism compared to critical scholars (Ahmed et al 2020; Ahmed 2018; Sirota 2017; Zembylas 2015, 2017b; Keet 2012, 2015; Cardenas, 2005), who raise concerns about the potential negative impacts of HRE and its dubious relationship to power. Since this chapter critiques the way HRE adopts largely a 'restrictive' orientation towards human rights, marginalising more 'expansive' conceptualisations (Goodale 2007: 7), this chapter focuses on classification and critical scholarship.

First, I will provide an outline of the main (and oft cited) models proposed by Tibbitts (2002), Flowers (2003) and Bajaj (2011a), and more recent analysis proposed by Coysh (2017), which focus variously on the aims, audience and ideological positioning of the purpose of HRE. A discussion of one of the most common cross-cutting approaches to the content of HRE programmes (education *about*, *for* and *through* human rights) is discussed and a rationale for using Dembour's (2010) framework to analyse the conceptualisations of *human rights* in HRE models and approaches is provided.

Tibbitts (2002), in her evaluation of global HRE outlines three models, which focus on the approach adopted: *values and awareness*; *accountability*; and *transformational*. She claims that the *values and awareness* approach seeks to familiarise individuals with legal frameworks, promoting the legitimacy of these legal instruments and encouraging commitment to these values. This is often done through a historical and philosophical lens in which global issues are examined, and it is often the model adopted by schools. According to Tibbitts (2002), the *accountability* model tends to be adopted by those in a professional context already affiliated with human rights issues (security forces, police, lawyers) in which primary attention is devoted to the law and the realisation of it in the context in which they are operational. The aim of this model is to further enable and enhance the work of these professionals in monitoring human rights violations and advocacy (Tibbitts 2002). The *transformational* approach, according to Tibbitts (2002), is commonly appropriated in contexts in which human rights are threatened or have already been denied. This model may combine other programmes such as conflict resolution and can be found in post-conflict societies or refugee camps (Tibbitts 2002). Tibbitts (2002) argues that if HRE is to contribute effectively towards the development of a human rights culture it must bring together aspects of these three models in the construction of HRE programmes.

Flowers' (2003) model is based on her contention that three groups portray definitions of human rights education differently: governments, NGOs and academics. Governments are driven by achieving aims and objectives and often adopt a legal tone. They place an emphasis on the 'rights' of human rights education as opposed to the educational element. Additionally, according to Flowers (2003), governmental constructions of HRE stress their responsibility as the state to oversee correctly the appropriate implementation of HRE. This can inevitably be forged in a way that works advantageously for the state powers involved (Flowers 2003). Unlike the definitions offered by state authorities, NGOs are far more willing to confront power structures through HRE. NGOs thus adopt a more subversive tone with the aim of empowering marginalised groups to prevent further violations of rights. However, Flowers (2003: 8) highlights the potential for this approach to lead to cynicism because of making promises which are not necessarily deliverable, observing that: 'to claim that HRE can lead to controlling corporations is to court disillusionment'. Similarly, states that make grandiose claims that HRE results in world peace are also potentially misleading and idealistic to the detriment of HRE (Flowers 2003). Finally, according to Flowers (2003), academics place a greater stress on the 'human' component of HRE and adopt a more abstract or theoretical approach. There is a preoccupation with the location of HRE within the broader curricular and whether it ought to break away from citizenship education as a subject in its own right. This group may well stress the importance of comprehending human rights; often it is implied by academics that human rights are a 'self-evident value system' and the assumption is made that they are universally applicable (Flowers 2003: 8).

Bajaj (2011a) also formulated a model which, unlike previous taxonomies, can be used to assess the ideological positioning behind an approach to HRE. She argues that most HRE programmes stem from ideological positionings, which are linked with the following three approaches: *HRE for Global Citizenship*; *HRE for Co-existence*; and *HRE for Transformative Action* (Bajaj 2011a). In brief, the *HRE for Global Citizenship* model includes conventions and legal instruments, stressing the universality of rights whilst situating learners as members of an international community with an emphasis on interdependency. The *HRE for Coexistence* approach prioritises narratives and the rights of groups who have been disenfranchised, and aims to foster empathy among learners. This model views HRE as a vehicle for reconciliation and may involve intergroup contact. It is often adopted in societies which have emerged from conflict. Additionally, the *HRE for Transformative Action* model centralises agency and solidarity to confront injustices. Examples of rights violations faced by vulnerable communities may make up part of the content; subsequent participation may include intervention in instances of injustice, collaboration with NGOs, or assembling in demonstrations. Importantly, these categories are not meant to be mutually exclusive, but elements from each can be combined within the one HRE initiative (Bajaj 2011a).

Coysh (2017) argues that HRE can take on four discursive orientations: technical, interpretive, critical and counter-hegemonic. These approaches rely upon different assumptions regarding 'whose knowledge counts, the exercise of power and how social change happens' (Coysh 2014: 23). Underpinning a *technical* HRE discourse is the construction of human rights as pre-existing 'facts' and the importance of transmitting these so-called neutral facts, such as human rights norms and standards, to learners in an accessible and relevant way (Coysh 2017). This approach relies upon two claims: firstly, that everyone is born with human rights; and secondly, that human rights as defined in the UDHR are universal (Coysh 2017). This form of HRE often practices a '*banking* style of education';[1] and whilst certain educators may strive to avoid this approach by employing more participatory methods, this, contends Coysh (2017), only acts as a masquerade.

[1] This is a term coined by Paulo Friere (1970), who uses a metaphor to describe learners as empty vessels which educators must pour knowledge into.

Guiding an *interpretive* orientation towards HRE is the notion that human rights can take on different meanings, but that these meanings can be negotiated to reach agreement. Therefore, for this approach HRE should involve 'reflective inquiry and deliberation' (Coysh 2017: 141). This orientation can be found in post-conflict contexts and in UN peace-building initiatives through efforts to highlight cross-cultural agreement between communities. This model may also involve efforts to identify how cultural traditions may harmonise with international human rights but also acknowledge where they do not. The interpretive approach, however, often regards institutions such as the UN as the legitimate authors of human rights and thereby may fail to recognise the '*hidden power*' that may exist within these institutional forms and within society (Coysh 2017: 34).

For Coysh (2017), the *critical* HRE orientation, unlike the *technical* approach, does not allot distinct roles to educators and learners, but rather views everyone as co-constructors of knowledge. It is inspired by critical pedagogical theory and propelled by the notion of praxis. A core aim of this approach is the notion of struggle and carving 'a space and voice for and engaging actively in it [struggle]' (Coysh 2017: 37). Consequently, this orientation demands that the disenfranchised become the 'primary authors' of the rights discourse as opposed to states and elites.

Finally, a *counter-hegemonic* HRE is characterised by its lack of respect for and trust of the human rights regime. Underpinning this orientation is the view that human rights are socio-historical constructions which are 'part of a dominant ideological hegemonic culture aimed at maintaining the status quo and regulating society' (Coysh 2017: 39). This orientation seeks to dismantle and disrupt forms of 'dominant knowledge', and education must provide learners with the ability to oppose 'colonization of the mind' by institutions at local and global levels (Coysh 2017: 43). It is unlikely that formal education can facilitate a counter-hegemonic orientation towards HRE due to its ambiguous relationship with the state.

As noted above, cutting across the HRE models, it is generally agreed by scholars and practitioners that the content of HRE should include learning *about*, *through* and *for* human rights (McEvoy and Lundy 2007; Lohrenscheit 2002): an approach endorsed by the UN in its Declaration on Human Rights Education and Training (UNDHRET) (UNGA 2011). In this construction of HRE, learning *about* human rights refers to the acquisition of knowledge about human rights such as the genealogy and principles of human rights, key international human rights documents, and how monitoring mechanisms work (Lohrenscheit 2002). Learning *through* human rights relates to the classroom and school culture as well as pedagogical methods and the need for these to embody the spirit of human rights (Tibbitts 2017b). Learning *for* human rights is the action-oriented dimension of HRE in which learners are empowered to take action for their own rights and the rights of others (Bajaj 2011a).

Discussions of this within the literature tend to be dedicated towards using these three components of HRE as a tool by which to *assess* a given HRE project (see for example Amnesty International 2017c; Froman 2015). Whilst this three-pronged structure is undoubtedly useful for deconstructing the content and delivery of HRE programmes, it does not however provide an adequate framework through which to engage critically with the particular conceptualisation of HRE (and indeed human rights themselves) favoured or promoted through such programmes. Rather, HRE, once institutionalised, can become driven by the agendas of governments and aid organisations which implement, develop and fund these HRE programmes (Bajaj 2011a).

What is apparent from this analysis is that models and approaches to HRE tend to focus on its *purposes* and *processes* (McEvoy and Lundy 2007), with more recent models attending to how HRE is *conceptualised*. Overall, less attention is given to how human rights themselves are conceptualised within HRE approaches.

IV. NARROW CONCEPTUALISATIONS OF HUMAN RIGHTS AND HRE: A CRITIQUE OF THE DOMINANT DISCOURSES

Exploring the content that is included and prioritised within different approaches to HRE offers clues as to the underlying conceptualisations of human rights (and HRE) which are shaping not only these individual models but also influencing global HRE discourse. It also offers insight into the extent to which learners are being given opportunities to engage critically with human rights and the broader human rights discourse, as well as whether they are being oriented towards action *for* human rights. As Ahmed (2021) points out, HRE approaches are not necessarily informed by the views and experiences of the subjects of HRE, but rather the aims of those who develop HRE programmes. The models discussed in the previous section (Coysh 2017; Bajaj 2011a; Flowers 2003; Tibbitts 2002) will now be analysed by exploring the following themes: first, the centrality of UN statements and international law; and second, the promotion of the UN's vision of HRE as a peace-building tool. Discussion of the latter reveals how this vision is dominated by a Eurocentric narrative which *decontextualises* human rights and presents HRE as a conduit for *preventing* future violations rather than as a tool for empowering learners to redress injustices.

The centrality of UN statements and international law can be traced in global HRE. HRE definitions and models preferred largely by international bodies, governments and academics privilege what could be referred to as a 'restricted' conceptualisation of HRE or, to use Coysh's (2017) term, a *technical* HRE discourse. This can be seen by the way most approaches to HRE (such as those that adopt a *values and awareness* model (Tibbitts 2002), or a *HRE for Global Citizenship* model (Bajaj 2011a), for example inter-governmental and governmental bodies (Flowers 2003)) seek to, firstly, familiarise learners with legal frameworks, UN statements, and international, regional and national rights documents, and, secondly, promote their legitimacy; and thirdly, foster commitment to these values.

This offers some clues as to how human rights are conceptualised in these approaches to HRE. According to Dembour (2010), natural scholars view human rights law as that which encapsulates and corresponds to human rights concepts. Similarly, deliberative scholars share a regard for the role of human rights law in guiding decisions made within the political realm. Furthermore, these scholars view the law as 'their typical if not only mode of existence' (Dembour 2010: 11). On the contrary, protest scholars are suspicious of human rights law and its relationship to power. The discourse school has a more nonchalant attitude towards human rights law, viewing it as no more significant than other laws. Additionally, natural and deliberate scholars both regard human rights law following 1948 as 'definite progress' (Dembour 2010). In doing so, they simultaneously endorse the UN as the 'author' and 'guardian' of international human rights (Freeman 2017: 10) without necessarily critiquing what the UN has authored and its legitimacy as a guardian.

Nonetheless, the way in which the natural and deliberative schools believe rights are conceived differs. For natural scholars, rights are *given* whereas for deliberative scholars, rights are *agreed upon*. In other words, for the natural school, human rights are universal entitlements which exist irrespective of whether they have been agreed upon by society (Dembour 2010). This provides a further indication that it is the natural school's conceptualisation of human rights, which is given primacy through these approaches to HRE. This is suggested by the way HRE often dismisses the discord which might exist between the lists of rights as codified in international law compared to the extent to which a learner's own society and government have actually agreed upon them. Therefore, learners are seldom given the opportunity to critically engage with rights concepts and explore other options available to them in this broader discourse, such as the protest scholar's view that rights are *fought for* or simply *talked about* according to the discourse school.

Bajaj (2011a), who also correlates HRE models including her own with Dembour's four schools of thought, helpfully points out that this notion of reaching agreement is often disregarded in HRE since learners are taught about rights as though they are absolutes. Consequently, whilst these approaches, often taken by international HRE initiatives, can stem from natural and deliberative conceptualisations of human rights, the implementation often resembles the natural school's approach to HRE due to the way they are presented as a *given*. This resonates with Dembour's (2010) own choice of religious analogy when depicting this school as human rights 'orthodoxy', along with her observations that these scholars have been historically responsible for defining the mainstream version of how human rights ought to be conceptualised. Arguably, making international human rights standards a central component of HRE also presents human rights from a universalist perspective in which rights were only 'meaningfully born' in 1948 (Stammers 2009: 22). This also has implications for the way in which scholars, governments and inter-governmental organisations (IGOs) will view the primary purpose of HRE.

I now turn to how the UN's vision of HRE as a peace-building tool has led to the promotion of a Eurocentric, decontextualised and preventative narrative.

It is generally acknowledged that human rights have the potential to address violent conflict and instigate stability (see McEvoy and Lundy 2007). Thus, HRE has increasingly come to be regarded as playing a key role in the rebuilding of societies emerging from conflict and in the promotion of peace (Ahmed 2021; Pinto 2014). This emphasis on the potential of HRE as a peace-building tool is also reflected across several HRE models. Flowers (2003), for example, contends that inter-governmental and governmental organisations offer definitions of human rights which stress the importance of HRE in promoting peace, stability and order. This resonates with the *HRE for Co-existence* model proposed by Bajaj (2011a), which views HRE as a vehicle for reconciliation and seeks to foster empathy among learners through a largely apolitical approach to human rights. It is often adopted in societies which have emerged from conflict. Similarly, *HRE for Transformative Action* (Bajaj 2011a) or *Transformative* (Tibbitts 2002) models also view HRE as having the potential to reduce violence and progress peace. Consequently, most HRE models recognise that HRE is seen as a tool which works to promote peace; however, how they seek to achieve this differs. It is helpful therefore to reflect briefly upon how this vision emerged within the UN's first definitions of HRE.

The emphasis on instigating peace among peoples was of central importance to the UN's initial definition of HRE since the world was emerging from the brutality of two World Wars. Alongside the drafting of the UDHR in 1948, attention was also given to the need to develop HRE. Article 26(2) of the UDHR outlines the requirement that education should be aimed at:

> The strengthening of respect for human rights and fundamental freedoms. It shall promote understanding, tolerance and friendship among all nations, racial or religious groups, and shall further the activities of the UN for the maintenance of peace (UNGA 1948).

Interestingly, a range of NGOs were involved in the drafting of the UDHR and it was during this process that the representative of the World Jewish Congress, AL Easterman, prompted the amendment of the original version of Article 26 to include the notion that part of the right to education should also include education about human rights (Roth 2009). Easterman claimed that the original version: '[P]rovided a technical framework but contained nothing about the spirit governing education which was an essential element. Neglect of this principle in Germany had been the main cause of two catastrophic wars' (cited in Roth 2009: 142). Once more, it is evident that the atrocities of the World Wars and those committed in the Holocaust, were linked closely to the UN's initial definition of HRE. Notably, the connection between the Holocaust and human rights is often made by human rights educationalists who portray these events as a catalyst for the drafting of UDHR (Morsink 2010). This aligns with the views of natural and deliberative scholars who regard 1948 a milestone in the development of human rights (Dembour 2010). This serves as a further indicator that more 'restricted' conceptualisations of human rights dominate HRE. However, simply tracing the lineage of rights back to key moments in Western history, such as the Holocaust, undermines other histories of struggles for rights which pre-date these events. Moreover, it conveniently disregards the fact that the Eurocentric rights narrative also developed out of the history of brutal colonialism (Zembylas 2017b).

The institutionalisation of human rights by the UN required the 'subjugation of particular types of knowledge' (Coysh 2017: 141). HRE was formally defined at the same time as the UDHR; however, it was not until the World Conference in Vienna in 1993 that it gained significant attention, resulting in the United Nations Decade for Human Rights Education being proclaimed two years later (UNGA 1993). Out of the World Conference, a plan for a global HRE was developed, which arguably led to the institutionalisation of HRE (Sliwinski 2005). This Plan of Action for the UN Decade for HRE (1994–2004) paved the way for the UN to control and regulate an official global construction of HRE (Coysh 2017). The UN's own form of HRE has been largely embraced without critique by both academics and practitioners (Coysh 2017). Consequently, not only has a narrow or technical conceptualisation of HRE been privileged, but also a Eurocentric narrative. Arguably, the Global North seeks to assert its ownership of the human rights discourse and in doing so promotes this Eurocentric conceptualisation of human rights as the legitimate version to be emulated by other traditions. That is why TWAIL-ers and decolonial scholars such as Barreto (2013a), Baxi (2007) and Douzinas (2000), Mutua (2002) argue that human rights need to undergo decolonisation (Zembylas 2017a). This argument will be unpacked later in this chapter. Prior to that, it is helpful to explore how promoting the UN's vision of HRE as a universal peace-building implement can also result in exposing learners to a decontextualised human rights discourse.

HRE for Global Citizenship approaches often lead learners to understand human rights in a 'de-territorialized' manner because of the way they are positioned as members of a global community (Bajaj 2011a: 492). Bajaj (2011a) also makes links between Dembour's four schools and her framework, claiming that the *HRE for Global Citizenship* model may appeal more to natural and deliberate scholars. Moreover, emphasising the role of HRE as a universally applicable peace-building tool also presents learners with a depoliticised rights narrative removed from their own personal context (Barreto 2013b). Flowers (2003) contends that governmental organisations also offer definitions of human rights which stress the importance of HRE in promoting peace, stability and order. This global decontextualised conceptualisation of HRE can appeal to governments which do not want to promote or nurture the more adversarial aspects of the rights discourse, which may in turn disrupt the status quo and thwart 'peace' (or in other words 'order') over civil society. Since governments are accountable to the UN for the implementation of HRE, it is unsurprising that the UN's vision of HRE has been largely incorporated into government definitions of HRE and the UN understandably applauds this. However, Cardenas (2005) scrutinises the ambiguous role of the state in furthering and developing HRE since once HRE is institutionalised the state can hinder the revolutionary aims of HRE. Models which uphold the UN's vision of HRE as a depoliticising peace-building tool are arguably less inclined to position their learners towards learning *for* human rights.

UN definitions of HRE are aimed at governing bodies therefore they are centred on a more top-down model of what HRE is and ought to be (Bajaj 2011a). Arguably, their approach towards educating learners about human rights has reflected their top-down approach more generally. Gerber (2004) argues that in the UDHR, the UN focused on making rights known to learners so that they would respect the rights of others rather than making rights known to learners in order to empower learners to contest rights violations. Gerber (2004) also maintains that the UN has largely continued to emphasise this more preventative aspect of HRE, which can be perceived as disregarding the potential agency of the individual.

As mentioned previously, the natural school is largely guided by UN definitions of human rights, and since most HRE programmes are arguably aligned to this school of thought it is unsurprising that such programmes have also embraced the UN's vision of HRE as a 'preventative' peace-building tool. Furthermore, this top-down orientation towards how rights are realised will impact upon whether learners are oriented towards action or not more generally, but also when it comes to engaging with conflict and pursuing peace. This also resonates with how Pinto (2014) describes Bajaj's (2011a) *HRE for Co-existence* approach as a 'preventative' model which is aimed at reforming the attitudes of learners towards the 'other' rather than aiming to empower learners to redress the structural causes of conflict. IGOs and governments are also more likely to adopt 'preventative' top-down approaches towards promoting peace through HRE such as the *HRE for Global Citizenship* or *HRE for Co-existence* approaches to HRE. Consequently, they are less likely to orient their learners towards action since this could pose a risk to existent power structures. HRE models and definitions which are universalist and 'declarationalist' (Keet 2010) may not enable learners to grapple with the inconsistencies that they may encounter between rights ideals and their everyday experiences. As a result, learners are not given the opportunity to interrogate asymmetrical power relations nor to engage critically with human rights discourse. This is problematic since it is arguably a learner's context which gives meaning to rights struggles in the first place rather than abstract legal documents (Zreik 2004).

Flowers (2003: 8) contends that academics have also enabled this UN-centric (top-down) depoliticised definition of HRE to become 'formalised' as they tend to view HRE as an 'ethical framework for universal application', rarely interrogating its theoretical foundations, but rather viewing human rights as a 'self-evident value system'. However, Flowers' (2003) categorisation of 'academics' should be defined more specifically as 'natural and deliberative academics', since there are scholars who do question the theoretical underpinnings of HRE. For instance, protest scholars are wary of human rights institutions – including the UN – and question their dubious relationship to power as well as their ability to deliver the human rights ideal (Dembour 2010). They argue that once institutionalised, human rights can be utilised as instruments to exert power over individuals rather than as a vehicle by which one can contest power (Sharma and Gupta 2006). This process is what Stammers (2009: 115) terms the 'paradox of institutionalisation'. He explores how power relations can become ambiguous since human rights can act as tools for good on the one hand and for the justification of the abuse of human rights on the other hand – often simultaneously (see also, Landy 2013).

Similarly, Ahmed (2021) refers to HRE as tactics and HRE as sovereignty. HRE as tactics refers to the way in which states, NGOs, educationalists, minoritised groups and the UN can all deploy HRE as vehicle to foster agency and enable action for human rights and as a means to hinder state power. In contrast, HRE as sovereignty refers to how human rights can be drawn upon to consolidate power or to justify certain actions. This can be witnessed among far-right civil society groups, states and corporations that draw on human rights discourse. Classification scholars may acknowledge HRE as sovereignty but tend to underplay its significance, instead recognising HRE as tactics to further the realisation of human rights for all (Ahmed 2021).

These analyses of how human rights discourse can be deployed as a tool to entrench power of certain actors, problematise Flowers' (2003: 8) claim that all academics accept HRE as a 'self-evident value system'. However, what her argument does highlight is how scholarship on HRE is dominated by natural and deliberative schools of thought, resonating with Dembour's (2010) observation of the traditional prevalence of the natural narrative within academic discussions. However, Dembour (2010) contends that deliberative scholars seem to be increasingly overtaking the prevalence of natural scholars. She also contends that protest scholars, whilst less prevalent than natural and deliberative ones, are more present in academic discussions than discourse scholars since they still have faith in and seek to advance the notion of human rights. Arguably, this is connected to the fact that human rights scholarship has been driven largely by two main disciplines: philosophy and law (Stammers 2009). According to Stammers (2009), philosophical traditions often focus on the canonised texts of male European thinkers and disregard grassroots social struggles. Legal scholars are also unconcerned with social activism unless this crosses over into the legal realm: they are concerned with legal texts. Therefore, it is perhaps unsurprising that a more 'restricted' conceptualisation of HRE seems to be privileged in scholarship models, and definitions and more 'expansive' approaches are sidelined (Goodale 2007).

Therefore, analysis of the content of HRE used by different models has illuminated how a natural school's conceptualisation of human rights underpins the majority of non-transformative HRE approaches. This dominant discourse exposes learners to a largely UN-centric, Eurocentric, decontextualised narrative which hinders the agency of learners and their ability to interrogate the theoretical foundations and the problematic aspects of rights discourse.

Bowring (2012: 63) argues that history has displayed that knowledge about human rights (whilst necessary) remains 'mere rhetorical froth, unless you fight for it'. With this in mind, do *transformative* approaches to HRE better position learners to critically engage with rights discourse and mobilise them to engage in human rights praxis?

V. EXPANDING CONCEPTUALISATIONS OF HRE THROUGH TRANSFORMATIVE APPROACHES

Transformative models of HRE tend to adopt a more bottom-up approach towards teaching about human rights. According to Tibbitts (2002), the *transformational* HRE model views an action-oriented dimension of HRE as an essential component. This can be likened to *HRE for Transformative Action* proposed by Bajaj (2011a), which centralises agency and solidarity to confront injustices. The aims of a *transformative* approach may differ slightly depending on the situation of the learners. If the learners are victims of rights abuses, this model of HRE may seek to empower them to challenge the oppressive power structures they face. Alternatively, if learners are not frequent victims of rights violations, they may be empowered to act on behalf of or in solidarity with marginalised groups in what Bajaj (2011a: 495) terms 'coalitional agency'. In a conflict-affected society, a *transformative* approach will seek to position learners towards action to reduce structural violence and confront rights violations (Pinto 2014). Nonetheless, regardless of the context, *transformative* approaches to HRE are concerned with learning not only *about* but *for* human rights. Thus, those who adopt a *transformative* approach to HRE may reflect the protest school's conceptualisation of human rights in which rights are claims which enable the oppressed to confront those in positions of power (Dembour 2010). Protest scholars contend that the fight for human rights is a perpetual struggle, a 'project always in the making' (Dembour 2010: 8) or as Bowring (2012: 63) articulates: 'human rights were born, and come back to life again and again, through an unending struggle against oppression, exploitation, inequality and discrimination'.

Flowers (2003) contends that NGOs are more likely to adopt a *transformative* approach to HRE, since they are more willing than the state to confront power structures through grassroots HRE initiatives. They can adopt a more subversive tone with the aim of empowering marginalised groups to prevent further violations of rights, including those committed by the state (Flowers 2003). However, certain NGOs might be reliant upon foreign aid or governmental funding, which means they must meet the objectives set out by their funders, and inevitably, this can entangle them in a specific political agenda. This has been the case in the Palestinian context, where NGOs, to meet the requirements of foreign aid donors, have depoliticised and de-historicised Palestinians and their struggle, and ultimately denied them political agency (Allen 2013; Landy 2013; Roy 2012). The Western development model has caused harm to Palestinians and, along with Oslo aid, has relieved Israel of the financial burden of ongoing occupation; it has also subsidised its colonial expansion in the OPT (Tatir 2023). Consequently, whilst NGOs may be more inclined to adopt transformative approaches to HRE this is not necessarily a given.

Coysh (2017) explores the complex position within which NGOs are often situated in relation to the global and the local. She argues that HRE discourse occupies three spaces: 'the global (UN), the intermediate (NGO) and the local (community)' (Coysh 2017: 151). She claims that NGOs are free to choose whether to adopt or resist the UN's centralised global discourse or to draw upon knowledge which already exists within an indigenous or marginalised community. Coysh also contends that the distribution of the dominant UN-centric vision of rights is dependent upon 'intermediaries' who can straddle the global and the local. She claims that NGOs have increasingly assumed this intermediary role. Thus, the relationship between the state and NGOs is not always a straightforward or harmonious one. Arguably, it has become more complex following the UN's promotion of the UN Decade for Human Rights Education in 1995–2004. Whilst this endorsement has proved beneficial for NGOs in terms of funding, coordination and collaboration regarding HRE, NGOs were assigned a subordinate role. Arguably, this has been another way in which the UN has assumed a lead role in determining the HRE agenda. This also offers another example of how other potential conceptualisations of human rights may have been marginalised in recent decades in HRE. Furthermore, this collaboration has placed NGOs in a potentially awkward position since they are involved in delivering HRE in schools run by the state whilst simultaneously scrutinising the extent to which the state protects, fulfils and respects the rights of individuals (Bajaj 2011a).

Again, in the OPT, since the establishment of the PA, there has been an ongoing rivalry between the quasi-state and HROs, which pre-exited the Oslo Accords (as discussed in chapter two). On the one hand, foreign donors began to favour the PA over the NGO sector and on the other hand, HROs began to extend their monitoring of human rights violations to also include abuses committed by the PA (Hajjar 2001). This demonstrates how the transformative potential of HRE may be hindered not only by conflicting agendas of governments, NGOs and funders, but also when human rights undergo institutionalisation. Although the assumption is often made that grassroots activism for human rights can resist institutionalisation, this is not necessarily the case (Stammers 2009). What may start out as a protest scholar's conceptualisation of HRE may morph into a more natural scholar's representation of HRE. The bureaucratisation of human rights at the hands of the elite is a preoccupation for protest scholars (Dembour 2010). Thus, whilst NGOs may be more likely to adopt a *transformative* model these aims might become compromised by their relationship to international, national and local sites of power. Additionally, NGOs are often preoccupied with employing participatory resources and methods at the expense of grappling with the more problematic aspects of human rights (Coysh 2017).

Finally, *transformative* approaches to HRE are concerned with learning *for* human rights. However, as outlined, even these emancipatory aims can become hijacked once institutionalised. Whilst practitioners and theorists may claim that their approaches to HRE achieve education *about*, *through* and *for* human rights, the majority of HRE definitions and models are underpinned by more 'restricted' conceptualisations of human rights that emphasise learners acquiring (a version of) knowledge *about* human rights. Thus, it is possible to see why, following the drafting of the UDHR, the UN's definitions of HRE became as Keet (2007: 139) describes, 'hermeneutically sealed', marginalising other conceptualisations of HRE that preceded 1948. As argued, UN statements and international conventions are portrayed as the most important aspect of HRE curriculum and pedagogy (Al-Daraweesh and Snauwaert 2013). Furthermore, the issue with centralising these international treaties is that they construct an image of human rights as Western absolutes that ought to be emulated by other non-Western cultures. The following section builds on arguments made in chapter two that human rights need to undergo a process of decolonisation (Zembylas 2017b; Barreto 2013a; Baxi 2002; Mignolo 2002), in particular how HRE also needs to be decolonised.

VI. EXPANDING CONCEPTUALISATIONS OF HRE THROUGH DECOLONISING THE DISCOURSE

Decolonial scholars contend that Third World conceptualisations and histories of human rights have been marginalised within broader human rights discourse. Even though human rights are contested concepts which can take on different forms in different contexts and moments (Baxi 2000), in a similar manner, HRE is also a 'transnational site of struggle which exists in a permanent relationship of provocation between domination and resistance' (Coysh 2014: 108). Just as the human rights system privileges Eurocentric histories, theories and interpretations of human rights, and fails to recognise that these narratives are deeply rooted in colonialism, the global discourse of HRE is also entangled with coloniality and modernity (Zembylas 2018; Yang 2015).

Okafor and Agbakwa (2001) offer insightful analysis that demonstrates how Eurocentric human rights discourse is present in different HRE approaches. They contend that the theories and practices of HRE have been shaped by three orthodoxies: the heaven–hell binary; the one-way traffic paradigm; and the abolitionist paradigm. Underlying the first typology is the assumption that the world is divided into heavenly societies which champion human rights and hellish ones which abuse them. States in the Global North are often portrayed as societies where human rights are respected and rarely violated whereas Third World societies are constructed as hellish locations infested with rights violations. The second dimension to this dichotomy exists in textual form. For instance, the international human rights instruments and standards are esteemed as sacred and absolute. On the contrary, texts which originate from other cultural and religious traditions which are also concerned with the dignity of humanity are constructed as 'hellish', such as the *Qur'an*. Okafor and Agbakwa (2001) also claim that this orthodoxy is employed not only by Western scholars but by Third World scholars as well.

Okafor and Agbakwa's (2001) second orthodoxy, the one-way traffic paradigm, refers to the way HRE is propelled by Eurocentric definitions of human rights. Therefore, knowledge about human rights is parachuted from heavenly states in the Global North upon the hellish societies in the Global South. Drawing on Friere's (1970) 'banking model', they argue that this orthodoxy can also be witnessed in the way in which HRE is taught in an uncritical manner, with knowledge transferred from expert teachers to ignorant learners. Similarly, within Third World contexts, elites who become human rights professionals can adopt this one-way traffic paradigm when it concerns instructing the rest of the society about human rights (Okafor and Agbakwa 2001).

The third orthodoxy – the abolitionist paradigm – refers to how local cultures and traditions that sit in tension with human rights must be removed since they constitute a barrier to the enjoyment of human rights and ultimately 'the good life' (Okafor and Agbakwa 2001: 584). A problem with this approach is that HRE becomes decontextualised, overly ethnocentric, and disrespectful. This paradigm assumes that cultural traditions and human rights are opposing forces and as though the international human rights scheme is completely untouched by culture. Western NGOs and HROs often assume the abolitionist paradigm. These orthodoxies all present a Eurocentric conceptualisation of human rights in which rights are universal and unquestionable.

Decolonial scholars call for HRE to be not only decolonised but also to be decolonising (Yang 2015). Zembylas (2018) outlines three strategies for decolonising HRE pedagogy and curriculum: the recontextualisation of human rights along with HRE; the critique of critical theory and critical pedagogy; and the incorporation of an ethics of emotion. The first strategy – recontextualisation of human rights – entails expanding human rights discourse to include the histories and theoretical contributions developed in Third World and Southern cultural contexts, such as the colonised (Barreto 2013c). In other words, space needs to be created for these counter-narratives not only in the discourse of human rights but also HRE (Zembylas 2017a). In the words of Barreto (2013a: 32), there is a need for the 'Eurocentric understanding of rights to escape its soliloquy and to enter a dialogue with other visions of rights'.

An example of this type of approach can be found in the work of Al-Daraweesh and Snauwaert (2013), who propose taking a critical and hermeneutical interpretive methodological approach to HRE pedagogy to address issues which arise regarding the applicability and adoption of human rights cross-culturally. This pedagogical approach consists of five aspects: historicisation, contextualisation, multiperspectivity, criticality, and partiality of human rights and HRE. This means learners engage with the historical, political, cultural and social underpinnings of HRE. They compare constructions of rights found within different local traditions and situate themselves within these diverse views whilst at the same time acquiring critical objectivity towards their own views on what constitutes a human rights culture, and simultaneously abstaining from portraying a different culture's vision of the 'good life' as inferior to others (Al-Daraweesh and Snauwaert 2013: 399). In doing so, this approach seeks to occupy a space between universalism and cultural relativism through a 'fusion of cultures' which is based upon 'comparable validity' and 'dialogical equality'.

As outlined in chapter two, the notion that human rights are unquestionably universal is an extension of Western imperialism; thus, rights discourse needs to be 'pluriversalised' (Mignolo 2006). In other words, the idea that humans have rights simply by being human does not have to be embraced as a given, but rather can be viewed as one possible interpretation amongst multiple interpretations of human rights. Pluriversalising HRE presents learners of all cultures an opportunity to interrogate theories of liberalism, individualism, rationalism, secularism and universalism inherent in the dominant human rights discourse. It can act as an important counter-hegemonic strategy required in the process of decolonising knowledge and rights discourse (Zembylas 2017a).

Zembylas (2018) proposes a second decolonial strategy towards HRE, one that involves critiquing critical theory and pedagogy, and is enriched with decolonial thinking and praxis. This is because a critical HRE, whilst important, does not go far enough according to decolonial scholars. Critical theory neglects the relationship between modernity and coloniality, thereby failing to acknowledge violence brought about by imperialism and history from the viewpoint of the colonised (Zembylas 2018; Broeck 2013). Instead, critical theory tends to underscore humanism as the central aspect of modernity. Tuck and Yang (2012) when discussing critical pedagogy, contend that decolonising strategies are not the same as critical pedagogical approaches. The latter situates the human as the unit of liberation, whereas a decolonising approach to HRE requires the notion of 'human' to be interrogated and dismantled (Yang 2015). The term 'man' was originally created by fifteenth- and sixteenth-century humanists as a way of differentiating themselves from 'the other', who in their view posed a threat. As Mignolo (2013: 45) expands: 'Easterners were defined by Westerners as if Westerners had the universal authority to name without being named in return'. Therefore, a decolonising HRE needs to go a step further and interrogate who qualifies as the 'human' of 'human rights'.

Adopting 'an ethics of emotions as an ethics of human rights and HRE' is the third strategy for decolonising HRE pedagogy and curriculum suggested by Zembylas (2018: 42). Decolonial and TWAIL scholars maintain that there is a connection between colonialism, human rights and human suffering (Barreto

2013b; Baxi 2000). They interrogate rationalism that is inherent in the Eurocentric rights discourse (Zembylas 2017c; Barreto 2013b) and instead seek to replace this with a rights discourse which includes the significance of emotion (Baxi 2002). As explored in chapter two, where attempts have been made to forge a relationship between suffering and human rights, this has been from a European standpoint. The emphasis has been placed on the pain Europeans experienced at the hands of totalitarian regimes and the suffering of the colonised inflicted by European empires has been dismissed (Maldonado-Torres 2021; Barreto 2013b).

Zembylas (2018: 45) explains that decolonising pedagogy in HRE entails acknowledging that pedagogies of emotion in school and local contexts are created by global human rights discourses. He argues that educators who seek to adopt a decolonising approach to HRE need to consider how 'learners' emotional attachments are strongly entangled with traumatic historical circumstances of human rights violations and material conditions', otherwise they risk diminishing their pedagogical efforts. He highlights how disenfranchisement can be embodied through a range of emotions, for example, apathy, hatred and humiliation (Zembylas 2013). He underscores that rather than assuming that resistance and empowerment is a given, a decolonising HRE pedagogy needs to sit with the fact that 'affective tension around issues of empowerment and resistance' may emerge and can be an important part of struggles for solidarity. Coming from another angle, Hart (2008) argues that children living in contexts of conflict experience the political in a more visceral way. It is possible to propose that they also understand and engage with human rights in a similar manner. Therefore, HRE has the potential to be expanded through including the role of emotion since rational understandings of human rights can enable the acceptance of the various forms of oppression.

Decolonising the HRE curriculum involves expanding the curricula content and design to include lineages of human rights that are often missing in mainstream narratives (Gilroy 2010). It requires including counter-narratives of the colonised that would cause Eurocentric knowledge to 'confront its barbarism and coloniality' (Zembylas 2018: 46). Zembylas (2018) proposes three decolonising approaches that can enable this: anti-essentialism, contrapuntal readings and ethical solidarity (Subedi 2013). First, an anti-essentialist HRE curriculum contests the Eurocentric readings of human rights, acknowledges the relationship between modernity/coloniality and Western ways of knowing, and foregrounds Third World theoretical contributions to the human rights discourse. Second, contrapuntal readings involve engaging with the dominant human rights discourse and its entanglement with colonisation and imperialism. As discussed in chapter two, Eurocentric human rights narratives emphasise the relationship between the state and society or governments and individuals; whereas Third World approaches consider the problematic relationship between empires and the colonies (Barreto 2013a). The third strategy of ethical solidarity is interested in how action-oriented empathy and solidarity can be generated. Zembylas (2018: 46) contends:

> To interrogate the trappings of sentimentality and especially narratives of pity, human rights educators and learners need to challenge the emotional investments and emotion-informed ideologies that underlie their responses toward suffering and seek to promote sympathy and solidarity that make a concrete difference in sufferers' lives.

In order to do this, critical awareness of how feelings of empathy are conjured at classroom level is deemed important, alongside consideration of how this can have different impacts upon those who suffer.

Despite the revolutionary potential of the human rights discourse and HRE, an institutionalised global HRE has been largely embraced as the 'official' approach. This conceptualisation, however, is Eurocentric, declarationalist and uncritical (Keet 2010). Therefore, HRE needs to be interrogated, renewed and decolonised (Coysh 2017; Zembylas 2017a; Keet 2012), not only by human rights theorists and practitioners, but by learners themselves. Nonetheless, young people are seldom given the opportunity to critique rights discourse, largely because they are presented with only one (Eurocentric) 'restricted' version which assumes its superiority over other conceptualisations within the rights discourse (Yang 2015; Coysh 2014; Keet 2012). Below, I briefly discuss the extent to which HRE in the Palestinian context is influenced by a Eurocentric liberal narrative and more 'restricted' conceptualisations of HRE. These themes will be revisited and expanded upon in light of the empirical findings in chapter seven.

VII. IMPLICATIONS FOR HRE IN THE PALESTINIAN CONTEXT

In the West Bank, Palestinian young people learn about human rights at school, whether they attend a private, UNRWA or government-run school. Although the MoEHE officially oversees education in each of these contexts, they follow the Ministry's National Education curriculum to varying degrees. In a government-run school, students will learn about human rights in civics education, which is taught once a week (Qazzaz et al 2010). Although UNRWA schools largely follow their host countries' curriculum, they do so to the extent that it abides by principles set out by the UN. Notably, when it comes to HRE, UNRWA has provided enrichment material for teaching about human rights known as the HRCRT (UNRWA 2013). This is either integrated into other subjects or taught as a distinct human rights class (UNRWA 2012). Private schools within the occupied West Bank enjoy more autonomy from the MoEHE and can follow different curricula including international ones. This illustrates how even within the same geographical context, HRE can be understood differently and cannot be confined to a distinct practice (Bajaj 2011a). Nonetheless, the ideological position of those developing and delivering the respective HRE will influence what is prioritised in terms of content, how the programme is delivered and the extent to which learners are oriented towards action *for* human rights.

In the OPT, most educational institutions are dependent on foreign aid (Velloso de Santisteban 2002), and this is, arguably, bound to influence the degree of non-Palestinian influence in terms of the content and delivery of HRE. For instance, following the Oslo Accords, the Curriculum Development Centre was founded in collaboration with United Nations Educational, Scientific and Cultural Organization (UNESCO) and received funding from the Italian Ministry of International Cooperation (Velloso de Santisteban 2002).

UNRWA schools are predominantly funded by UN state members, the EU and other regional governments (UNRWA 2022). Moreover, their own HRE programme is supported by the United States Bureau of Population, Refugees, and Migration (BPRM) (UNRWA 2016). It is also shaped by contemporary global educational practice, as outlined in the HRCRT Teacher's Toolkit: 'This toolkit builds upon past experience teaching human rights in schools but also is careful to address human rights education within an updated, commonly understood global framework of human rights education' (UNRWA 2013: 6). Consequently, the ideological position of those who have developed the HRCRT programme is informed largely by international influences and is unsurprisingly UN-centric. Similarly, government schools also emphasise UN statements and the universalism of the rights discourse as evidenced by the textbooks.

The task of creating the first Palestinian curriculum was given to the Currciulum Development Center – a team led by educational reformist Ibrahim Abu-Lughod. This team were interested in pedagogical reform as well as formulating a curriculum. Their plan proposed grounding content included in classrooms with the real-life situations faced by Palestinians (Brown 2018). Their plan unapologetically criticised rote-based learning and instead promoted an innovative pedagogy which sought to employ democratic practices, believing that these would inevitably evoke creative vision and develop critical-thinking skills within the classroom (Brown 2018). This team bypassed the more official authorities and directly consulted the views of teachers, graduates, religious leaders and other members of Palestinian society to inform the curriculum (Mazawi 2011). However, the initial plan was rejected by the MoEHE on the grounds that it was unrealistic, not financially viable and possessed a Western bias (Nicolai 2007).

Subsequently, a less 'radical' plan was drawn up and submitted in 1998. This alternative plan concentrated on more administrative rather than pedagogical matters. Nonetheless, the MoEHE did go on to incorporate more 'moderate' aspects of the former plan, such as the introduction of civics education (Brown 2018). Significantly, HRE was introduced into civics education and contemporary issues. Ali Jarbawi, who was part of the team and involved in the development of civics education and social studies, expressed the challenges faced by the team tasked with creating a new curriculum, asking the oft-cited question: 'Which Palestine should we teach?' (Mazawi 2011: 174). He also raised questions about the complexities faced when discussing Israel in the curriculum. Moreover, the revised plan, which was adopted and continues to this day, avoids certain topics relating to the Palestinian political context and ruptures within Palestinian history (Rohde 2012).

Following Oslo, the orientation of the Palestinian national movement shifted from an anti-colonial struggle to a state-building effort (Dana 2015). Consequently, education became a vehicle by which these ideological aims were and continue to be foregrounded. Whilst Abu Lughod's plan was deemed to contain a Western bias, arguably the MoEHE, by rejecting this plan, also forsook the knowledge of the Palestinian people for a more Eurocentric approach resulting in a less relevant HRE (Abu Moghli 2020).

As the name suggests, the HRCRT initiative also displays elements of the *HRE for Coexistence* model (Bajaj 2011a). There is an emphasis throughout the programme on learning skills for conflict resolution and fostering 'attitudes of tolerance' (UNRWA 2013: 18). Othered groups in the textbook include those who are discriminated based on gender, religion or disability. Notably, relations between Israelis and Palestinians are not part of the focus. The programme states that it has chosen to explicitly include 'conflict resolution' and 'tolerance' alongside HRE because it 'contributes to UNRWA's vision of violence-free, peaceful schools' (UNRWA 2013: 18). Since Oslo, UNRWA has acted as a vehicle for the UN's agenda of promoting an idealistic narrative of peace as opposed to meeting needs on the ground among the Palestinian refugee communities (Albhaisi 2021). Therefore, whilst this HRE model includes aspects of *HRE for Coexistence*, it does not have a focus on the broader Palestinian–Israeli 'conflict', but rather on how human rights can be healing amongst school children who live *within* a context of ongoing violent occupation.

Additionally, due to Oslo agreements such as the Declaration of Principles (DOP), three parties monitor the development and teaching of the curriculum: the PA, Israel and the United States (Velloso de Santisteban 2002). Consequently, this not only harnesses the MoEHE's autonomy regarding developing HRE, but it also means it is accountable largely to Western sites of power, most importantly their occupier. HRE in the Palestinian context has intentionally sought to hinder struggles for self-determination and to replace a culture that is considered 'violent and in need of rectifying' according to the global human rights regime (Abu Moghli 2020: 21).

Pinto (2014) in her analysis of the HRCRT, helpfully points out that whilst the aims of the HRCRT are modelled upon the 2005 World Programme for HRE's three-pronged definition of HRE (*about*, *through* and *for* human rights) it omits the 'action' or *for* element. Since Israel and its closest ally, the USA, monitor HRE, it is unsurprising that learners are not learning *for* human rights since this may disrupt the oppressive status quo. Consequently, it is possible to argue that Palestinian HRE has been colonised even prior to exploring how they privilege a Eurocentric rights narrative.

Tarrow (1992: 22) argues that the approach to HRE will be largely informed on how a specific nation-state 'wishes to socialize its children', but this is not necessarily the case in the Palestinian educational context. This is because the

MoEHE is operating with limited autonomy since it is accountable to the tripartite monitoring groups noted above. To reflect on Tarrow's (1992) words, the Palestinian HRE is arguably influenced by how their occupier and Palestinian elites seek to socialise them.

A combination of factors, such as reliance on international donors, the PA's state-building efforts and external monitoring of the curriculum, suggest that the natural school of thought (Dembour 2010) is largely underpinning HRE in Palestinian school contexts. However, the life experiences of Palestinian young people can cause them to question the legitimacy of the UN and the Global North as guardians of human rights, as will be discussed in subsequent chapters. Moreover, the fact that natural scholars view human rights developments since 1948 positively clashes with the Palestinian historical narrative since for them 1948 marks the *Nakba*. Therefore, it is unsurprising that UNRWA and government-run schools adopt models of HRE that present learners with a largely depoliticised and decontextualised narrative about human rights.

Zreik (2004: 78), a Palestinian legal scholar, argues that Palestinians 'have lost not only their rights and their land, but also the context that enables them to demand these rights in a way that makes sense'. Consequently, it should come as no shock that HRE in the Palestinian context also largely draws upon the Western liberal tradition and in doing so promotes this Eurocentric conceptualisation of human rights as the legitimate version that must be emulated. Drawing on her research on UNRWA's HRE in Gaza, Albhaisi (2021) concludes that less is known about Palestinian learners' own interpretations of human rights when it comes to their lived experiences and identities.

VIII. CONCLUSION

A global HRE, which is declarationalist, Eurocentric and underpinned by theories of liberalism, individualism, rationalism, secularism and universalism has been institutionalised by the UN and uncritically adopted by governments, many academics and NGOs. HRE in the OPT has also been colonised as a result of the lack of autonomy they enjoy over their education system and their dependence on foreign aid. This has meant that a depoliticised, decontextualised, UN-centric global HRE has been largely embraced.

HRE more generally needs to be interrogated, decolonised and renewed (Zembylas and Keet 2018; Coysh 2017; Keet 2012) by learners as well as theorists and practitioners. In the context of settler colonial violence where rights violations prevail, it is even more pertinent that youths are given opportunities to engage critically with the broader human rights discourse, to question notions such as universalism and rationalism, and to be empowered to participate in human rights praxis. Therefore, this book contributes to these discussions and aims to amplify their lesser-known interpretations of human rights. This is important because Palestinian young people's views are often excluded: firstly, as those who have endured a history of colonialisation from various foreign powers; and secondly, as those whose voices are often marginalised because they are young. And it is their counter-narratives that can enable Eurocentric knowledge to square-up to its coloniality (Zembylas 2018).

Informed by empirical research, the next three chapters consider how Palestinian young people's understandings of human rights are influenced by what they learn through their everyday lived experiences *outside* school. These chapters explore the three layers of marginalisation that Palestinian young people face in relation to their human rights: the occupation which denies them their *humanity*; the Palestinian pseudo-state that denies them a *voice*; and patriarchal structures which deny them *agency*.

The following chapter focuses on the first layer of marginalisation that youths are forced to encounter: the Israeli occupation.

4

Human Rights as a Vehicle to Struggle against the Occupation: Reclaiming the 'Human' of 'Human Rights'

I. INTRODUCTION: SETTING THE SCENE

IT WAS DARK as I travelled back to my apartment after a day interviewing youths in another city in the West Bank. As soon as I went through the checkpoint, a short distance from my apartment, I joined a line of traffic. Congestion at this time of night was unusual. I turned left (the only route I could take because of the separation barrier) and realised the reason for the delays. Teenage boys with *keffiyehs* wrapped around their heads hurled stones with slings towards the nine-metre-high wall. In the rear-view mirror, I noticed a burning tyre being used as a road block. I followed the lead of the car in front and carefully drove on the opposite side of the road, around the demonstrators. Youths were taking part in demonstrations that evening in response to the shooting of Jihad al-Jafari, a 19-year-old culinary student from Dheisheh refugee camp (Al Jazeera 2015). He had been shot in the chest at close range during a camp raid. The Israeli military had then prevented anyone from attending the injured youth, blocking an ambulance from entering the camp.

When demonstrations like this appear in Western media reports, these encounters are often referred to as yet another 'clash', and often missing is the question 'why is the Israeli military entering a Palestinian community in the first place?' Also absent in commentaries on Israel–Palestine relations when violence erupts is any sort of context – be that recent, historic or political.

This chapter explores how life under occupation influences how young people (primarily) and their educators understood, discussed and deployed human rights. The youths interrogated the 'human' of human rights and questioned why the West often gets to decide who qualifies as the beneficiaries of human rights. This chapter considers how the youths asserted themselves as the *agents* of human rights by rejecting the humanitarian frame that has been imposed upon Palestinians and reintroducing the political in their struggle. Human rights discourse in Western commentaries tends to be abstract, legal and associated with rationalism and removed from the victims of rights violations, whereas the narratives within this chapter will jar against some of these Eurocentric discourses as they reintroduce the dimension of suffering to human rights. Living under military occupation meant that the youths offered a desanitised discourse around human rights. This chapter concludes by looking at the ways in which young people and their educators exposed and countered Orientalist attitudes that prevail in mainstream human rights discourse and which perpetuate their marginalisation as Palestinians. Interwoven throughout this chapter is how the occupation denies Palestinians their humanity, and how Palestinian youths reclaim it.

II. RECLAIMING THE 'HUMAN' OF HUMAN RIGHTS

Over time, the occupation has come to be accepted by much of the international community and Israeli society by the way that Israel has managed to successfully reconfigure Israel–Palestine relations as a 'conflict' that is between Muslims and Jews exclusively, as opposed to an anticolonial struggle (Browne and Bradley 2021; Roy, 2012; Karam, 2010). This reconfiguration of Israel's settler colonial project into an ethnic-religious conflict began in early Zionism, which was influenced by secular Eurocentric racialised notions of nationhood (Khalidi, 2009), and on the other hand a religious belief that the establishment of a Biblical Jewish homeland was a fulfilment of prophecy (Barakat, 2018; Lloyd, 2013). The combination of these two frameworks were 'meant to reassure the European powers that the Zionist colonization of Palestine would be a civilizing project' and that 'the "Divine right" of the Jewish people to settle Palestine would be carried out by a people in close proximity to Europeans, who were racially superior to the indigenous/uncivilized Arab inhabitants' (Shalhoub-Kervokian 2014: 279). In contemporary Zionist discourse, Palestinians have been assigned the label of 'Islamic terrorist' (Karam, 2010: 68). This has been largely accepted by Western states since it complements the neo-Orientalist discourse that has been adopted by those engaged in the War on Terror following the 9/11 attacks.

Framing the 'other' as terrorist has become a highly effective way of delegitimising the aims of opposition groups and dehumanising members of these groups since terrorists do not behave like humans and ultimately do not need to be treated in a humane way (Chagankerian 2013). Since there is a lack of consensus in defining terrorism, political powers can take advantage of this to advance their own political agendas. Consequently, Israel has managed to categorise any kind of Palestinian resistance as a terrorist act and a security threat. To draw on Lloyd's words (2013: 72), 'these besieged territories are envisaged as themselves besieging', rather than occupied. Israel has used young people's participation at demonstrations against the occupation as a justification for the surveillance, detention and even killings of Palestinian youths (boys especially, but not solely). This has also enabled Israel to reconfigure these young people as terrorists who pose a threat to national security and, in doing so, deny them both their childhood and their rights (Jiménez 2023; Shalhoub-Kevorkian, 2019). When examining the 'whom for' aspect of human rights, Mignolo (2013: 45) explains the term 'man' was originally created by fifteenth- and sixteenth-century humanists as a way of differentiating themselves from the 'other' who in their view posed a threat: 'Easterners were defined by Westerners as if Westerners had the universal authority to name without being named in return' (as discussed in chapter two). This Orientalism that dichotomises those who qualify as human and those who do not (according to the West) is still experienced by Palestinian young people to this day.

The youths I interviewed emphasised the ways Palestinians have been vilified within Israel–Palestine relations. Whilst they did not explicitly use terms such as Orientalism, they highlighted the neo-Orientalist mythologies that have been built around their identities (as Muslims, Arabs and Palestinians) by the West, which have in turn disqualified them as the 'humans' of human rights. This was apparent when Rula (student, PS) reported that she had experienced discrimination when travelling. She believed that this had been because her mother was wearing a *hijab*. She highlighted that the world forms judgements based on the outward symbols of those who practice Islam. This was possibly because she was aware of how the *hijab* is seen by the West as a controversial signifier, which for some is a symbol of oppression imposed by men and has become associated with those belonging to more traditional forms of Islam (Hatem 2003). She went on to discuss how this discrimination had impacted her overall belief in the human rights system, commenting: 'I don't believe in human rights, because people think that if I'm a Palestinian then they must think that I'm a terrorist' (Rula, student, PS).

Rula's strong rejection of human rights seemed to be linked to an underlying belief that those who promote human rights also deny these rights to Muslims and Palestinians. She explained how this stereotyping that she had been subjected to as all three (a Muslim, Arab and Palestinian) 'really hurts' (Rula, student, PS). Her reflections were traceable in the narratives of her peers – that Palestinians report they have been disqualified as the beneficiaries of human rights because of how they have come to be depicted as Islamic terrorists.

The youths in the BGS also interrogated not only who qualifies as the 'human' of human rights, but also who gets to decide who qualifies. Abdullah (student, BGS) questioned the international community's decision to delegitimise past Palestinian resistance movements, stating: 'Many Palestinian revolutions happened in Palestine and always many world countries stand against us. So, we as Palestinians are treated differently – in a bad way'. He perceived the world as not merely indifferent but actively opposed to the Palestinian collective struggle for their rights. This left Abdullah (student, BGS) marginalised and reinforced an overarching theme across their narratives that Palestinians consider themselves the exception to the global rule when it comes to being counted as the beneficiaries of rights.

Similarly, his classmate Laith (student, BGS) also interrogated why Arabs, including Palestinians, are constructed as terrorists. He asked: 'So why is it when Arabs or Palestinians do peaceful demonstrations or claim their rights, they are considered terrorists?' Laith (student, BGS) emphasised that these demonstrations are 'peaceful' and that the demonstrators pursue human rights; therefore, he described Palestinians as those who simply seek fair treatment and the enjoyment of rights. The way he described Arabs and Palestinians makes the fact that they are perceived as terrorists for these innocuous apolitical actions seem all the more ludicrous. He seemed aware that the Palestinian political agenda serves as a hindrance to their struggle for rights since it results in them being denoted as terrorists.

However, Laith (student, BGS) did not divorce the political from the Palestinian struggle for rights. In fact, he was particularly vocal as he debated with his peers who were sat beside him the tension that exists between what constitutes acts of terrorism as opposed to revolutionary movements, and who gets to decide what differentiates one from another. He also interrogated why global powers have historically chosen to categorise Palestinians as terrorists. He did so by comparing the West's perception of the uprisings that swept across the Arab world to the Palestinian national struggle. Interestingly, he directed his question at me and asked specifically for my personal opinion on the nature of the Arab Revolutions: 'What happened in Syria, Tunisia and Morocco- was that terrorism or just?' (Laith, student, BGS). It was as though he used me as a vehicle to interrogate the West's definition of terrorism versus legitimate struggles for human rights. He scrutinised what he perceived to be the partisan attitude of the West that supports certain movements such as the Arab uprisings and opposes other forms of resistance such as the Palestinian national movement.

As mentioned previously, due to the lack of agreement when it comes to defining terrorism, states can conveniently apply this label to the 'other' to achieve their political aims. This can be witnessed in the rhetoric of Western powers, but also Arab leaders. For instance, President Bashar al-Assad has referred to opposition groups in Syria as terrorists (Merz 2014) and depicted his regime as the protector of the 'correct' form of Islam (Khatib 2015: 344). Labelling Palestinians as terrorists has helped Israel to delegitimise the Palestinian political cause and simultaneously justify their own (Bar-Tal and Salomon, 2006). Laith (student, BGS) went back further in history to compare the way human rights have been operationalised in favour of the Jewish people as opposed to Palestinians. He questioned: 'When the Jews claimed their rights after the Holocaust, human rights stood with them and helped them to get their rights, but why is this not applicable with Palestinians?' (Laith, student, BGS). He personified human rights, describing them as having a mind of their own able to capriciously choose to stand with certain groups of people and against others. In doing so, he thereby interrogated the supposed neutrality and universality of human rights. He afforded the Jewish people their historical narrative of loss when he indirectly compares their diaspora to the Palestinian one. However, he was left questioning why Palestinians are considered less worthy of rights than other groups who have encountered forced displacement and discrimination, such as the Jewish community. His comparison is of course intentional given the fact the establishment of the state of Israel led to the injustices he continues to face decades later.

As explored in chapter two, the establishment of the state of Israel was portrayed as a 'humanitarian solution' to the atrocities of the Holocaust, which allowed the early Zionist settler colonial enterprise 'an aura of legitimacy' (Perugini and Gordon 2015: 46). It was apparent from these boys' discussions that they were aware of how this shroud of legitimacy has in turn delegitimised the Palestinian struggle in the eyes of the international community, their claims to the land and their narratives of pain both past and present (Shalhoub-Kervorkian 2014). The way Laith associated the Holocaust with human rights also reflects the way in which the Holocaust is often linked traditionally to the UDHR (Morsink 1999) and foregrounded as a key event in Eurocentric readings of human rights (as discussed in chapter three). Another boy named Fawaz (student, BGS) from the same school, also made this association when he stated that human rights originated from 'Hitler's time!' despite later saying that he was only joking. Nonetheless, these comments were indicators that some of these boys had likely encountered the 'textbook' version and Eurocentric framing of human rights in their school's HRE.

This was also apparent in Laith's (student, BGS) criticism of the role of the UN in promoting human rights: 'United Nations are the ones who implement human rights and also the ones who invade them'. By questioning the partiality and integrity of the UN, he also delegitimised it as an institution that promotes values which underpin much of the Western worldview. In doing so, he contested the misconceptions held about Palestinians as people and their role of aggressor within the so-called conflict. Whilst the UN is an intergovernmental organisation, he positioned it as an institution more akin to a state which acts discriminately. Girls from the refugee community such as Nour (student, UNGS) also situated the UN in a similar manner, stating: 'The United Nations should give us our rights as many Palestinian children are deprived from their rights and cannot live their childhood also they live with anxiety and fear'. Children living in refugee camps, such as Nour, are accustomed to having many of their basic needs, such as their education, healthcare and social services, provided for by the UN agency UNRWA. Therefore, it is unsurprising that the UN is seen by the youths as a type of state that is responsible for implementing human rights more generally.

Returning to Laith's (student, BGS) remarks, his critique of the hypocrisy of the UN reflects arguments made within the literature around the perception of the UN system. As Freeman (2017: 10) explains, the UN was 'the author and guardian of international human rights standards', but also 'an association of governments' that were violating human rights. In Laith's (student, BGS) commentary he also allotted responsibility to the UN in current Palestinian–Israeli relations where it has been forgotten. Morsink (1999: 78) notes that when the drafters of the Declaration were discussing the rights of Palestinian refugees that there was a 'gentleman's agreement' not to engage in discussions of a political nature surrounding the UN's controversial involvement in the proposal to partition Palestine that became 'the proximate portal of the Nakba' (Khalidi 2009: 26). In his detailed analysis of UN General Assembly resolution 181(II), Imseis (2023) argues that Palestine's 'legal subalternity' was reified in the UN system and signalled the beginning of a dilemma in which international law would be held out within reach of Palestinians only to then be repeatedly withheld. Laith's (student, BGS) critique displays awareness of this dilemma, though is articulated differently. He was interrogating the trustworthiness of the UN as guardians of rights, partly because of their legacy in his current experiences of settler colonialism and partly, because of the way he incorrectly positioned them as an organisation that not merely promotes rights but also implements them.

Throughout discussions at the BGS, the youths rejected this imposed stereotype of the Palestinian as terrorist, first by reintroducing the political into their struggle for rights, and secondly, by criticising the West's inconsistency when it comes to deciding what constitutes legitimate political struggle versus terrorism through their analyses of the West's approach to events such as the Arab uprisings and Zionist enterprise past and present. Therefore, they were scrutinising not only who qualifies as the 'human' of human rights but also who holds the power to decide who counts as such.

Another way that adult and youth participants reclaimed Palestinians as the 'humans' in human rights was through a counter-hegemonic strategy of self-dehumanisation. For instance, youths and their educators repeatedly used the comparison between Palestinians and animals in order to articulate how they have been made to feel sub-human by Israel and further ostracised by the international community. When being asked to denote human rights more generally, Hiba (student, PS) immediately wrote that it was funny that animals have more rights than Palestinian people (see Figure 4.1).

Figure 4.1 'Animals have more rights' (student, PS)

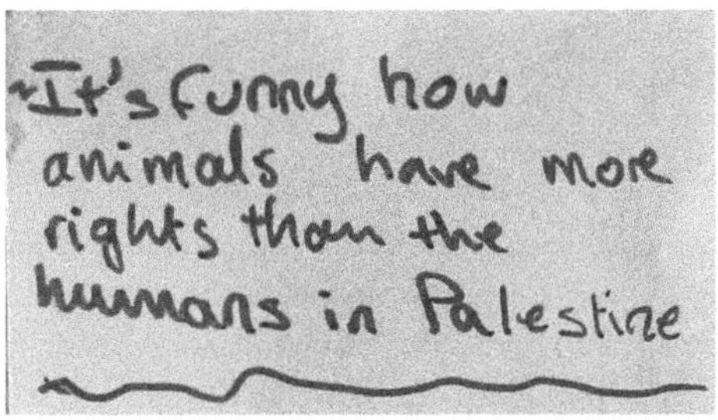

Hala (teacher, UNGS) also used this comparison to contrast the rights of Palestinians and animals: 'On Western TV you see dogs have more space to play'.

Comparing the right to play that dogs in the West enjoy compared with Palestinian refugees has the potential to lose some of its impact on a Judeo-Christian audience. This is because dogs have a low status in Islamic tradition (Polinsky 2022); thus, comparing refugees to dogs further stresses the degradation to which her community has been subjected. Arguably, these two participants were not only describing Palestinians as sub-human, but as almost sub-animal.

Another way in which participants denoted Palestinians as sub-human was through the use of simile and metaphor. These linguistic choices achieve different effects. By way of example, to state 'we are *like* animals' using a simile achieves a different impact than if one were to state, 'we *are* animals' using a metaphor. Riham (teacher, PS) employed a simile to compare the life of the occupied to that experienced by vermin.

> Sorry for this example, but we are here like rats in a hole. People watch us that we are trying to live but we are in a prison … we are trying to let the whole world see that we are people, we are humans (Riham, teacher, PS).

Firstly, she prefaced her comparison of Palestinians to rats with an apology. Arguably, this indicated her reluctance to embrace the animalisation to which she along with her people have been subjected. Furthermore, she chose to use a simile as opposed to a metaphor because whilst her people have been made to feel sub-human, she refuses to relinquish their humanity. The words 'hole' and 'prison' were used to describe specifically the way in which freedom of movement is severely curtailed for those who live in the OPT and the monotony of life under occupation. Notably, she used the animalisation of Palestinians as a tool to shame the international community by de-normalising what has come to be accepted in the international arena. She also reinstated her people as humans deserving of dignity as a way of also challenging the apathy of the international community.

Anwar (student, UNGS) also dehumanised the self; however, she did so by describing Palestinians as faceless statistics as opposed to animals. She chose to utilise a metaphor when articulating her view of how the world places different value upon the lives of Palestinians and those in the West:

> In Western countries, if someone dies, so they make like a massive issue of it, which is a big issue, but if we Palestinians were killed whether it was a hundred to a thousand then it's normal and OK. Palestinians are numbers (Anwar, student, UNGS).

She held the view that the world has come to normalise the occupation to the point that the value of a Palestinian life is ranked lower than the life of an individual from the West. This is something which the youth-led NGO We Are Not Numbers has sought to counter following the 2014 Gaza War and in current violence in Gaza. Whilst she critiques this attitude shown towards Palestinians, she does not in turn de-value the life of a non-Palestinian, since she states that if someone is killed regardless of their ethnicity, it is important. She ends by employing a metaphor – 'Palestinians *are* numbers' – and thus demonstrates how she along with her people have been dehumanised. Whilst this, at first glance, may imply a sense of resignation to the imposed constructions that have been placed upon Palestinians, she made this comment sardonically.

Anwar (student, UNGS), through her use of metaphor, achieves the impact of drawing attention to the absurdity of the degradation that Palestinians have been made to experience. Consequently, these participants dehumanised the self as a strategy to articulate, first, how they have been made to feel under occupation, and secondly, to challenge the oppression that they face that would not be accepted if it was another population undergoing such injustices. In doing so, they simultaneously de-normalise what has come to be accepted by Israel, Israel's allies and neighbouring Arab states. Further, they sought to reconcile the conflict between their understanding of how rights play out worldwide in comparison to how they play out in the OPT (see also chapter seven).

When considering the 'for whom' dimension of human rights, the youths also discussed whether contingencies should be placed on the rights of their occupier.

III. QUESTIONING THE OCCUPIER AS THE 'HUMAN' OF 'HUMAN RIGHTS'

A Eurocentric account of human rights is preoccupied with the relationship between the state and society, and governments and the individual, whereas a Third World perspective considers the relationship between empires and the colonised (Barreto 2013c). In accordance with a Third World approach, young people in this study considered the relationship between the occupier and the occupied. This became apparent when young people were asked during the walking debate whether all humans everywhere should be given the same human rights. The majority of participants initially made universalist claims such as Nabil (student, PS), who articulated: 'Everybody should have their rights poor, rich, Black, White, anybody should have their rights'. However, when they were asked a second time if there was anyone they could think of who maybe should not have rights, youths across the school contexts often listed terrorists, prisoners and murderers. This idea of citizens not deserving their rights when they have acted irresponsibly is not an uncommon way of categorising the deserving of human rights entitlements (Shor 2019). However, because these interviews took place in a society impacted by political violence among a people group who face the denial of human rights on a regular basis, the conversation moved away from simply focusing on whether 'bad people' deserve rights towards whether the main withholder of Palestinian rights – the occupier – is deserving of human rights.

There was no singular viewpoint on this among participants. The way the occupier was categorised by participants varied and often informed who the deserving and undeserving Israelis were when it came to human rights entitlements. For instance, some youths, such as Jiries (student, PS), made a clear distinction between Jews and Zionists, and wanted to make this clear to any potential readers:

> Some people say that Jews are the one who are Zionists ... but ... they're wrong because there are a lot of Jews that supports us ... but the problem is that the Zionists ... that planted this idea in the Israeli community that's why I just want to make sure that everyone who reads Jews or Zionists can separate between the two.

When working with the research advisory group at the analysis phase of the research, one of the young people explained the way in which Palestinians' view of the Jewish community evolved as a result of the 1948 *Nakba*. A YPAG member explained that Palestinians 'stopped looking at Jews as it's like a religion but more as the source of their pain so they became against Jews, not all of them. Some Palestinians believe there is a difference between Jews and Israelis' (female research advisor, YPAG 1). This analysis was helpful in terms of providing local knowledge on how Israelis are defined differently by different young people in various schools. It also posed a challenge to the incitement debate that suggests that the Palestinian curricula incites hatred towards the Jewish people (Brown 2018; Bernard and Maître 2006). Instead, the youths articulated how they were opposed to Zionist ideology and those whose vision of a Zionist Jewish homeland requires the displacement of indigenous Palestinians. They also acknowledged that some parts of the Jewish community stand in solidarity with them (Darweish 2017).

A similar distinction was made by some of the girls at the UNGS. Initially, they had agreed that everyone was entitled to human rights, but then went on to have this discussion:

> **Majd:** Maybe Israel?
>
> **Interviewer:** You don't think they should have rights?
>
> **Majd:** No, they are taking our rights.
>
> **Interviewer:** So, because they are taking your rights, you think they shouldn't have rights?
>
> **Majd:** Yes, yes.
>
> **Randa:** The state of Israel is not humanitarian; they are not operating in a human way (UNGS).

In this exchange, Israel is deemed undeserving of rights by the participants, who suggest that human rights are for humans, not for those who act inhumanely – as the state of Israel does towards Palestinians. Here, they reverse the logic that Israel has applied to them by suggesting that to be a recipient of rights you need to behave like a human. However, this conversation continued, and another participant made a further distinction between Israelis who are worthy and those unworthy of possessing rights based upon historical and political factors:

> **Interviewer:** So, do you all agree that Israelis should not take their rights?
>
> **Maryam:** No, they have their own rights, because not all of them are bad ... Our issue is with the ones who took our lands.

Nadiya: The Israeli Zionists.

Maryam: So, some of them must have their rights, the Jews don't have a problem with us.

Nadine: No, because not all people in Israel are the same and they have their rights as well. We are not against Jews but against Israeli Zionists (UNGS).

By stating that not all Israelis 'are the same', and 'not all of them are bad', Maryam again attached contingencies upon the rights of Israelis whose Zionist ideology would involve their displacement, as opposed to more broadly, those who belong to the Jewish faith or who live in Israel. To gain further clarification, I asked these girls whether they thought an Israeli young person their age should have human rights. They all said yes; however, another distinction was made:

Lina: There is a difference between civilians and soldiers.

Nadiya: But in the Gaza war they didn't differentiate between civilians and soldiers, Israelis target civilians and most of those who were killed were children, women and old people (UNGS).

This whole debate ended with a criticism of Israeli's inability to recognise unarmed civilians during the (then recent) 2014 war in Gaza. Nadiya (student, UNGS) therefore returns to a narrative of rights earned by the fulfilment of humane behaviour. It is important to remember that these girls (along with most of the youths interviewed) lived in PA-controlled areas of the West Bank where Israelis are officially not permitted to enter. Therefore, their interactions with Israelis would have been with soldiers at checkpoints or military raids or in other areas of the West Bank.

This distinction was not made between Zionists, soldiers or citizens by Yasser (student, BGS). Instead, he proposed that 'those who agree with killing Palestinians are different than other ordinary people' and thus are disqualified as the beneficiaries of human rights. Instead of breaking down his categorisation of Jewish people or Israelis in more detail as the girls did, Yasser broadened the category of the undeserving by including those who also condone the murder of Palestinians. This could arguably refer to other groups who are mandated to serve in the Israeli military, such as the Palestinian Druze. Or it is possible that he even encompasses those from further afield such as nation-states who by their inaction or support for Israel also fall within this category of those who are undeserving of rights. However, this initial dismissal of rights for those who misuse their rights, and more specifically Zionist Israelis, was refuted by Laith (student, BGS), who made a more universalist claim that rights 'should be given to everyone' since bad people – even the occupiers – are still humans and based upon that are still entitled to human rights regardless of their ethnicity, political policies or religion.

Even though the young people encountered settler colonial violence and rights violations on a regular basis, there were still some who displayed an unwavering belief in the universality of rights based upon the fact that everyone who is human deserves rights – even if they do not behave humanely. Although girls from the GGS clearly identified the occupation as a significant barrier against their enjoyment of rights, not one young person from this school indicated that Israelis should not have rights. In fact, they used very universalist language and encompassed many members of society, such as children, the disabled and – more surprisingly – those whose behaviour does not warrant rights: 'There might be some people who don't deserve to take rights, but they should still take their rights. Everyone has rights' (Rama, student, GGS). Therefore, whilst Palestinians are often disqualified as the 'human' of human rights, and whilst some participants disqualified certain Israelis and those who support the state of Israel as the subjects of human rights, there were still individuals who challenged this based upon a belief in universalism. This theme of interrogating the universality of human rights in the context of military occupation will be revisited in chapter seven.

IV. ASSERTING THEMSELVES AS THE *AGENTS* OF HUMAN RIGHTS

Palestinian children and youths have been decontextualised by being portrayed as not only terrorists but also as victims of a humanitarian crisis as opposed to a political one (Jiménez, 2023; Landy 2013). The 'humanitarianisation' of the OPT has transformed Palestinians 'from a people with political rights into a humanitarian problem for which the international community becomes largely if not wholly responsible' (Roy 2012: 78). This narrative has been adopted and promoted primarily by the international donor community and NGO sector following the signing of the Oslo Accords. As Pitner (2000: 35) explains, two-state solution proposals along with initiatives centred on 'peace and co-existence' appealed to foreign donors. Humanitarian initiatives involving Palestinian children were of particular interest to donors since children can be perceived as politically neutral subjects or as those who have simply become caught up in the 'humanitarian' crisis (Challand 2008).

Projects involving Palestinian children have been underpinned by the trauma discourse and yet the underlying cause of the trauma – the occupation and its colonial violence – remain unaddressed (Marshall 2013). It is assumed that if Palestinian children's trauma is not treated then they will inevitably turn to violence even though the source of the trauma is not named. This creates 'an image of a threatened but also threatening child' (Marshall 2013: 285). Representing Palestinian children as some sort of psychological issue that requires intervention from the international community works to decontextualise them, which serves Israel well since it allows their settler colonial violence to go largely unchecked. Whether portrayed as a threat to Israel's security, or as voiceless victims of a humanitarian disaster, this allows Palestinian children to 'occupy a liminal space in which their suffering is visible to the world, but they remain uncounted' (Shalhoub-Kevorkian 2015b: 238).

The youths in this study rejected the way in which they believe the Palestinian community as a whole (both refugee and non-refugees) has come to be represented as a helpless beneficiary of aid sustained by the donor community (Nayak 2006). Instead, the young people rejected the imposition of the humanitarian frame and asserted themselves as the agents of human rights. The young people achieved this by alluding to the way in which this humanitarian approach to their situation has obscured meaning for their rights claims. Further, they critiqued the international community and confronted the dominant narratives which deny Palestinians agency, using 'voice' as a reminder that they and their fellow Palestinians are political agents with stories that are worthy of an audience. Some of the young people were under no illusions as to the politically crippling effect of humanitarianisation. Adel (student, PS) directly scrutinised the work of UNRWA, claiming that:

> They're supposed to … talk about human rights. They only give you something to eat as if, you know, 'you're human, we care for you', but they don't listen to opinions, they don't listen to stories. Many people here in Palestine have … hard stories, and very sad stories to tell but nobody cares about that. No, they care only for giving them something to eat and 'it's ok, you have rights'.

She expressed her frustration with this organisation, which she believed treats Palestinians as victims of a humanitarian crisis as opposed to a historical and ongoing political one. For Adel (student, PS), the Palestinians' right to articulate the injustices suffered carries more importance than the delivery of aid when the latter is perceived as a form of political pacifism. This resonates with arguments made in decolonial theory that suffering is a key aspect in rights discourse of the colonised (Barreto 2013a). For Adel (student, PS), it is the stories of dispossession which give meaning to rights discourse in the first place.

Basel (student, BGS) was also critical of the way in which a humanitarian frame has been imposed upon him and his peers by Israel and other nation states:

> The occupation only wants us to think about eating, drinking, sleeping and going to school to memorise things without questioning anything. In Palestine, we are fooled by thinking that we have our rights but actually we don't have any of them.

He argued that Palestinian children are the subjects of the occupation's aim to produce an uncritical populace. He claimed that attempts to quash their political agency are made by granting them certain social and economic rights. He also suggested that many Palestinians had fallen prey to this tactic. Notably, neither of these young people attended refugee schools and yet they felt that they are all victims of this depoliticising approach. The way they have come to be misrepresented as victims of a humanitarian crisis, de-historicised and dislocated from their political context, is another reason why the young people sought to assert themselves as the 'agents' of human rights. Due to the way in which they have come to be misrepresented, the young people used their voice in the hope that it will increase their visibility globally. They were not afraid to confront global powers who perpetuate these dominant narratives, as Adel (student, PS) exemplified:

> People are sleeping about Palestine ... they think that ... it doesn't really belong to the Palestinians. That's why maybe they don't want to listen ... they don't want to hear anything about it because they don't want to really believe that it's ... a Palestinian land and not an Israeli [land].

By asserting Palestinian's rootedness to the land, Adel and her peers redressed the way that Palestinians have been reconstructed as 'intruders in their own land' (Roy 2012: 80). She viewed the international community as those who are passive, and who deliberately close their ears to Palestinian narratives of loss. Listening would mean they would have to engage with the colonial question around Israel's claims to the land which would prove disruptive to the current convenient status quo and could expose their entanglement in the Zionist enterprise.

Adult and child participants regularly referred to how the world continues to rob Palestinians of their humanity as indicated by their general indifference towards the suffering they experience. They described Palestinians as an exception when it comes to enjoying rights, as Amina, principal of the UNGS articulated: 'We feel that we are the least people in the world who are living ... without the human rights' (Amina, principal, UNGS). Participants depicted themselves as the neglected party within Palestine–Israel relations, as Sabina (student, UNGS) remarked 'Nobody cares for the Palestinians', and Hiba (student, PS) commented 'we're not equal, we are different from other children in the world'.

Riham (teacher, PS) highlighted how the occupation has become generally accepted over time by the international community, stating that 'people stopped watching us'. Hiba (student, PS) used the motif of voice to capture the marginalisation that they encounter at a global level: 'In general, the world doesn't listen ... to what Palestine's saying ... it's like, "ok a land under occupation, I don't care" ... we need human rights too'. According to Hiba (student, PS), the occupation has become normalised internationally to the extent that it condones the ensuing rights violations. She illustrated this by using her own voice to speak on behalf of the world. She ended her criticism with an urgent demand on behalf of the Palestinian people for human rights.

Furthermore, the humanitarianisation of the OPT has also resulted in normalising the occupation, and by extension the rights violations of Palestinians. According to humanitarian law, the occupier is responsible for the welfare of the occupied. However, Israel has shirked its duty towards the Palestinians because the international donors have assumed this role on its behalf and as a result have failed to contest the malignancy of the occupation. As Darweish and Rigby (2015: 133) argue:

> Foreign donors have been acting, however unintentionally, in a manner that reinforces the occupation as it is foreign funds that help to maintain the basic services which according to international law, should be the responsibility of Israel.

This irony was captured by Bashar, a Palestinian senior educator in UNRWA, who highlighted the unusual paradoxical position of the Agency, which is trying to plan and fundraise for the future whilst simultaneously hoping they will soon no longer have to exist:

> So, on one hand we are like a temporary organisation but on the other hand we are providing a service that's normally [offered by the] government … because we have been here for the last sixty-two, sixty-three years, I think the feeling that we are staying is becoming more and more [laughs] embedded in our thinking (Bashar, senior educator, UNRWA).

Whilst discontent with the humanitarian model, his comment indicates the general sense of resignation which exists within the Agency regarding the humanitarian model of dealing with the refugee community. His laughter implied cynicism towards the notion that a just resolution to the refugee crisis will be secured anytime soon. As Landy (2013) argues, this humanitarian approach to the Palestinian situation aims to achieve justice for the Palestinians within the current political norms without having to acknowledge the political reasons that led to the current crisis. Whilst this apolitical rights discourse may have been adopted by NGOs in the region, the adult and child participants largely rejected such an approach. Instead, they articulated their struggle for rights in a way that reintroduced the political and historical backdrop to current injustices they face as Palestinians. It is their context, which as Zreik (2004) argues, enables Palestinians to claim their rights in a meaningful way.

V. DESANITISING RIGHTS DISCOURSE

Eurocentric human rights theory is abstract, sanitised and distanced from stories of pain (Baxi 2002), as discussed in chapter two. In their discussions, the young people desanitised human rights discourse by approaching it from a non-rationalistic way and instead intertwining the violence of the occupation with suffering. They did this by describing everyday encounters (some imagined, some witnessed and some experienced) between Israelis and Palestinians. These scenarios took place in locations such as refugee camps, checkpoints and at demonstrations, which act as reminders that this is a relationship between the occupied and the occupier, as opposed to two warring parties. Throughout these encounters they presented rights from the perspective of the victim of rights abuses.

One of the imagined encounters between Israelis and Palestinians was described by refugee girls who discussed how children in their camp like to play the 'soldier–citizen game' and that they do this because they are imitating real life. The fact that Palestinians are assigned the role of 'citizen' and Israelis 'soldier' alludes to the way they position themselves as targets of their occupier's colonial violence. For child participants living in refugee camps, these games were re-enactments of events that they experience inside their camps. These children are more likely than non-refugees to be exposed to rights violations perpetrated by the Israeli forces since, for instance, raids occur within refugee camps regularly (see chapter one). This was exemplified when Lina (student, UNGS) and her friends described an encounter that they had experienced the night before the focus group discussion took place. The following exchange illustrates how their encounters with suffering inform their understanding of human rights:

> **Nadeen:** Like we as Palestinians living under occupation, like yesterday Israeli soldiers were shooting guys spontaneously with live bullets.
>
> **Dayna:** They invaded the camp last night.
>
> **Ahlam:** Yeah, they came at 10:00 pm and hit a pregnant woman.
>
> **Nadeen:** They were searching for someone, and they just broke into her house, and they pushed her out of their way.
>
> **Ahlam:** Last night they were so angry as they were shooting anyone in their way
>
> **Lina:** My cousin was on the roof of our house just looking around to see what was happening and he was shot in his leg. Now he is in the hospital because yesterday he went into surgery.
>
> **Nadeen:** There was another guy who was shot in his knee.
>
> **Dayna:** They shut off the electricity in all the houses in the camp. We were scared
>
> **Nadeen:** The last two months we suffered from this on a daily basis.
>
> **Girls:** [speaking at once] We are used to this and are forced to be used to this.
>
> **Nadeen:** Once, a group of Israeli soldiers broke into our house aggressively. It's too scary (UNGS).

The girls' account of this raid exposes the asymmetry that exists in Israel–Palestine relations and counters the dominant narratives discussed above about Palestinians being instigators of violence, since it was clearly the armed Israeli soldiers who forced their way into the camp and shot people indiscriminately. The military also have the power to switch off the electricity and break into civilians' homes. Their account also contests the way Palestinian children (and adults) have come to be portrayed as terrorists since a pregnant woman is physically attacked and the children were woken up whilst in their beds. Notably, what seemed to frighten the girls more than the firing of live bullets was the way the soldiers were able to bring darkness into their homes. This is significant because it displays how the occupation's violence during this night-time raid affected them personally. However, these girls did not set out to make these arguments, but rather sought to share an experience, which they had lived through less than 24 hours before I interviewed them.

It is important to point out that this raid took place in a camp situated in Area A of the West Bank, which is supposedly under PA control and off-bounds for Israelis. The girls' account poses a question that is missing in debates on children's rights in the Palestinian context (Shalhoub-Kevorkian 2015a): why were the soldiers in a Palestinian community to begin with? Furthermore, according to these girls, they are forced to learn more about human rights from the perspective of the victim due to the way children are often targets of settler colonial violence. As highlighted in chapter one, Lina (student, UNGS) ended the exchange by asking me: 'Yeah, so what do you expect from us? We learn about rights because of what is happening to us daily'. It was as though she questioned my expectations (as someone from the West) when it came to the factors that inform how they learn about rights. Her friend Malak (student, UNGS) added that the problem with human rights is that 'it's only on papers and not practised'.

Another group of young people enrolled in the PS shared their recent experience of loss involving a friend who was killed (see Figure 4.2). During the discussion Hiba (student, PS) said she wanted to share about:

> The unlawful killing of a 16-year-old boy who was our best friend and there's a video that shows exactly how he was killed and that shows ... he didn't do anything. So, for me here, the human rights ... they're not doing something.

Figure 4.2 'I can't see my friend, he is dead' (female student, PS)

Having witnessed the video in which he was killed fuelled the youths' sense of injustice, but also brought human rights and their emancipatory potential into question since they were unable to protect their fellow teenager's right to life. Youths in this (private) school referred to other youths, especially girls who had been detained in Israeli prisons for taking part in demonstrations. Jiries (student, BGS) reported that a 14-year-old girl named Malaak had been arrested and later released on suspicion of holding a knife at a checkpoint.

Other young people desanitised human rights by describing encounters that they had observed between the Israeli military and Palestinian schoolchildren at checkpoints: 'Sometimes we see Israelis using violence on the children of Palestine ... some children, they doesn't *[sic]* want to go to school because maybe this time ... the Israelis will hit them or do something bad' (Nabil, student, PS). He also exposed Israeli soldiers not only physically harming children but also hindering them from accessing their right to education. Nabil (student, PS) did not state the exact context he was referring to or whether he was speaking from his own experiences, but some of his peers had stated that they had to travel to school from other enclaves of the West Bank. It is also well-known that children in Hebron (the second largest city of the West Bank) must cross checkpoints to attend school. This is because following Oslo, Hebron was divided into H1, which came under PA control and constituted 80 per cent of the city, and the remaining 20 per cent, known as H2, remained under Israeli control (OCHA oPt 2019). To this day there are around 21 permanent military checkpoints in Hebron (B'Tselem 2019b). Palestinians still live in H2 under military law, whereas Israeli settlers live under Israel's civil law in this same area.

Similarly, Wissam, a teacher in the BGS also chose to discuss the interactions that take place at checkpoints between the Israeli military and Palestinian civilians:

> This is about the mood of the soldiers – if the soldiers tell them that 'ok, no one passes'... you can see about a hundred cars ... waiting for two or three hours ... What if for example, there's a pregnant lady who wants to go to hospital – a very weak old person, a student who wants to go to university? (Wissam, teacher, BGS).

Once again, the way that Palestinians have come to be portrayed is challenged, this time by an educator. Unlike the interactions described by the young people, who emphasised the physical aspect of settler colonial violence, he emphasised how it can also be psychological, their freedom of movement being dependent upon 'the mood' of particular soldiers on certain days. His definition of an unpredictable occupier also helps him realign the structural relationship between Israelis and Palestinians. However, as in the young people's accounts, he too consciously includes people who are often considered the most vulnerable in society, such as a pregnant woman, an elderly woman and a student. Including these people emphasises the humanity of Palestinians and counters how Palestinians have come to be misrepresented. Once again, the Israeli soldiers are constructed as rights-violators who prevent the rights of Palestinians to move freely, to access medical care and education. Furthermore, the mere mention of checkpoints also serves as a reminder that the Palestinian people within these encounters are people who live under a military occupation and whose mobility is controlled by Israel (Clarno 2018; Tawil-Souri 2012).

Negative stereotypes imposed upon Palestinians were also countered during a lesson I observed that took place in the BGS. The teacher cited the Fourth 1949 Geneva Convention and then went on to describe how Israelis do not apply it and instead target and shoot the cars of Palestinian doctors and civilians. The Fourth Geneva Convention applies to civilians in occupied contexts, and it is well documented that Israel has not recognised the application of this Convention in the OPT (UN Economic and Social Commission for Western Asia (ESCWA) 2014). Nidal (teacher, BGS) explained to the class that 'fighters are the ones who hold guns, but we don't have guns like fighters'. Nidal's understanding of what constitutes a fighter was linked to the possession of arms. He subsequently claimed that Palestinians do not therefore qualify as fighters since they are unarmed and in doing so, he also dispelled any commonly held myths that Palestinians are terrorists and instigators of violence. Instead, he pointed out that Israelis such as soldiers and many settlers (civilians living in illegal settlements in the West Bank) carry guns on their person and therefore are the actual fighters. Whilst the term 'terrorist' is a contested one, a terrorist act can be defined as one which targets civilians as opposed to individuals who represent the state (Ganor 2010). Highlighting the way that Israelis target innocent civilians, adult and child participants implicitly raised questions whether Israelis are the actual terrorists – though no participants used this term when defining Israelis.

The young people also demonstrated how their right to freedom of movement is hindered by Israel's military forces through their drawings (see, for example, Figures 4.3, 4.4 and 4.5): human rights are presented from the standpoint of the violated in a way that reintroduces the notion of suffering.

Figure 4.3 Israeli soldier (female student, GGS)

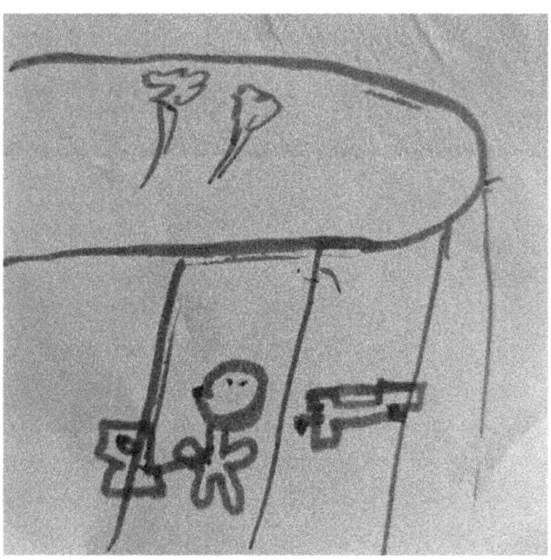

Figure 4.4 Demonstrators (male student, BGS)

Figure 4.5 Separation wall (female student, GGS)

In these images the young people indirectly redressed the stereotypes held about Palestinians as the confrontational party within the so-called conflict, as Israelis are instead depicted as the instigators of violence since they are armed with guns and a tank is seen firing into the crowd of unarmed protestors. Palestinians are portrayed here as non-violent since they do not hold weapons, but a single flag. Furthermore, they are depicted as the victims of rights abuses since they have been shot whilst trying to exercise their right to assemble. In these drawings, young people also reintroduced the suffering dimension into human rights. This was a strategy to appeal to the emotions of the outside world, which they feel has become detached from the victims of human rights violations, as Fadi (student, BGS) stated: 'It's important to keep struggling as maybe we will be heard one day, or someone will feel with us.'

Finally, these relayed encounters highlight how Palestinians learn about human rights from the perspective of those whose rights are violated, as opposed to enjoyed. The accounts of the young people resonate with Embrick and Williams' (2023) observations that Palestinians are both racialised and alienated in 'a settler colonial racial capitalist system of oppression' that 'works to render Palestinians both invisible (read: they are not oppressed) and as terrorists (read: they are the oppressors)'. The youths challenged these dual ways they have come to be misrepresented.

VI. COUNTERING ORIENTALIST NARRATIVES WITHIN HUMAN RIGHTS DISCOURSE

Engaging with the 'for whom' dimension of human rights also entailed the youths engaging with the 'where from' aspect of human rights (Barreto 2013a). Palestinians have been engaged in political struggle for decades against various foreign occupying powers; therefore, they were quick to react against Orientalist narratives within human rights discourse since it is entrenched in colonialism and imperialism (see chapter two). Adults and young people that were interviewed often resisted the colonisation of the *rights* in human rights by dismantling the Western hegemony over rights discourse, through rejecting the idea that human rights are a gift from the West (Baxi 2007), and by reclaiming human rights theory from a Palestinian perspective.

Palestinians are aware of the neo-Orientalist attitudes in which the West constructs itself as the subject which is able to judge, subdue or save the East (Abu-Lughod 2002; Said 1978). The young people I interviewed countered these imperialist narratives that prevail in rights discourse and were critical of how human rights can have an ambiguous relationship to power. Nabil (student, PS) and his classmate Adel believed that human rights was a Western concept and alluded to how human rights can be deployed by the West to exert power over others:

> **Nabil:** Because the West is stronger, you know, in some way he controls the world.
>
> **Adel:** Like the East here thinks that the West is the smartest people … They think that they're smart. That's why the West controls the people in the East and tells them what they should do under human rights but … if we're open-minded enough we won't think they should control us and tell us what to do (PS).

They offered their analysis of Orientalism in human rights discourse through their discussions of the power relationship between the West and the East, and how human rights are invoked to uphold this Western dominance. Nabil (student, PS) highlighted how the West is the dominant partner within the relationship, describing it as 'stronger', and subsequently afforded it the place of the subject by claiming that it exercises control over the rest of the world. Adel (student, PS) also described how the West 'controls' the East and 'tells them what they should do' – even through the vehicle of human rights. Furthermore, she used the superlative 'smartest' to depict the impression the East holds of the West. However, she refused to embrace this narrative herself. Conversely, she equated open-mindedness as the key to subverting Western moral imperialism; however, by doing this she ironically perpetuated this Orientalist narrative since an assumption is made that the East is not enlightened in the first place.

Nawja (student, PS) also resisted the moral imperialism of the West under the guise of human rights when she questioned the inconsistencies between the practice and rhetoric of the West concerning human rights. She commented: '[human rights] do come from the West but they're not reflected. They're only reflected on media like "yeah we did this, whoa we're America!"' Meanwhile, Nawja (student, PS) viewed rights as Western constructs and seemed at ease with this; she was not afraid to scrutinise the human rights performances of the West. She also undermined the way the United States boasts about its rights record by mockingly speaking on its behalf and subverting its claim as the champions of human rights. Conversely, the majority of the participants did not view human rights as Western imports and in fact considered this suggestion offensive.

Mignolo (2013) argues that the proclamation in the UDHR that humans everywhere were equal and entitled to rights was the First World's 'gift' to the Second and Third World. This attitude that human rights flow from the West can still be found within rights discourse to this day (Subramanian 2009). Throughout their discussions, educators and youths rejected the idea that human rights are a gift of the West to the East, as Abdullah (student, BGS) contended: 'We are humans who know how to differentiate between what is right and what is wrong. We know human rights since we are humans and so it's not a Western idea'. Abdullah (student, BGS) employed what decolonial scholars would term 'epistemic disobedience' (Mignolo 2009: 160) (discussed in chapter three) in the way he contested the notion that knowledge production in relation to human rights arises exclusively from the West. However, he based his argument on the notion that humanity is a transcendental entity and that humans (simply because they are human) have the same vision of what constitutes the 'good life'.

When interviewed, educators also rejected the notion that human rights are a gift from the West, as exemplified by what Bashar (senior educator, UNRWA) had to say: 'This is what I believe, that human rights is not something that … was parachuted on people, [it's] something that has been prevailing in societies since there were certain rights … even in … ancient cultures'. He rejected the notion that human rights are Western imports and instead viewed their genesis as not necessarily Eurocentric nor conceived in 1948 following the drafting of the UDHR. Rather, he conceptualised rights as arising historically in different civilisations. His argument reflects aspects of the Protest school (Dembour 2010) since he rejected the notion that rights are a 'top-down "civilising" process' (Stammers, 2009: 24) or that which has come from the West and has been 'vernacularised' in the West Bank (Merry 2006). He also interrogated the assumption that only knowledge generated by the West about human rights is legitimate.

Elsewhere during the interview, he resisted the imperialist attitudes found within human rights discourse. He stated: 'Palestinians like all other societies … they were not living in a jungle, they are not animals, they are human beings and … they have equal rights' (Bashar, senior educator, UNRWA). He demystified the essentialist mythologies which have been built up around Palestinians by the West by countering the view that Palestinians are 'inferior, uncivilized, barbaric, and violent', which enable the normalisation of the occupation and denial of their rights (Embrick and Williams 2023). Interestingly, he did this by invoking the universalist argument that humans are all equal and all have rights. Bashar's view of humanity was aligned with a Western construction of what it means to be human (Mignolo 2013), since he bought into the notion that humans are equal when the reality is Palestinians are not. Similarly, Naseef (principal, BGS) also sought to dispel myths that Palestinians are unfamiliar with rights concepts, arguing: 'We are educated people and part of our culture is to know about human rights and to defend [them]'.

Perhaps, because I am from the West, these educators may have felt the need to dismantle any Orientalist assumptions I may have had around the rights discourse. These educators also rejected the 'one-way traffic paradigm' proposed by Okafor and Agbakwa (2001) (discussed in chapter three), which refers to Western constructions that human rights are imposed upon 'hellish' societies in the Third World.

Many participants not only rejected the idea that human rights are Western imports, but also went on to reclaim human rights theory from a Palestinian perspective.

The Human Rights Conflict Resolution Tolerance Education Teacher's Toolkit, which is used in UNRWA-run schools, outlines in its vision statement that 'human rights education builds on Palestinians culture, it is not something imposed from elsewhere' (UNRWA 2013: 10). When asked why it was important to include this line, Bashar (senior educator, UNRWA) explained that UNRWA was dependent upon foreign aid to execute such an initiative; he stated, 'immediately there was resistance'. He continued:

> Immediately, people linked it up to politics … to the international community – 'they don't want us to fight for our rights and … fight the occupation'. So, it's important for the people to see that what we are talking about is part and parcel of the culture as well as the religion (Bashar, senior educator, UNRWA).

Therefore, it seems that the need to encourage society to 'buy into' the HRE programme led UNRWA to emphasise the idea that human rights are not a Western imposition, but inherently Islamic and Palestinian at some level.

Moreover, Amina (principal, UNGS) raised her concerns about the threat of Westernisation in Palestinian society. She commented:

> We are not learning them [human rights] from the West or the East. No, no. But even though, all of us, children, young, eldest people believe … now that [the] West is trying to put its culture here as it is there … if you want to give me … ideas, thoughts … No … I will not accept it, I will just accept what … goes with my culture (Amina, principal, UNGS).

Notably, she claimed that 'now' there is a consciousness within all echelons of Palestinian society of Westernisation. She also dismissed the idea that rights come from the East as much as from the West. Therefore, anti-Western sentiment is not necessarily part of a relativist challenge to the universality of human rights, but more a decolonial strategy which seeks to dismantle the presumption that ownership of the doctrine of rights belongs to the West (Mignolo 2013). Instead, this educator conceptualised human rights as that which flows from Islam. She ended the interview by stating:

> According to our culture, as Muslim people and Palestinians here in Palestine … we are persuaded that our rights … come from Qur'an and our Prophet Muhammad (Peace Be Upon Him (PBUH)) and … not from the East or the West. Our faith, it's a part of our culture that the human rights exists. We are not learning them from the West or the East. No, no (Amina, Principal, UNGS).

This rejection of Western culture resonates with an argument made by Johnston (2015), who claims that universality of human rights has been feared by some religious Muslims as a 'Trojan horse' of secularism that seeks to marginalise Islamic voices in public debate (see chapter two). Therefore, it was apparent that many of the participants – both educators and youths – countered Western imperialism via human rights by reclaiming human rights not only as Islamic constructs, but culturally as their own or essentially Palestinian, thus, addressing the 'from where' aspect of human rights (Barreto 2012a).

VII. WISHING TO SPEAK ABOUT THEIR MARGINALISATION AS PALESTINIAN YOUTHS

Settler colonial violence disproportionately impacts Palestinian children and young people. In the words of Hussein (student, PS) on life under occupation: 'Children are suffering more'. Young people depicted life as an occupied people as 'a challenge' in and of itself because of the threat of death that continually stalks them, their families and wider community. Although they did not explicitly employ the term *settler colonialism*, they were very familiar with Israel's 'logic of elimination' (Wolfe 2006: 387), which targets Palestinians, or as Fadi (student, BGS) put it: 'The occupation wants to delete us'. Young people referred to the constant fear that they will one day receive a phone call informing them that a friend or relative has been arrested or killed. They were also fearful of house demolitions or of being killed themselves. Young people's drawings also captured this sense of living in fear of the future (see Figure 4.6).

Figure 4.6 Martyrs (female student, GGS)

Manal (student, PS) drew an image of a child lying under the stars (see Figure 4.7)

Figure 4.7 Child lying under the stars (female student, PS)

When asked to explain what this picture represented, she explained that the subject in the image is a child trying to fall asleep at night. She expanded:

> **Manal:** You know when you get your point at the middle of the night you dream about death, memories of awful things that happened?
>
> **Interviewer:** Like nightmares?
>
> **Manal:** Yeah or maybe like things that will happen (PS).

She described the psychological effects of war with a sense of normality. This can be observed by the way she addressed me and assumed that I too would be familiar with the experience of how living in a context of political violence negatively impacts sleep. According to Manal (student, PS), they were reliving events which had already taken place whilst simultaneously living in fear of what might happen in the future. The ongoing settler colonial violence that takes place in the West Bank and Gaza was often at the forefront of the minds of these young people irrespective of their socio-economic status, as Figure 4.8 illustrates.

Figure 4.8 'I imagine blood' (female student, PS)

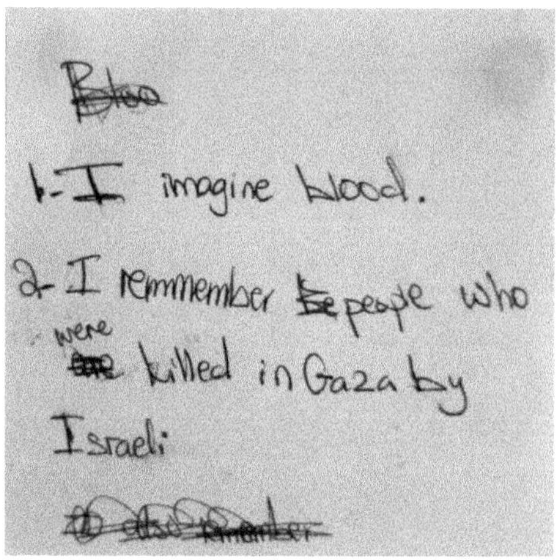

The youths consistently demonstrated solidarity with the Palestinian community in Gaza despite being geographically dislocated from them as a consequence of Oslo, the siege and Israel's settler colonial project. It was apparent that the occupation was having a significant impact on the lives of the young people I met, whether they lived in refugee camps, villages or cities. And yet, apart from the social workers and school counsellors, it seemed as though they were rarely being asked by adults about the effects of this on them. Sabina (student, UNGS) stated that if she knew adults would listen then she would want to 'Tell them about our feelings, everything in our minds and everything we feel'. At the end of another discussion, Elissa (student, PS) reflected: 'I think the reason why we have so much to say is because we've been holding our feelings inside because nobody asked us what we think … it's the first time somebody asked'.

These comments underscore that children are often unequally affected by political violence (Jiménez 2023; Lundy and McEvoy 2007), and yet their perspectives are rarely consulted in society or research. As Hart (2004) contends, children do not necessarily reproduce the views of adults around them, nor do they offer deficit views. Or in the words of Marwan (student, PS) '[adults] don't understand that we are mature enough to understand our world'.

VIII. CONCLUSION

Life under occupation has a significant influence upon young people's understandings of human rights and how they talk about human rights. They use human rights discourse as a vehicle not only to make sense of this layer of marginalisation in the first instance, but also to challenge it. Whilst they may not have done so intentionally, they employed several decolonial strategies as they interrogated the *human* and the *rights* of 'human rights'. The youths and their educators not only explored the 'what' of human rights but also the 'from where' and the 'for whom' dimensions of it (Barreto 2012a). They issued a challenge to the way the West has distanced itself from the victims of human rights abuses. Through their narratives of pain, they offered an invitation to those beyond Palestine to draw close to the suffering dimension of human rights that is so often purged from Eurocentric rights discourse. Ultimately, they exposed the fact that whilst the dominant rights discourse claims that all humans are born equal, this is not necessarily the case for Palestinians.

Although young people named the occupation as the main obstacle to their rights, they identified another layer of marginalisation against which they must struggle against: the authoritarian Palestinian pseudo-state which denies them a *voice*.

5

Human Rights as a Vehicle to Critique the Authoritarian Palestinian Pseudo-state: Reclaiming Voice

I. INTRODUCTION

IN JULY 2023 Israel carried out a military attack involving the use of drone strikes on the densely populated Jenin refugee camp, the first of its kind in the West Bank since the Second *Intifada*, which ended in 2005 (McKernan 2023). Footage emerged of thousands of residents fleeing the camp – images that were reminiscent of scenes from the *Nakba* of 1948. Following the attack in the PA-controlled enclave, President Mahmoud Abbas visited the camp, arriving in a helicopter (a journey that would have taken him around two hours by car). Whilst Fatah supporters welcomed his arrival, other residents were less enthusiastic and instead viewed it as too little too late and merely a photo opportunity. According to one news report, mourners at the funeral of one of the victims of the invasion chanted: 'Get out! Get out!' at three highly ranked PA officials (Al Jazeera 2023). This is because the PA failed to protect the camp against Israel's offensive in an area that is meant to be under PA control and that Israelis are not supposed to enter.

As a result of the Oslo Interim Agreement, the West Bank was carved up into three areas known as Areas A, B and C. This arrangement should have only lasted five years and was meant to lead to the withdrawal of Israeli occupation and the establishment of a Palestinian state (Zeid and Thawaba 2018). However, to this day, Area C, which makes up 60 per cent of the West Bank, remains Israeli-controlled. Roads, settlements and military instalments in this area have come to act as 'strategic corridors' which succeed in dislocating Palestinians from one another and their lands (Gordon 2008: 36). Area A consists of Palestinian cities which are governed by the PA and today make up 18 per cent of the West Bank (Singer 2021).

Oslo also led to the uneven distribution of land and dismemberment of the West Bank, and relieved Israel of its responsibility towards Palestinians living there, but allowed it to maintain its control over them. The PA assumed the responsibilities of a state but lacked the sovereignty to behave like one (Zreik 2004). Following Oslo, the establishment of the PA along with an influx of foreign aid, a small Palestinian elite emerged consisting of the political ruling class, NGO officials and capitalists from the diaspora (Clarno 2018; Farsakh 2005). The formation of this group of elites was enabled by the PA's neoliberal economic approaches, which are essentially shaped and governed by Israel, the US, and the World Bank and International Monetary Fund (Clarno 2018; Khalidi and Samour 2011). They are often the beneficiaries of the occupation, unlike many people living in the West Bank whose freedoms are severely restricted and who face high rates of unemployment and poverty (Farsakh 2005, Clarno 2018). Consequently, Palestinians living in these enclaves experience not only colonisation, but also inequality and repression. Therefore, it was unsurprising that the oppressive practices of governing officials, the violent acts of the security forces, and criticism of the human rights performances of those representing the Palestinian state were topics that emerged frequently during discussions with young people especially those from non-elite backgrounds.

This chapter is oriented around these themes and the overarching argument made by the youths that those from political ruling classes deny the powerless a voice in society. It concludes by considering how the youths occasionally chose to restrict their own voices so as not to undermine the state-building efforts of the PA – however imperfect they may be. Throughout these conversations, the young people used the motif of 'voice' to capture their marginalisation. It is helpful to bear in mind that for the young people, at times, 'voice' was used to depict the right to a literal voice, but often it was used as a symbol for other civil and political rights.

II. VOICE IS HINDERED BY THE POWERFUL

Whilst the young people I spoke to did not use the terms 'bureaucracy' or 'bureaucrats', they seemed well acquainted with the administrative rituals practised by those in positions of power. These practices often achieved a distancing effect which succeeded in alienating mainly those who did not make up part of the elite members of society. This is illustrated in this exchange between students in the UNGS:

> **Sabina:** When you go to someone who is in charge to tell him an idea, he will give you an appointment … then he will keep on delaying the appointment and finally if you manage to see him maybe he will not listen to you.
>
> **Isra'a:** Maybe they listen but they will not really act upon this (UNGS).

These officials were perceived as inaccessible due to their repetitive rituals of delaying appointments. Engaging with these officials was often viewed as futile since they did not listen or act upon the concerns of those who approached them. Similarly, girls who attended the GGS identified those in positions of power as obstacles, more specifically, to the voices of Palestinian youths. When asked what a young person could do if they felt their rights were being threatened or in danger, Lama (student, GGS) responded that they could 'ask for help from people in high positions'. But this was rebuffed by her peer Zahra (student, UNGS), who was quick to say: 'But it's not possible to go to people in high positions because they will not take our opinions seriously as we are so young'.

Voice was used to capture the marginalisation that children and young people face when it comes to being heard and taken seriously by fellow Palestinians – even in relation to rights violations. Referring to those with influence as those in 'high positions' again reflects the image they hold of the hierarchical structure of the Government. The fact that citizens have 'to go' to these people implies that they position themselves at a distance in relation to those in and working for the PA. It was these encounters with bureaucrats that shaped their perception of a state that seems inaccessible to people like them and one which acts as a barrier to their realisation of their right to a voice. The PA, through their authoritarian style of governance, have intentionally created a gulf between the realm of the state and civil society (Allen 2013). This gap is experienced in particular by children from lower income families who attended government-run schools and those from the refugee community who were enrolled in UNRWA-run schools.

The monetary interests and cronyism of the PA is a source of much debate for the Palestinian people, especially amongst those who do not benefit from political connections with the PA. This was a topic of conversation with those I met during my time living in the West Bank, but it was often uttered in hushed voices out of fear of who might be listening. Educators in non-private schools avoided making these critiques not because they lacked opinions, but because they were aware of the surveillance they and their colleagues are subjected to by the PA via the MoEHE and its spies. However, young people who were interviewed were less afraid to question the internal corruption of those who represented the state, as summed up in Rama's (student, UNGS) comment: 'Those in charge are not interested in human rights as much as money'.

Most of the youths who attended government schools were from families who faced economic hardship. This was reflected by the emphasis they placed throughout their discussions on economic concerns and their prospects of unemployment. It was therefore unsurprising that they perceived those in positions of authority as being responsible for perpetuating the inequalities they face within society. Farah and Khadija explained:

> **Farah:** Sometimes those in charge or in the [Palestinian] Authority use their position … to give somebody or his relatives a job when he doesn't have the skills needed for it.
>
> **Khadija:** Or for example, expensive schools … not everybody can enrol but high people like ministers can (GGS).

For these young people, this cronyism affects their future opportunities. These sentiments were reiterated by girls from the refugee community, who were also suspicious of those who would use their connections with the politically powerful even to circumvent the law:

> **Hadeel:** If the son of the President had an accident with his car and hit someone, it's okay because he's the son of the President, but it would be a problem for a normal person who commits the same accident.

> **Amal:** Also, jobs, they don't give jobs to the people who need them, but they give them to the richest people. In the past, there was help and services for the poor people to keep an eye open for them (UNGS).

Frequently, the youths referred to the controversial practice of *wasta*. Historically, intermediary *wasta* was used to peacefully address conflict between individuals or groups and was an effective tool for achieving a truce in a tribal setting (Cunningham et al 1994). Intercessory *wasta* is a powerful mechanism that is still used in Arab societies. This form of *wasta* allows people to gain favours based upon their connections with those with influence – often those in government roles. The young people that I interviewed were critical of this form of *wasta* using the colloquial term *vitamin w*. They viewed this practice as a form of bribery and corruption, which serves the interests of those in places of economic and social power. *Wasta* also lends itself well to oppressive forms of bureaucracy since those who use *wasta* can avoid the administrative trappings that others would have to face. For instance, successful employment is reliant upon these connections rather than qualifications, as Amal (student, UNGS) explained: 'getting a job is not based on qualifications but on vitamin w … You know it's just vitamin w that has ruined the people'. Furthermore, a mediator is often involved in securing favours for the person he or she seeks to represent. This also can result in silencing the voices of those who are not easily heard to begin with. Arguably, if individuals were enjoying their rights, especially their right to express their opinions, there would be no need for the use of *wasta*. Ultimately, this practice employed by those in government roles or connected to those in positions of influence leads to the reproduction of inequalities within society.

Youths who attended the BGS also spoke of nepotism and claimed that possessing a voice was dependent upon possessing power. As Akram (student, BGS) explicated: 'If I want to express my opinion, I need to have an important position (power position) so I can get what I want'. His peer, Omar (student, BGS), responded: 'If I have a problem with someone who is in a powerful position, I would not get what I want'. They explained these 'facts' with a tone of resignation, which contrasted with the more confrontational attitude of the refugee girls. This reflected the overall register of the discussions with the boys. Largely, they seemed to hold the most pessimistic attitudes towards human rights and had a fatalist attitude towards not only their present circumstances but also their futures. Lack of voice was used not only by the boys, but also by the girls (from non-elite families) to capture the sense of marginalisation they faced, but which they expect to encounter in the future because of their social status or their lack of *wasta*.

Therefore, the gulf between civil society and the state seemed even more apparent to the young people who were not connected with those from the ruling political classes. Class hierarchies within Palestinian society influenced the way the youths made sense of the complex political relationship between the PA and the occupying power (Jiménez 2023). This chasm between them and the state hinders their voice and ability to participate in society. Whilst the young people's analyses suggested that the state often functions to ensure that the voices of the powerless are marginalised, they also exemplified how young people were not deterred from using their voices to critique what they deemed to be the unjust actions of the powerful.

Human rights can be used not only to challenge power, but to consolidate it. As Douzinas (2003: 172) observes: 'A close look at the history of state and empire building indicates that natural/human rights claims always accompanied the project of state building'. Human rights discourse is invoked by political leaders across the globe – even those leading so-called rogue states (Allen 2013). Governments or those engaged in state-building can participate in human rights rituals and enact human rights performances so as to appear legitimate to international actors, at UN assembly meetings as well as locally among the people they govern (or intend to govern). The PA also engage in human rights activities and rhetoric to appear to behave like a state and to secure international financial support.

For instance, the PA became an International Criminal Court member in 2015 and applied to join 15 international human rights conventions and treaties (Erakat 2015; United Nations 2014). In her book, Allen (2013) recounts a frank exchange that took place between the head of police in the West Bank and Gaza and a Palestinian UN worker engaged in human rights training for PA security forces. In this exchange, the head of police commented:

> I don't send my cadre to your training because of you or because of human rights, but for my reports to the Europeans … As director of police I do respect human rights, but I want cars and arms. I want something out of this (Allen 2013: 131).

The youths that I interviewed were not beguiled by the face the PA seeks to present, but were cynical of the PA's human rights performances. The refugee girls scrutinised the spoken and written word versus the practices of those acting on behalf of the state – especially the current President Mahmoud Abbas. In certain authoritarian regimes, ironic mockery can enable subjects to criticise the state safely (Anderson 2013). The youths employed mockery when describing Palestinian politicians, as Hadeel (student, UNGS) did when criticising the rhetoric of the PA: 'They always say, "the Palestinian Authority is in the people's service". So where is this service when you have a problem?' She scoffed at the strapline used by the PA and then reformulated her own rhetoric to question their legitimacy as a representative of the people. In doing so, she constructed the realm of the state as a distant entity from civil society. This resonates with Sharma and Gupta's (2006: 14) claim that subjects can be 'critical of the premium placed on the written word by state officials, and resist the hierarchicalism and procedurialism inherent in bureaucratic practices'.

Cynicism of the written word among the youths also included the role of human rights instruments. This was evident in a discussion about gender inequality when Basel (student, BGS) cast doubt on the President's conduct versus his rhetoric in relation to the rights of women when he commented: 'Our President signed the agreement for human rights, but nothing is applicable, and I doubt he's applying it in his home'. Basel (student, BGS) viewed the President's act of ratifying human rights documents as another form of performance since he doubted the appropriation of these rights in practice. He also employed the use of scorn by questioning the President's embodiment of rights in his private life. This implied that he was not convinced that the President truly intends to deliver the written promises of which he has signed.

The young people were not only sceptical of the written word of state officials but also their spoken word. Lina (student, UNGS) was very vocal throughout discussions when it came to criticising Arab politicians more generally. She claimed that: 'They go on TV and preach about human rights and the first thing the Arab leaders do is just say words when nothing can be applied in reality'. Interestingly, she chose the word 'preach' to describe the way in which politicians invoke human rights discourse. This implies that they are not merely drawing on the language of human rights, but seem to be passionately promoting them when they address mass audiences. She later clarified that she was referring to the PA's President and was clear to differentiate him from his predecessor, Yasser Arafat (something which other students were also keen to do). She also explained that she believed that their rights would be fulfilled in the future 'if they change the president'. Young people regularly implied that human rights are unrealisable not only due to the military occupation, but also due to the obstacles presented by their own political leaders and factions within Palestinian politics. Allen (2013: 132) describes how governments deploy human rights rituals and rhetoric as 'a necessary window dressing that is hung to prettify, and sometimes to block the view of what is really happening inside'. When interviewed, young people seemed to be keen to expose how the state attempts to 'prettify' itself as a smokescreen for rights violations taking place behind the scenes.

The construction of those who represent the face of the state as barriers to rights was also articulated in the walking debate that the young people took part in. During this activity, statements were made to which youths had to agree or disagree. In response to the statement: 'A lot of people talk about human rights here in Palestine, but nothing happens', Nadine (student, UNGS) indicated that she strongly agreed with the statement and explained: 'Yes, no one listens to us, even our President. If our President would listen to us, then something might change'. This further demonstrates that these young people longed for not only a global audience but also a local one since they believed that their participation could deliver some of the emancipatory potential found within human rights discourse.

III. VOICE IS HINDERED BY THE FEAR TACTICS OF THE STATE

In the 1980s and leading up to Oslo, the Israeli economy began to change from a welfare economy to a globalised one (Clarno 2018). Israel's dependence upon Palestinian labour diminished as a result of this neoliberal restructuring of its economy along with Oslo. In turn, this enabled Israel to shirk some of the financial cost of military occupation and facilitated the flow of international donor's money into the OPT (Tawil-Souri 2012). Following Oslo, Israel also outsourced its security to a force populated by Palestinians, easing them of some of the financial burden of military occupation and leaving Palestinians to restrict other Palestinians' participation at demonstrations against the occupation (Desai 2021; Tawil-Souri 2012). It may come as no surprise that girls from the refugee community categorised the PA along with the occupation as another force against which they must struggle to claim their rights. This was evident during one of the discussions in which they were asked to write and then discuss the unique barriers they face when it comes to enjoying human rights as Palestinian young people. Several of the girls wrote down lists which included the Occupation, the PA and aspects of their culture. One of the main reasons why the PA were categorised this way by participants was due to their role during demonstrations against the occupation. As Majd (student, UNGS) explained: 'I would like to participate in a peaceful demonstration, but I know it's not allowed as I know the Palestinian Government will stop us'.

After Friday prayers, many Palestinians walk from the mosque to take part in protests at interfaces such as checkpoints or the separation wall across the West Bank. What is controversial for many is that the Palestinian security forces take up their positions facing the Palestinian demonstrators and, therefore, stand in between the people and the Israeli soldiers. As a result of this symbolic physical stance taken by the PA, they are seen as yet another barrier against which they must struggle to achieve rights. Basel (student, BGS) clarified how participation in demonstrations is restricted by the use of force: 'The Palestinian Authority works with Israel in preventing any attempt of claiming our rights through demonstrations. They prevent resistance and threaten people with being imprisoned or hit'.

The right to assemble freely in the form of demonstrations is a common form of 'offensive resistance' that has been practised by Palestinians for decades (Darweish and Rigby 2015: 61). This form of popular protest re-emerged as a response to the construction of the separation wall that commenced in 2003. Historically, young people, often known for throwing stones, have also played a significant symbolic role in these clashes with armed Israeli soldiers, who fire tear gas grenades, rubber bullets and skunk water. The youths' participation has helped create the desired visual image of 'David versus Goliath' (Darweish and Rigby 2015: 61). Nawja (student, PS) talked about the treatment of a girl called Lena by Israeli forces:

> Lena didn't really affect anyone she was just like throwing rocks to express her opinion NOT at people, she's just you know, like throwing rocks and she was held by her hair actually. She fell down and she was pulled by her hair.

Nawja was careful to note that by throwing stones Lena had not sought to harm anyone, but used them, interestingly, as a vehicle to exercise her right to freedom of expression. Consequently, to hinder freedom of assembly in the form of demonstrations can be perceived as a barrier to expressing one's opinion, and a challenge to aspects of the historical collective struggle that many have engaged in throughout the years. It can also be interpreted as undermining the visual representation of an asymmetrical conflict that Palestinians have strived to show the world. Additionally, due to the ongoing central role of youths in this collective act of resistance, preventing demonstrations understandably affronts the young people's preferred form of political participation. Again, this was a focal point of discussions among the refugee girls: 'Our youths go out and defend the camp, but they don't get their rights because the Authority comes and suppresses them' (Anwar, student, UNGS). This was reiterated by Lina (student, UNGS), who explained that 'our police prevent and stop our guys from making a peaceful demonstration or don't listen to them'. Prefacing both 'police' and 'guys' with 'our' captures how Palestinians have been conscripted into Israel's neoliberal settler colonial enterprise (Clarno 2018) since Palestinians working for the security forces are hindering their own people from mobilising against the occupation.

Whilst refugee girls often named the PA as a barrier to their rights, they did not offer explanations as to why they think the Palestinian police might be acting in this way. In contrast, the boys who attended a school made up of those from refugee camps and villages offered different interpretations as to why the PA try and prevent demonstrations. In fact, more generally, they were keen to unravel their thoughts concerning the ambiguous relationship between the state of Israel and the PA. Amjad (student, BGS) constructed the PA as collaborators with Israel under the current presidency:

> In 2001, there was a Resistance to the occupation but after the death of President Yasser Arafat, our current president chose to negotiate with Israel. Consequently, we are not supposed to struggle or raise our voice against Israel because Israel will offer us a 'good life'.

Amjad refers to the Second *Intifada*, a predominantly violent form of resistance in which individuals were recruited by militia groups to take up armed struggle against the occupation (Darweish and Rigby 2015). He marks the death of Arafat as a key turning point, which led to the PA prioritising cooperation with, rather than resistance against, Israel. Because of the negotiations, he claims that he, along with other members of civil society, have been robbed of a voice of protest and ultimately their political agency since they are 'not supposed to struggle' anymore. Furthermore, because of this complex political partnership, the Palestinian people have been encouraged to accept the oppressive status quo of life under occupation because a privileged minority has been able to benefit off the back of it – 'Israel will offer us a good life'. He of course uses the pronoun 'us' with irony. Therefore, according to Amjad's analysis, the PA discourage popular resistance because they want to protect the vested interests of the few. Their critiques echo academic analyses such as Desai's (2021: 58) observation that 'neoliberalism has reinforced class hierarchies in which some bourgeois "natives" have become collaborators with their colonizers based on their shared market interests across settler states'.

Alternatively, Hassan (student, BGS) offered the following analysis of the ambiguous relationship between the occupation and the PA, depicting the PA as the powerless partner whose hands are tied:

> Sometimes our government cannot give us our rights because we are occupied and depend on the occupier to supply it to us. For example, if we are a poor family and need help from our government, our government will not be able to help if Israel is putting financial pressure on them.

Hassan pardoned the Palestinian Government and reminded his classmates that the Palestinian people and the PA alike live under occupation. He suggested if the PA were to encourage the mobilisation of the people through demonstrations, Israel would respond by further crippling the Palestinian economy; for example, through suspending the transfer of taxes on imported goods collected by Israel on behalf of the PA (see Darweish and Rigby 2015). Israel has been known to withhold these transfers as a punitive measure in response to other acts of resistance, with a direct impact on basic services such as healthcare and education (Roy 2012). Discussions demonstrated that these boys from non-elite backgrounds had experienced on the ground the consequences of this form of financial punishment, as Abdullah's (student, BGS) comment illustrated: 'If the occupation puts financial pressure on the government, then our governmental schools will be shut down. Many times, we had school strikes because there are no salaries for teachers'.

Abdullah and his peers went on to provide examples of how punitive measures had impacted healthcare provision as well as education. Tariq (student, BGS) offered a similar account and linked it back to why the PA therefore try to prevent Palestinians organising in the form of demonstrations:

> The Palestinian Authority is under pressure by the occupation because the Israeli occupation; for example, it will not give salaries to Palestinian workers in response to any form of Palestinian resistance. Consequently, the Palestinian Authority will try to prevent any demonstration or ways of resistance to keep the situation in Palestine under control.

The poorer members of Palestinian society would be more likely to bear the brunt of Israel's reprimands if the PA were to encourage popular resistance. This could explain in part why the boys were so aware of the power dynamics at play between the PA and Israel. Whilst the youths from the private school also described demonstrations as a central way of protesting against the occupation, they did not once refer to the PA as a barrier to their right to assemble. Typically, boys attend demonstrations whereas girls are discouraged by their parents from taking part for cultural reasons (see chapter six), hence possibly why the students at the GGS did not discuss the role of the PA at demonstrations. However, the girls from the refugee camp were more accustomed to frequent raids and lived in the centre of a site where demonstrations took place weekly. Therefore, whilst they might not have been free to participate in protests for reasons related to the honour code, they witnessed this interplay between the Israeli forces, Palestinian police and protestors (their brothers, cousins, fathers and uncles) yards away from their homes. Unlike the boys, these girls did not theorise about the motivations of the PA, but rather constructed them as the violent local arm of the occupation.

The PA were also viewed as a barrier to the realisation of rights due to the way they instil fear into the population through surveillance. Youths from the refugee camp and the BGS used the word 'punishment' frequently when discussing the consequences of voicing one's opinion about the PA. Lina (student, UNGS) also explained that: 'If someone … criticises our President, the Palestinian Authority will come directly and punish them'. Furthermore, her classmate Shefa'a (student, UNGS) discussed the way in which their right to privacy, freedom of conscience and expression is hindered by state surveillance:

> In our community if anyone criticises the government or the Palestinian Authority in Palestine it's not something good because there are many spies who might transfer what was said and then they will get arrested. So, it's prohibited to express your opinion or criticise the President.

Whilst the youths did not use terms such as 'neoliberalism' in their discussions, it was apparent that they were making sense of how neoliberalism and settler colonialism in the West Bank intersects and manifests in their day-to-day lives (Jiménez 2023). Despite their awareness of the possible consequences of using a political voice, youth participants from non-elite backgrounds were willing to exercise their right to freedom of expression when it came to critiquing those in positions of power within the state during focus group discussions. Even though the PA have intentionally created a gulf between civil society and politics, which has led many adults to become politically disaffected, many of the youths were not afraid to exercise their own political voice and questioned those who seek to subjugate them. This resonates with the view that the Palestinian people have a unique long legacy of popular political struggle for the recognition of their rights (Kazziha 2010). Notably, the young people's willingness to use their political voice was not matched by most of their educators. This may however reflect the fact that discussions took place in schools in which the realm of the state also exercises influence.

IV. VOICE IS HINDERED AT SCHOOL LEVEL BY THE STATE

It became apparent that the state's influence also extended beyond the wider community and into the realm of the classroom via the MoEHE. In her ethnographic study of the Turkish state, Navaro-Yashin (2002) proposes that the state is not bound to one locality, but rather 'faces of the state' that appear in different guises such as through the media, monuments, letterheads, or through the practices of the police. In the West Bank, principals of government schools sat at desks over which hung large pictures of the current President Abbas and his predecessor, President Yasser Arafat. After a discussion with boys from the government school, Basel (student, BGS), who had been critical of the oppressive practices of the state, got my attention before pointing to a framed photograph of the current President, which was on the floor waiting to be mounted on the wall, at which he laughed mockingly. This was something that an educator from his school or a UNRWA-run school would not have felt free to do publicly. This act reflected a trend throughout conversations with the youths – young people seemed to possess a courage to express their political opinions and oppose the injustices enacted by the PA in a way that their educators did not.

Although UNRWA schools are accountable to the MoEHE, these visual representations of the 'state' such as political figures, flags and slogans are not found on the walls of the UNRWA schools because of the Agency and its commitment to neutrality. Installation inspections are carried out in their buildings including schools to ensure they are aligned to the 'Humanitarian Principles'.[1] It is in part due to this neutral stance that the discussion of politics is discouraged at school. Bashar, a senior educator who had worked for many years at UNRWA, acknowledged the conflicting values faced by his Palestinians colleagues at the Agency: 'In UNRWA we are a UN organisation, we need to observe all the time the neutrality … although we are national staff and we are impacted … every minute of [by] what's happening' (Bashar, senior educator, UNRWA). However, for Bashar, loyalty to the Agency seemed to override his personal opinions in a way that was not necessarily imitated by other Palestinian educators at school level. This was also encapsulated when elsewhere during the interview he asserted: 'I'm a Palestinian, I work in UNRWA, I should observe the UN values'.

The state, via the MoEHE also prohibits political discussion in schools. As Naseef (principal, BGS) confirmed when asked about his facilitation of student voice at school: 'I held an open meeting with 12th grade students to listen to their problems from their right to express their opinions in terms of anything – except their political opinion as it's forbidden with all schools'. However, what was forbidden in reality was the discussion of *internal* political affairs in school. That is, young people and their teachers had no qualms about discussing the broader political situation of the Israeli military occupation. For instance, in one lesson that I observed at the UNGS, the teacher stated that the occupation intentionally shoots the cars of Palestinian doctors, and students discussed how Palestinian prisoners are subjected to medical experiments without their consent at the hands of Israeli captors. Moreover, the MoEHE *Civics Education* textbook, which was used in government and UNRWA-run schools (at the time this research was undertaken), contained examples of the freedom to explore issues connected to the occupation. In a unit entitled 'Solidarity Among People' various activities discuss the rights of disabled people, including one which states: 'Invite one of the people with special needs (disability resulted from INTIFADA war) to talk about his experience. Discuss with him [*sic*] the demands to enhance the solidarity with people with special needs' (Qazzaz et al 2010: 43).

Similarly, during a lesson I observed in the GGS, Sally (teacher, GGS) connected the rights of those with disabilities with settler colonial violence, by giving a personal account from when she was at school: 'There were two students in my

[1] See UNRWA's statement on 'Neutrality' on their website https://www.unrwa.org/neutrality and their statement on 'Staff Conduct & Neutrality' https://www.unrwa.org/staff-conduct-neutrality.

class at school who were disabled because they were shot the legs by the Israeli army. Should we shut them away?' Therefore, in practice, what is actually prohibited in both government and UNRWA schools is not political discussion in general, but the discussion of intra-Palestinian politics. If conversations with educators had not been carried out on the school premises, removed from fear of surveillance, then maybe they would have offered their own critique of the PA and its policies.

Prior to interviewing the youths, I consulted the Palestinian YPAGs. One of these YPAGs had predicted that educators would not necessarily feel free to share their views on the internal political situation because of the MoEHE's surveillance at school level and concerns over losing their jobs, or their schools being closed. This forecast came to pass most obviously during an interview that was conducted with the civics teacher at the UNGS named Hala. Midway through the interview, Hala (teacher, UNGS) recruited the assistance of the vice-principal. She did this by shouting out the question, claiming she was not as experienced as her senior colleague, who was sitting at a desk in a different part of the same open-plan office, to answer. This resulted in the other staff member joining the discussion towards the end. The question that she felt she was not experienced enough to answer was: 'Do you think there are places where Palestinians' rights are respected?' This did not seem like a question that required years of teaching experience to answer. Rather she was either motivated to avoid answering the question out of fear of giving the 'incorrect' answer or alternatively, she did not believe in the answer she knew she was supposed to give and therefore allowed her colleague to answer, who replied promptly: 'The Ministry of Education' (UNGS).

Elsewhere in the BGS, the Principal, Naseef (principal, BGS) also answered the same question with this uncannily similarly worded answer and without hesitation: 'The Ministry of Education'. These examples illustrate how educators' voices are hindered at school level by the state. At the time I reflected on why, if it would cost these educators their jobs, would they speak critically about the PA for the sake of an interview? The teachers' concerns were not unfounded. For instance, in the February of 2016 (the year after I conducted the work for this book) a general strike was coordinated and involved thousands of teachers travelling from different West Bank cities to assemble outside the Prime Minister's office in Ramallah. The PA's security forces responded by setting up checkpoints to prevent teachers travelling to the demonstrations in Ramallah (Wilson 2016). These actions to hinder the teachers' freedom of movement, assembly and association were criticised as having resembled the tactics often deployed by the Israeli military (Abu Moghli 2020). In the following days, pupils joined their teachers at these strikes in an act of solidarity.

Conversely, educators at the private school seemed much more at ease when it came to discussing internal politics and the practices of the Ministry of Education. Whilst private schools enjoy relative autonomy from the requirements of the MoEHE, there are still certain instances where they must consult the MoEHE. During one interview, Elias (vice-principal, PS) recounted that he had organised an annual school field trip to a nearby city in the West Bank only to have his plans rescheduled by the MoEHE. The school was required to apply for written approval by the Ministry. The application was denied (only a few days before our interview) because the co-educational school had proposed to take boys and girls together on the same day. Instead, the MoEHE had insisted that they must take the girls and boys on separate days. Elias (vice-principal, PS) vented his frustration during the interview and slammed a pile of MoEHE papers down on the desk, as he exclaimed: 'Imagine, imagine? Yeah! I cancelled the trip. It's best for me to cancel rather than to follow their instructions actually'. He felt at ease not only in discussing his recent dealings with the MoEHE, but also in his refusal to pander to their demands when it went against his own convictions and his school's ethos.

However, it also demonstrated that there are spaces where the MoEHE can exert control even over the actions of staff and pupils in private-run schools. There was only one instance where a government school teacher Sally (teacher, GGS) mentioned the President in an interview, stating that 'we can disagree with our President and give our opinion about his work. It's important to be respectful though'. Whilst she upheld that Palestinians enjoy a degree of freedom of political expression when it comes to the President, she attached 'respect' as a condition to this. Either Sally was muting her political voice out of fear, or she was accustomed to attaching this responsibility upon this particular right.

The youths also offered insights into how the state's control is exercised over their educators. Some of the young people speculated that fear drives their teachers not to enter political discussions with them, whilst others claimed there would be consequences. Majd (student, UNGS) offered this commentary: 'In school, teachers can't talk about him [the President] and the government or the [Ministry of] Higher Education will arrest him if he talks about them'. Some youths had been informed by teachers that they would risk losing their jobs or even that schools would face closures if they were to enter political debates with their pupils. Arguably, the teachers could have been using the way they felt threatened to indirectly caution their students in return when they sought to discuss Palestinian political affairs. In other words, they exercise their control over the child's political voice in the classroom. However, the youths did not interpret their teachers' actions this way. Instead, they displayed understanding towards their teachers.

It seemed that the teachers, under the auspices of the MoEHE, performed in the school premises 'as if' they were loyal and complicit subjects to the state (Navaro-Yashin 2002: 171). However, the pupils at these schools did not perform the same role. Instead, many of them offered explanations as to why their teachers are assigned the role of the 'cynical subject' (Žižek 1989). Arguably, one of the reasons why young people desired a political voice was because of the way in which it was denied at school. Throughout our conversations, the youths were eager to use their voice to express their political opinions about the future, as well as the current President and the ruling elites, which they ordinarily were not at liberty to do.

V. VOICE IS SELF-HINDERED BY THE YOUTHS: FEAR OF BEING SEEN TO HINDER STATE-BUILDING EFFORTS

Whilst many of the young people from non-elite backgrounds criticised the unfair practices of the PA, there was at times a reluctance to contest their oppressive practices considering the broader injustices caused by the occupation. As Hala (teacher, UNGS) commented: 'There are things out of our hands, even out of the hands of the Palestinian Authority because of the occupation'. Turning a critical eye inward can be difficult for Palestinians either because of fear of punishment, as explored above, or fear of being accused of hindering the state-building efforts. Moreover, in the wider context of ongoing political violence at the hands of a common 'oppressor', it was difficult for some youths to expose their fellow Palestinians' conduct – even when at times it too could be oppressive. The following dialogue which took place between girls who attended the GGS demonstrated this reluctance to critically analyse internal obstacles to their enjoyment of rights:

> **Ghada:** Sometimes it's hard to tell because we have never experienced a life without occupation, so we have never known how our life would be without it. I personally haven't lived in a country where there is no occupation to know if I'm taking my rights or not in my country.
>
> **Zahra:** I'm against her opinion, sometimes our rights are not respected and it's not due to the occupation.
>
> **Dinah:** No, you cannot say that the occupation affects our life.
>
> **Zahra:** If we had no occupation, we don't have freedom in many things (GGS).

Whilst challenged by her peers, Zahra (student, GGS) made a distinction between the rights that are denied because of the occupation and freedoms which are restricted by other factors such as the authoritarian practices of the PA and the patriarchal aspects of Palestinian culture. However, Ghada (student, GGS) and Dinah (student, GGS) equated criticisms of these other factors with denying the severity of life under occupation.

There was a notable lack of commentary offered about the President, governing officials and security forces by participants who attended the PS. However, there was one girl, Nawja (student, PS), who spoke positively about the President:

> When you have a president that goes up to fight for us even though he failed many times, yet he keeps trying and he finally got us to be like now we got 194 and we got to be a country that is fighting for our rights. He made us a country.

Here, she was referring to the campaign led by President Abbas that saw the state of Palestine recognised as an Observer State to the UN in November 2012. However, whilst she uttered her praise for the President, her peers in the room seemed uncomfortable while she spoke; they mumbled, rolled their eyes and sought to interrupt her. Nonetheless, she spoke with such confidence and succeeded in speaking over them. She argued that the President had been a resilient mediator between the populace and the international community:

> Mahmoud Abbas, who is our President, and he goes to the UN like multiple times, and he failed multiple times, yet he kept on going, that means he does respect our rights and he does want us to become better people.

She concluded, 'he's done our best, the President'. Nawja's (student, PS) enthusiasm for the President seemed to cause her to compromise some views she had articulated earlier in the discussion. Several of her peers had said that those in positions of authority, including Palestinian politicians, did not listen to young people. However, Nawja became defensive, and commented:

> I don't think they're supposed to listen to someone that isn't like above the legal age yet because we aren't that aware. Like when you look at somebody that has been working and studying about politics like a lot, they know a lot more than us so. As my opinion, I don't think that they should listen.

She seemed to deny herself and her peers a political voice in exchange for loyalty to the President. She set restrictive criteria to exclude those below the voting age, and those who had not studied politics from a right to a voice in political matters. This contrasted with earlier comments where she expressed her frustration with the fact that her school limits those who are able to participate in demonstrations to certain grades, claiming: 'Age shouldn't be a concern … because everybody has the right to reflect how they feel'. In another instance, she also spoke about the important political role of youths both globally and in the Palestinian context, arguing:

> The younger people are the people affecting the world today. Like I forgot what the girl's name was but the girl that got shot in the head in Pakistan that survived … Like something like that really motivates. They [adults] see that you can fight, and they should notice that the younger people are fighting, like when you look … at the Palestinian issue, you will see that the majority of people in jails or that are having huge conflicts with the occupation are of the younger generations.

According to Nawja's conflicting comments, when it concerns opposing the Taliban or the Israeli occupation, young people ought to, and indeed do possess a credible political voice. However, when it comes to being heard by local Palestinian politicians, young people should not expect to be heard. In arguing in such a way, she also silenced the voices of her peers who reacted through winces in response to her claims. They did not speak out in support of what she said at any time, nor did they overtly contest (verbally) what she had to say or offer a critique of the policies and practices of the Palestinian officials.

There was only one student from the PS who scrutinised the inaction of the Palestinian Government when it came to rights abuses committed by Israel in the Gaza War that had taken place months before the discussions. Camilla (student, PS) commented: 'Our government acts as if like they don't care whether we are occupied or not'. However, she opted to employ the more generic word 'government' and on other occasions did not specifically mention the President by name nor the PA. Camilla also remarked on the ambiguous relationship between the PA and Israel when it comes to protecting the rights of Palestinian children, noting that 'Israelis are killing kids and the government is not letting Israel pay for it'. Overall, the youths at the PS did not engage in discussions about the PA nor the President to the extent that those from non-elite backgrounds did.

As a non-Palestinian, it was helpful for me to turn to the analysis of the research advisory group made up of refugee youths (YPAG 2) especially when it concerned internal political matters. At one point they offered their insights into why youths living in, for example, the city of Ramallah would be less critical about the President and the PA than their peers living in other parts of the West Bank. They proposed that because Ramallah is considered the cultural capital of Palestine and is where the President resides, considerably more financial investment is pumped into it. Therefore, they deduced that the people who live there are more 'satisfied', to draw on their words. One of the research advisors wondered whether people were more fearful to criticise the President because he resides in Ramallah and seems physically closer. They also questioned among themselves whether the PA acts 'better' in Ramallah in comparison to where they live.

A different member of YPAG 2 suggested that these young people's parents probably worked for the Government because many people who live in Ramallah are employed by the PA. YPAG 2 therefore offered possible insight into why there was comparatively less criticism of the PA articulated by certain students. This links back to previous discussions around those belonging to or associated with the political classes possessing a voice. In other words, it is more difficult for the children of those who belong to this political class to be aware of the unjust practices of the state if they are more closely bound to it, possibly benefit from it and definitely less likely to suffer at the hands of it.

Most young people did not go as far as to champion the President as Nawja did, but many viewed the PA being at the mercy of Israel given the broader political situation of living under occupation, as Jamila (student, GGS) explained: 'Our country tries to give people their full rights, but the occupation plays its role'.

The members of YPAG 2 also debated who they found it easier to criticise – the PA or the occupation. Opinions were split, with one girl stating that she found it more 'painful' to criticise the PA because it was akin to criticising one's family. Another girl felt that change needed to take place from within and spoke about the need to get one's 'own house in order' first. This dialogue amongst the research advisors offered me valuable insights into the reluctance and frustration Palestinian young people face when it comes to negotiating their way through internal political complexities in the context of a wider ongoing occupation. At times, young people were hesitant to identify the PA as a restricting factor to their civil and political rights because of the fear of being seen to jeopardise state-building efforts in the broader context of the struggle against a common occupying regime. This reflected Allen's (2013) explanation that the PA have capitalised on this complexity. Alternatively, because of the scale, duration and intensity of the occupation, the PA enjoys a certain amount of immunity from criticism for some of its conduct towards its own people.

In a final session with one of the research advisory groups, the young people compiled a child-friendly summary of their peers' views for dissemination. This summary identified the barriers facing Palestinian youths at various levels when it comes to their enjoyment of rights (see Figure 5.1).

Figure 5.1 Youths in Palestine (YPAG 2 child-friendly summary of the findings)

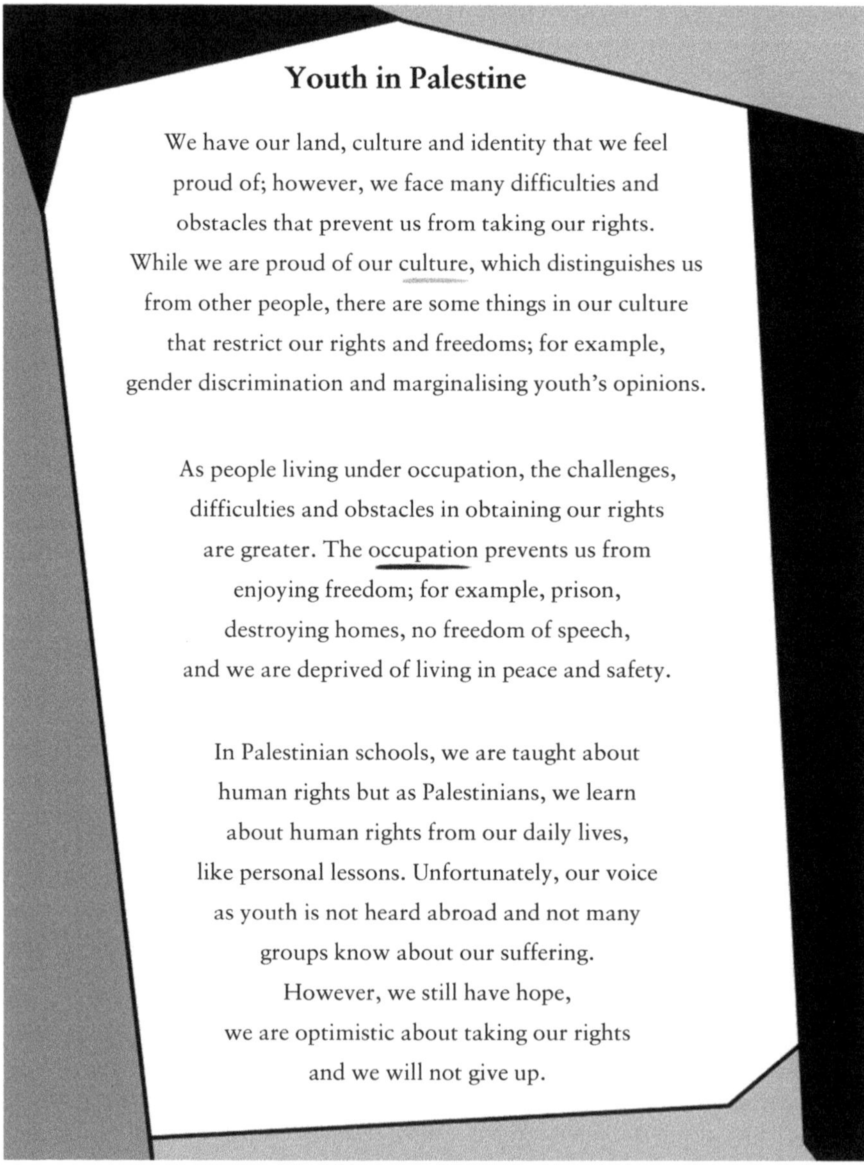

Two of the three layers of marginalisation are explicit in this summary: the occupation (see chapter four); and patriarchy (this will be explored in chapter six). But what is interesting is the layer of marginalisation they decided to omit – their critique of the PA – even though this was a prominent source of discussion among their peers and the data they analysed. Sometimes it is the 'unsayable' that reveals more about the child's voice than what is verbally articulated (Spyrou 2011: 157). Excluding their criticism of the Palestinian pseudo-state is not to suggest that they were being disingenuous about the other layers they included, such as the occupation and patriarchy. Rather, their omission highlights the need to consider the particularities of the context in which these voices were produced – an educational setting that was under the surveillance of the PA through the MoEHE.

How the research advisory group chose to represent their peers' voices was steered by power imbalances they encounter as those living under an authoritarian-styled state rather than power imbalances between them: these YPAG members (refugee girls) were all very vocal when it came to the oppressive practices of the PA. As I have argued elsewhere, I believe they made a reasoned decision to omit discussion of the PA to protect themselves, their peers and educators since they were aware that those working for the MoEHE might read their summary (see Jiménez 2021). The research advisors, like some of the interviewees and focus group participants, may also have wished to avoid being perceived to hinder any state-building efforts, as flawed as they might be.

Nonetheless, throughout discussions, the youths displayed a depth of understanding about the political intricacies in which they live: a pseudo-authoritarian state which has limited autonomy because of a military occupation and reliance on the international donor community. It also exemplified how the young people do not merely root their understanding of human rights in the context of the occupation, but also in other intersecting injustices they encounter in their everyday lives.

VI. CONCLUSION

Whilst the state seeks to silence those belonging to the non-political ruling classes, non-elite youths were not content to play the role of complicit subject, but instead used the language of rights to critique the oppressive practices of the PA and their governing officials, spies and security forces. Unlike their educators, they seemed freer to expose how political discussions are monitored inside school. However, expressing one's opinions about the state can also be viewed as undermining state-building efforts. This occasionally led the young people to hinder their own political voices when criticising the state that, like them, is also under military occupation. Ultimately, they too long for a Palestinian state, although not necessarily the one that has come to be imagined and that has come to represent them. Consequently, they were not afraid to unmask some of the practices of the PA that make it difficult for their rights to be realised, or in their words, their voices to be heard.

The Palestinian youths wished to take part politically because they know they have important contributions to make, adults have become increasingly politically disaffected, they are prohibited from discussing internal political affairs, and because they have been alienated from the elite gerontocratic politics of the PA (Tuastad 2017).

The young people underscored another layer of marginalisation that threatens the rights of girls and children: the patriarchal aspects of Palestinian culture which denies them agency.

6

Human Rights as a Vehicle to Challenge Patriarchy: Reclaiming Agency

I. INTRODUCTION

There are two main arguments when it comes to the relationship between human rights and religion: first, that religion is incompatible with a secular international human rights scheme; and second, that religion has the potential to motivate struggles for protecting human dignity and challenging injustice (Banchoff and Wuthnow 2011). What emerged from conversations with the youths and their teachers was that these two opposing viewpoints existed within Palestinian rights discourse. However, unlike in Western debates (Johnston 2015), the dominant view among participants tended to be that religion complements human rights concepts.

Sections II and III of this chapter examine the range of perspectives among the youths and their educators on the relationship between religion (namely Islam), patriarchy and human rights. Patriarchy in Arab and Islamic societies can manifest itself in hierarchies of age as well as gender (as discussed in more detail in chapter two). It is also helpful to consider the locally contextualised definition of patriarchy according to the young people. In the YPAG's child-friendly summary of the findings. The opening lines of this summary (see Figure 5.1) captures the layer of marginalisation discussed in this chapter and offers indications of how they defined patriarchy:

> We have our identity and culture that we feel proud of. However, we face many difficulties and obstacles that prevent us from taking our rights. Despite the fact that we are proud of our culture, there are things in our culture that restrict our freedom. For example, discrimination between the sexes, and ignoring the youths' opinions (extract from YPAG 2 child-friendly summary of the findings).

Therefore, sections IV and V focus on how young people have deployed human rights as a tool to understand and challenge patriarchal attitudes that hinder both the rights of women and girls, and the rights of children and young people.

II. HIGHLIGHTING AREAS OF DISSONANCE BETWEEN ISLAM AND HUMAN RIGHTS

Of the 11 adults I interviewed, only three educators – Sally (teacher, GGS), Elias (vice principal, PS) and Osama (teacher, PS) – emphasised areas of dissonance between aspects of Islam and human rights. These educators viewed Islam as a religion that can hinder the rights of certain marginalised groups within Palestinian society such as women, children, Christians, Marxists and atheists.

Sally was from a Christian background and identified herself as an observant Christian. She worked as a civics teacher at the GGS where all the staff and pupils were from Muslim backgrounds. During my conversations with Sally, she identified areas of dissonance between aspects of Palestinian cultural traditions, Islamic religious beliefs and human rights. She commented: 'Culture and religion restricts rights for young people'. She focused on the discrimination of children and young people, girls, and how the Islamic religion can hinder freedom of expression and conscience.

However, her opinions fluctuated regarding the role of culture in determining the universality of human rights and, at times, she articulated cultural relativist attitudes. Referring to her pupils at the all-girls' government school, she explained: 'They get 70 per cent of their rights, but there are things that are limited because of the culture, let's say the Islamic culture, but it's not in a wrong way because this is culture' (Sally, teacher, GGS). On the one hand she emphasised that 'Islamic' culture can act as a barrier to certain rights, yet justified this culture by describing it as not 'wrong'. In her lesson (which I observed), she made a more apparent cultural relativist argument when she said: 'There are things in religion, some rules that take away our rights, but we need to follow them – it's not the same as Israelis abusing our rights and taking them away' (Sally, teacher, GGS).

Although she acknowledged the way that religion can deny individuals their rights, she was quick to situate this in the broader context of how rights are abused by the occupation. She was not the only educator who used the occupation as a way to distract from rights violations committed by Palestinians – sometimes as a strategy to excuse patriarchal practices (this will be discussed later). Moreover, what Sally articulated when she was teaching her class contrasted with remarks she made in her interview: 'As a Christian teacher, I can see clearly. They [her Muslim students] can't criticise religion' (Sally, teacher, GGS). Unlike in the lesson, she differentiated herself from her pupils by identifying herself as a Christian and suggested that this enabled her to hold a more objective perspective.

Was it the case that her wavering attitudes towards the relationship between religion and human rights reflected her own personal journey as a (self-identified) observant Christian navigating her own religious views with human rights as a civics teacher in an entirely Muslim school? When she was asked to discuss the unique human rights challenges faced by students in her school, without hesitation she stated 'the culture' and then clarified what she meant: 'The Islamic culture, for example, if one of the girls wants to express her opinion in front of her father, she cannot because she was told that by her religion' (Sally, teacher, GGS). She suggested that Islam upholds the patriarchal system, which denies girls the right to express themselves in a family setting. Her comments echo the notion that patriarchy in Arab and Muslim-majority societies is concerned with how men 'as fathers', as opposed to brothers, exercise control over women (Joseph 1994). She also claimed that adults use religion and the fear of questioning it as a tool to silence the voices of girls and possibly those who would seek to challenge patriarchal structures.

When asked to share the most important aspects of human rights she would like her pupils to grasp, she responded: 'That they can express their opinions, take decisions, not let their parents control their personality just because they are girls, also to disagree with things in the community' (Sally, teacher, GGS). For Sally it was important for her female pupils to learn about human rights in a way that would enable them to disrupt the oppressive status quo within the patriarchal system. She centralised children's participation rights in the hope that girls may consequently confront the dominant narratives of adults in the home and the wider community so as to make their own decisions about their own lives.

During interviews, male educators Osama (teacher) and Elias (vice principal) at the PS were also concerned about the role of Islam in curbing the rights of girls. They discussed the *hijab*, often portraying it as a symbol of oppression. However, they approached this from different perspectives. Osama, was a social studies teacher at the private school, single and in his twenties. Although he was from a Muslim background, he made it clear that he was secular and was critical of the role of religion in Palestinian society. He told me that he was from and still lived in a refugee camp. When discussing women's rights with me he said that he was looking to the moment when all Palestinian women would have the freedom to choose whether to wear the *hijab* or not as an indicator of the extent to which human right more generally were being upheld in Palestine. Osama constructed the veil as a signifier of patriarchy, informing me that it is older men such as fathers who decide whether their daughters must cover their hair or not.

Elsewhere in the interview he highlighted the generational discrepancies that he saw between the views of young people and the older generations towards women's rights. He told me that older generations believe that women have to stay home and cook, clean and watch TV, thus indicating the double jeopardy that Palestinian girls face in the OPT. The *hijab* is a symbol which carries not merely religious significance, but also political meaning. Whilst in the West, it is often perceived as a 'loaded sign of oppression' (Hatem 2003: 94), in Iran during the Islamic Revolution of 1979, wearing it was an act of resistance against the Shah (Fathzadeh 2020). Its meaning shifts in different contexts and times.

We have seen this more recently in France, where pupils and teachers have gone on strike and Muslim human rights organisations have challenged the French Government's decision to ban the *abaya* (along with other religious dress) in state schools (Al Jazeera and News Agencies 2023; Nazeer 2023). In Iran where the *hijab* is mandatory, women and schoolgirls have removed their *hijabs*, chanting the slogan 'women, life freedom' (BBC Newsnight 2022). These protests were sparked by the murder of a Kurdish 22-year-old woman, Mahsa Amini, who died whilst held in custody by 'morality police'. Therefore, as Golley (2004: 525) argues, 'wearing the veil and discarding it in different situations should be seen as symbolising political struggle and women's political agency'. Palestinian Muslim women and girls also choose or refuse to wear the veil, although it must be acknowledged that some do not have this choice either way. However, for Osama (teacher, PS), he perceived the *hijab* as a form of female subordination. Arguably, this reflects his broader view that religion and human rights can be awkward bedfellows.

Osama's male colleague, Elias, the vice principal of the PS, also discussed the *hijab* with me. Elias told me that he was from a Christian background, but unlike Sally (educator, GGS), he did not stipulate whether he was an observant Christian or not. When he discussed the *hijab*, he described it as a potential threat to the Christian community, since for Christian Palestinian women not wearing a *hijab* is a visual marker of their cultural identity as a minority group. Therefore, being forced to wear it would be seen as an attempt to deny their right to express their Christian cultural identity. He explained:

> I'm worried in the future, if we have what Gaza have ... it's very terrible, in Gaza they have boys alone and girls alone, no co-education ... all women teachers have to wear ... the *hijab* ... I don't know [if] this is [a] challenge in the coming future, if we are going to be in such a ... situation (Elias, vice principal, PS).

He then let out a deep sigh and said: 'Yeah, the religion'. The fact that he used Gaza as an example shows his fear of the Islamist agenda, since the Gaza Strip has been under a Hamas-led government since they were democratically elected in 2006. Throughout the interview, he described conservative Islam as the cause behind the inequality that Palestinian women experience, claiming:

> I'm a Christian by the way. The Islamic religion puts some restrictions on human rights, yes ... I don't know in details but ... socially the man, he has the superior power on the woman. He has the rights, his wife she doesn't ... she doesn't have the right to sit with men in the same setting (Elias, vice principal, PS).

He used the word 'religion' and then clarified that he was referring to Islam when discussing the way in which he perceives it to curb the rights of women. Notably, he, like Sally (teacher, GGS), also chose to identify himself in the interview as a Christian before offering comments on the way he views the relationship between Islam and human rights. Throughout the interview, he expressed concerns as a member of a Christian minority regarding the role of (Islamic) religion in not only the West Bank, but also the Middle East more generally. He told me:

> Regardless of whether we have a Palestinian state … if religion will be dominant as … in other places, I'm sure this is a big challenge for us not only as a school but as [a] society (Elias, vice principal, PS).

Palestinian Christians have felt increasingly sidelined within the nationalist movement because of the rise of an Islamist opposition along with their decline in numbers (Patierno 2015; Lybarger 2007). According to Lybarger's (2007: 786) ethnographic study, before Oslo, Palestinian Christians played a key role in the pursuit of an independent secular state, but now feel as though they are no longer represented and wonder 'whether the nation still has a place for them'. It is helpful to bear in mind this political dimension when analysing how Elias (vice principal, PS) viewed conservative forms of Islam negatively. Furthermore, he also broadened his criticism of the role of Islam in politics beyond the Palestinian state by comparing the freedoms which Palestinians enjoy to other parts of the Middle East. He reflected:

> Comparing ourselves – Palestinians to other places, other countries in the Arab World, I can say that we are in a good shape. I know other places I read about … are very closed, they're not open and what's happening right now in the Islamic World – it's a good indicator of how they think or how the mentality is … going backward to hundreds and hundreds and hundreds of years (Elias, vice principal, PS).

It is important to remember that this interview took place when *Daesh* was gaining momentum in the region and during a time in which this group had targeted Christian minorities such as Egyptian Copts (see Black 2015). Both Christian and Muslim participants were aware of the close proximity of *Daesh* in the region and made reference to this movement often during our conversations. So, whilst he seemed to view the Islamist agenda with a degree of fear, it is important to state that this seems to be more motivated by the events that were taking place in the region during the time of these discussions and the fact that he was from a minority group within the OPT.

Notably, Osama (teacher, PS) was also suspicious of the role religion was playing in Palestinian state-building efforts. He argued that other political voices were curbed by the dominance of religion in Palestinian society. He claimed that in his school a student or teacher can be an anarchist or a Marxist, whereas their views would not be tolerated outside of the school gates since in his words: 'Society believes in God' and God and religion is seen as 'the only solution to their lives'. Elsewhere, he contended that not only Palestinians but the whole Arab World needed to 'get over' religion, describing those who believe as 'under control' and unable to think freely. He not only understood Islam as a religion that curbs rights to freedom of expression but also freedom of conscience. He was the only educator from a Muslim background in this study who conflated patriarchy with Islam and explicitly described religion more generally as a stumbling block to the enjoyment of human rights.

On the contrary, Riham (teacher, PS), his colleague and the Christian religious education teacher claimed that religion and human rights complemented one another:

> If you don't understand what is written in the Holy Books – Muslim or Jewish or Christian it will not work, but if you are open-minded and reading [in context] … you will see it's not something that will stop you from taking your rights because most of the human rights are taken … from the religion[s].

Whilst she believed that human rights and religion can work in harmony, she also acknowledged that religion had the potential to act as a barrier to human rights if religious texts are taken out of context. She was the only educator in the study to view the origins of human rights in the three main Abrahamic religions (Banchoff and Wuthnow 2011). However, Osama and Elias (her male colleagues), as well as Sally, who taught at the GGS, did not disentangle patriarchy from Islam, instead viewing Islamic religion as that which can marginalise the voices of women, children, non-Muslims, and those with alternative political views within Palestinian society (Elboubekri 2015). Young people from the PS also expressed similar concerns that the intersection between Islam and human rights can be problematic.

As outlined in the introductory chapter, I worked alongside two young person's advisory groups (YPAGs) made up of Palestinian youths who closely represented the young participants. When I consulted them before conducting fieldwork, they suggested that their peers may exercise more caution discussing their views on Palestinian political issues and religion, especially if an adult was within earshot. They did not advise me to avoid discussing these sensitive topics, but rather suggested strategies that would enable the young people to participate in these discussions (see Jiménez 2021). The YPAGs' advice indicated, even before I had spoken to participants, that young people, if they felt safe to do so, may counter the narratives of adults when discussing patriarchy, religion and politics.

When it came to religion, the youths who attended the PS were the only child participants who attributed the marginalisation that Palestinian women face with Islam. They all agreed that Palestinian women did not enjoy equality with men, stating that women are viewed as 'half a man' (Nadia, student, PS), which they attributed to 'the religion issue' (Jiries, student, PS). When asked to clarify whether this was because of both Christian and Islamic religious beliefs, they immediately attributed the discrimination Palestinian women face as a consequence of solely Islam. Nadia (student, PS) stated: 'Islam is a huge issue yeah, it makes people's minds conventional. VERY conventional'. This was followed by laughter by others in the room as though they knew this was a controversial line to take.

At times their conversations reflected the secular-religious divide which exists within Palestinian society. When asked whether human rights sit in tension with aspects of their *culture* (note that the word religion was not used in the question) they immediately discussed Islam and depicted it not only as a variant of patriarchy, but also as the source of the discrimination of women. Jiries (student PS) told me: 'When it comes to women, it's bad … because the Palestinian law is based on religion and Islam makes it bad'. His female classmate Nadia (student, PS) added: 'We represent ourselves as secular, but we're [rest of society is] not, we are, like our law is based on Muslim ideology … Religion's a huge concern, it's very big and it's not just us'. It is this group of students' predominantly secular leanings which seem to drive their negative portrayal of religion. These young people described religion as 'a huge concern' arguably because of their political beliefs or family connections as elites with links with secular nationalism. There has been a fear among those associated with the PA (predominantly secular *Fatah*) of the rise of the Islamist nationalist opposition within the OPT (Brich and Lampridi-Kemou 2013).

Similar to their teacher Osama (teacher, PS), these participants often depicted Islam as a religion which seeks to silence the voices of those who scrutinise it against other values such as human rights, as this conversation indicated:

> **Jiries:** Because we have the fear of speaking about religion issues, especially in the Arab World.
>
> **Nadia:** It's a huge problem.
>
> **Jiries:** It's complicated.
>
> **Nadia:** It's not just here, in Iraq and Syria.
>
> **Salim:** It's … we have freedom of speech but not when it comes to religion.
>
> **Nadia:** Yeah, it's a very sensitive topic (PS).

Whilst these students seemed at ease criticising aspects of religion, they also acknowledged that this was a delicate and complex issue not only in the Palestinian context but in the wider region. Nonetheless, they felt that their school was a space in which students felt free to debate religious issues or to voice opinions which were critical of religion. This is arguably exemplified by the fact that they were the only group to critique areas of dissonance between religion and human rights. Their teacher Osama (teacher, PS) also attested to this, claiming that his students enjoy a unique freedom to discuss religious matters compared with youths in other schools: 'I can talk with them about religion, we can talk about it without the '"holy" thing … But in another school they cannot'.

When the YPAGs analysed their peers' conversations relating to these school differences, research advisors from YPAG 1 drew attention to the role religion plays in the context of occupation. They argued that refugee children who attend UNRWA-run schools are more exposed to settler colonial violence with

Israeli soldiers, thus making them more likely to 'resort to religion as a coping mechanism'. One of the research advisors suggested that 'no one in their sane mind' would be able to deal with the stress of the violence the refugee community experience without believing in 'a higher being' and having a hope that what they face is not all there is to life. This may help to explain in part why the young people I interviewed who attended government and UN-run schools tended to view their religion, in its true form, as a haven from rights violations.

III. HARMONISING ISLAM AND HUMAN RIGHTS

There were also educators and young people (from non-private schools) who harmonised Islam with human rights. As discussed in chapter two, there are mainly two schools of thought that emerge when it concerns the relationship between patriarchy and Islam – 'those who believe that Islam as it is today is fair and just to women, and those who believe that Islam *as it is practised today* is utterly patriarchal, but that *true* Islam is not' (Al-Hibi 1982: 207). In the interviews I conducted, the educators who taught in non-private schools tended to lean towards the first perspective, while the young people from non-elite backgrounds attending these schools gravitated towards the latter. Because of the scale of the rights violations committed by the occupation, adults often presented a utopian view of Palestinian society and in doing so risked sidelining rights that are hindered by patriarchal traditions. Whilst young people may have conflated Islamic theology with Palestinian culture, they drew attention to the areas of conflict which arose between human rights and the patriarchal aspects of Palestinian culture. The range of perspectives among educators and the youths will be discussed respectively.

During discussions, non-private school educators repeatedly conflated Islam the religion with Palestinian culture. When asked about the relationship between Palestinian *culture* and human rights, Hala, a civics teacher at the UNGS, responded passionately: 'It goes well with Islamic teaching and our Book. It's all part of the Islamic religion and culture. It can't be split and it's not contradictory' (Hala, teacher, UNGS). Notably, the question posed focused on culture, not religion, and yet Hala responded by referring to Islamic thought. She also constructed human rights as that which cannot be divorced from Islamic religious beliefs, denying the existence of any tensions. This was a narrative which was particularly dominant among the UNGS educators. For instance, Amina, the principal of the UNGS, also used the words 'Islam' and 'culture' interchangeably when arguing that there are no 'clashes' between human rights, Islamic religious beliefs and Palestinian cultural traditions, and that 'all Muslims' know that. She went on to state: 'If we want to talk about the human rights, immediately, we say – look at what our Prophet says, look at the *Qu'ran* … we teach them human rights through our culture and it exists actually in our culture' (Amina, principal, UNGS).

Similarly, Bashar, the senior educator at UNRWA, when answering the same question also initially argued 'I never saw an area where it clashes'. However, unlike Amina (principal, UNGS) and Hala (teacher, UNGS), he was at times willing to concede practices that do not uphold the rights of women:

> There might be some areas of life for example, they will come and say, 'well equity', that someone passed away then all children … should have equal rights … while in Islam it says that the male has double [the inheritance] of the girl (Bashar, senior educator, UNRWA).

In using the pronoun 'they' he distanced himself from the argument that others have been known to make around the inequality of inheritance laws. Subsequently, he diluted the severity of this practice by going on to claim that 'it does not reach the level of [a] clash'. He concluded his thoughts by broadening this debate beyond the Palestinian context by assessing the teaching of HRE in other cultures around the world, claiming that:

> Conflict is inevitable … take it [HRE] to any country and it will conflict with some of the culture, or some of the traditions, or some of the religious beliefs … that conflict is not huge, it's minimal. The issue is how you address it (Bashar, senior educator, UNRWA).

Whilst his view shifted during his answer, he seemed content to make light of inequalities which result from some of the customs practised in Palestinian society, and in doing so failed to acknowledge areas of conflict between for example Islamic inheritance laws and human rights. But he, along with his UNGS colleagues, may have been challenging what Okafor and Agbakwa (2001) describe as the 'heaven–hell binary' orthodoxy (as discussed in chapter three). This is the notion that the world is made up of heavenly societies (in the Global North) that uphold rights and hellish ones (in the Global South) that violate them. According to this binary, certain cultures and religious texts such as the *Qu'ran*, are viewed as 'hellish' as opposed to the international human rights instruments, which are deemed sacred. Therefore, the UNGS educators contested this by elevating Islamic teachings and religious texts as the source of human rights.

Nonetheless, by refusing to acknowledge any areas of dissonance which might arise between human rights and aspects of their religion or culture, educators also ended up presenting a somewhat utopian view of Palestinian society.

Due to ongoing settler colonial violence, sometimes the oppressive practices that take place *within* the Palestinian community get overlooked. Unsurprisingly, patriarchal aspects of culture which produce rights violations may not seem as pressing in the light of an ongoing military occupation. This led some of the educators to believe that once the occupation ends, all their rights will be fulfilled, as Wissam (teacher, BGS) claimed: 'If the political situation in Palestine is settled [meaning establishment of a state and an end to the occupation] … I think that our rights is [*sic*] going to be given automatically in all sides of life'. He also maintained that in Palestinian society 'human rights are applied, totally'. During the interview he largely idealised Palestinian society as one in which there are no rights violations at all, comparing his society with the surrounding Arab states ruled by authoritarian regimes as a reference point. Other educators also argued that if the occupation ended, Palestinians would be superior to other neighbouring countries, as typified by Naseef's (principal, BGS) comment: 'We expect if we're not living under occupation, we'll be the best Arab country'. During a lesson on human rights (which I observed) at the BGS, Nidal (teacher, BGS) dismissed the notion that Palestinian women enjoy fewer rights than men. He rhetorically asked his class:

> Give me an example of a girl who withdrew from school at 10 … Because we have compulsory education, we care about women's education more than men … As Palestinians, we give her rights … There was a woman in the elections at the same time as Yasser Arafat. In Saudi Arabia … women can't drive cars, but thank God, it's not like that here. In mixed schools, most teachers are women, therefore, there's equality.

According to a UNICEF (2022) report, 94 per cent of Palestinian young women living in the West Bank and Gaza complete basic education by age 20, and 62 per cent complete secondary education. Education is viewed by Palestinians as a mode of resistance to the occupation that has sought to hinder children's rights to education over the decades (Habashi 2008). Education was viewed in this way by the young people I interviewed. It was described as a 'weapon' against Israel by one boy, and Jamila (student, GGS) stated: 'Israel gets angry when we are getting educated'. This is what Nidal (teacher, BGS) was most likely to be referring to when he said that Palestinians prioritise girls' education. However, the choice of the phrase 'give her rights' implies that women are dependent on (presumably) Palestinian men to bestow them with rights. This contrasted with the overarching narrative which dominated discussions: that rights are 'struggled' for (Dembour, 2010). These narratives, which situated Palestine in relation to other Arab states, also implied that some of the educators mainly associated human rights with resisting the occupation as opposed to challenging other forms of oppression within Palestinian society itself such as patriarchal practices.

Educators (all male) in the BGS also appeared to subvert the 'heaven–hell binary' (Okafor and Agbakwa 2001), constructing Palestine as a 'heavenly' community and, by implication, Israel as the 'hellish' society which perpetrates rights violations. However, this dichotomy, whichever way it is used, poses the danger of downplaying rights violations that occur in the so-called 'heavenly' communities. It is likely that this ideal portrayal of Palestine was appropriated since it can be difficult for individuals who are part of an oppressed community to critique the oppressive acts committed within that community.

Nevertheless, the young people I interviewed spoke out against aspects of Palestinian culture (and occasionally Islam when viewed as an expression of patriarchy), which negatively affect their enjoyment of rights. Young people from non-elite backgrounds did not shy away from wrestling with some of the tensions that exist between human rights and patriarchal aspects of their culture. Most youths who attended government- or UN- run schools viewed religion as not only compatible with human rights but the source of them, as Basel (student, BGS) contended: 'God gave us rights and created us with dignity so why would anyone take this from us? We were created free'. Rama (student, GGS), similar to Riham, the RE teacher at the PS, maintained that human rights can be found not only in Islam but all 'religions', arguing that 'all prophets talked about human rights'. These narratives contested dominant views in Western debates that propose that religion is at best, irrelevant to human right and at worse, is entirely incompatible with human rights (Johnston 2015).

Both male and female youths from non-elite backgrounds argued that religion does not pose a threat to human rights, but is problematic in the way that it is interpreted or practised. As Basel (student, BGS) put it: 'Religion is good, but the way people apply it is wrong. Religion gives rights, but people don't apply religion in the right way'.

Islam in its 'true' form and if applied correctly was viewed as an ally to Muslim girls and women among some female participants, as this exchange demonstrates:

> **Isra'a:** If our religion is applied we would take our rights, it encourages us.
>
> **Sabina:** Our religion is easy, not a difficulty and fits well with human rights.
>
> **Amal:** If they are applying what is written in our religion we would be able to take all our rights.
>
> **Isra'a:** They don't apply the constitution of Islam; if people do apply it they will live well (UNGS).

These girls also issued a challenge in this exchange to those who do not practice what is written in scripture. Whilst it is not stipulated who exactly 'they' are, arguably, it is Palestinians who carry out patriarchal practices which are not expressions of *true* Islam. Their argument resonated with claims made by feminist theologians that it is the male-dominated interpretations of the *Qur'an* that are problematic rather than the content of the *Qur'an* itself (Golley 2004; Majid 1998).

Some female participants were also keen to disentangle Islam from patriarchal values and practices. Enas (student, GGS) explained that 'in the past they were killing young girls once they were born but the Prophet Muhammad (PBUH) prevented that so we can see that religion is the source of human rights'. She referred to the practice of infanticide of female children that became prohibited upon the arrival of Islam and according to the *Qur'an* (Saaed 2015). Her classmate Shatha (student, GGS) also argued that 'The Prophet Muhammad (PBUH) said that men and women should be treated equally'. Many of the girls who attended non-private schools viewed Islam as a movement which is historically associated with bringing about rights to women in particular. This reflects the discourse of modernist Islamic religious scholars who often emphasise that the status of women greatly improved as a result of the dawn of Islam (Sidani 2005) and the Islamic feminist argument. As discussed in chapter two, a criticism of this approach is that these reformists avoid engaging with areas of dissonance that exist between types of oppression women experience in the local context compared to their rights-respecting interpretation of Islam (Bouachrine 2014; An-Na'im 2011a; Ahmed-Ghosh 2008). However, young people did not shy away from contesting the discrimination they currently experienced or expected to encounter in the future as women. Largely, the youths claimed that it is their *culture* which clashes with human rights as opposed to religion, as Basel (student, BGS) boldly stated: 'Our culture doesn't know the meaning of human rights!'

Young people also invoked human rights discourse as a vehicle to make sense of the marginalisation they faced as girls in Palestinian society and to contest patriarchy.

IV. PATRIARCHAL ATTITUDES TOWARDS WOMEN AND GIRLS

As part of discussions, the youths engaged in a walking debate where they were asked to agree or disagree along a continuum with different statements about human rights. When asked to respond to the statement 'girls enjoy the same rights as boys in Palestine', the vast majority of the young people walked towards the 'disagree' side of the room, giving examples of how women and girls are discriminated against in different spheres of life. Similarly, participants were asked to write down what they knew about human rights. What was striking was that, unprompted, male and female pupils from the PS included words which referred to the rights of women such as, 'sexism', 'feminism', 'women's rights' and phrases such as, 'women should have the same rights as men' and 'as Palestinians, we don't have that much of human rights, like we don't have rights for women'. Whilst they were the only school to include women's rights in their initial definitions, the discrimination Palestinian girls and women face surfaced regularly in young people's discussions about human rights.

Youths who attended the UNGS and BGS acknowledged that men exercise economic control over women when it comes to employment and ownership of land and property. Young people across the schools all referred to the inheritance laws, which, when adhered to, apportion sons twice that of daughters (Naik 2021). As Milad (student, BGS) commented: 'She's also deprived of her right of inheritance'. The Women's Centre for Legal Aid and Counselling (WCLAC) conducted research in 2014 in the West Bank. According to their survey, even a woman's claim to her inheritance in line with *Shari'ah* law (half of what her brother is entitled to) was rejected by 56 per cent of male siblings (Al-Jubeh et al 2014). This indicates that it is patriarchal attitudes that hinder women's economic equality rather than Islamic law (Hattab and Abualrob 2023).

Other ethnographic studies in the region explain that many women will defer their right to their portion of inheritance to their brother in their support of patrilineality and as a way of securing protection for the future (see Hasan 2002; Rubenberg 2001; Joseph 1996). This was also reported by the WCLAC (Al-Jubeh et al 2014: 5), which explained that shame, legal challenges and 'fear that their families will break off relations with or physically assault them' stops them from claiming their right of inheritance. However, the girls in this study did not seem to defend this practice of waiving this right. Additionally, the patriarchal kinship system seemed to affect the girls in ways that were not simply economic; Shatha (student, GGS) told me that 'adults love boys more than girls, a woman would be more loved if she is pregnant with a boy rather than a girl'. Because of the patrilineal kinship system in Palestinian society (which can be more strictly adhered to in camps and villages) women face pressure to continue the patrilineal line through giving birth to sons as opposed to daughters. While the girls I interviewed were familiar with this system, irrespective of where they lived, they were largely critical of the way it denies girls and women equality and their rights.

Girls from the PS also offered depictions of how they viewed women to be conceptualised within marriage and denied agency. Hiba (student, PS) claimed that women are denied a voice: 'Women are not allowed to express themselves'. Her peer Adel (student, PS) followed this comment, stating:

> Here in Palestine, they don't see the woman as a soul, as a human. They see her as a machine … to do what they want with her, it doesn't matter her opinion, no, she's just like a machine, she's like a slave. What they [men] want her to do, she must do it.

These girls argued that women are dehumanised, as 'machines' and 'slaves', whose primary purpose is to meet the needs of men and reproduce. They explained that this succeeds in robbing women of a soul, a voice and ultimately agency.

This group of participants also referred to the practice of child marriage in certain Palestinian villages where girls as young as 14 may be forced to marry. In the OPT, the minimum age for marriage was raised to 18 for both boys and girls (apart from in exceptional cases) in 2019 after President Abbas issued Decree Law No 21 (The New Arab 2019). The Decree was welcomed by human rights activists, women's organisations and non-traditional Muslim scholars (Marzouk 2022; Al Zaain 2021). Alternatively, the Decree was met with opposition from religious and tribal leaders who urged the public to protest against the Decree, warning that this would inevitably lead to the implementation of the CEDAW (Melhem 2019). Demonstrations against the Decree gained momentum in Hebron, a more conservative area of the West Bank (Salameh 2010). During discussions, a group of refugee girls also referred to Hebron when they told me how some families deny their daughters a right to education: 'Some people don't want a girl to be educated' (Sabina, student, UNGS). Sabina's classmate Anwar (student, UNGS) elaborated: 'There are some ignorant people who let their daughters marry early'. According to Palestinian Central Bureau of Statistics (PCBS) (2022), underage marriage has decreased since the Decree was enforced. However, 11.9 per cent of marriage certificates issued include those below the age of 18. This would explain why young people at the PS as well as pupils and educators in the GGS and UNGS were preoccupied with the issue of child marriage (PCBS 2022).

Male youths who attended the BGS highlighted how patrilineal kinship affects notions of identity around women:

> **Majdi:** Whenever something goes wrong we always blame women.
>
> **Interviewer:** Why?
>
> **Wael:** This is our culture.
>
> **Laith:** In our Arabic culture, we know a woman by her family, for example, we say a sister of, a wife of, a daughter of. We don't deal with her as an individual who has an existence by herself. She's always considered a follower of someone (BGS).

These boys did not reproduce patriarchal discourses, but offered an analysis of the way in which women are regarded within their communities. They attributed the fact that women are perceived as the property of another man to the Arab culture, indirectly referencing patriarchal kinship where women's identities are bound up in their kin rather than their own individuality. For instance, a married woman will still belong to her father's kin group, who in turn will retain responsibility for her (Joseph 1996). They also critiqued the way in which women can be treated as scapegoats. This is most likely a reference to the discourse of shame and honour and how women are held responsible even when they are innocent. This was also reiterated by Nadiya (student, UNGS), who asserted: 'If a girl did something bad then she has brought shame on the family but if a boy did the same thing then he's a boy'.

Overall, refugee girls were the most critical regarding the shame–honour system and offered their critique of the highly controversial practice of honour violence, as the following exchange demonstrates:

> **Sabina:** In the court if someone kills somebody else he can be in jail for nearly ten months and after that period they let him out easily.
>
> **Interpreter:** Do you mean the killing based on what is called the 'honour of the family'?
>
> **Sabina:** Yes, the killing of women.
>
> **Isra'a:** Yes, they put perpetrators in jail for two months and then give them an excuse like they have mental health issues (UNGS).

Based on the ease with which they discussed honour killings, it is possible to infer that it is a custom that is not unfamiliar to them. Honour killings take place in the Palestinian community and are carried out by male agnates such as fathers, uncles, brothers and sons of the woman who has been accused of conduct that has violated *their* family honour (Hasan 2002). In the August of 2019 (four years after fieldwork for this book was conducted), a group of women took part in a rally in front of the Palestinian Prime Minister's office in response to the suspected honour killing of 21-year-old Israa Ghrayeb from Bait Sahour, a village just outside Bethlehem (Begum 2019). The year before that the Women's Centre for Legal Aid and Counselling (WCLAC 2018) reported that 13 women in the West Bank had been killed as a result of honour killings.

Interestingly, the girls I interviewed did not explicitly condemn the fact that women are killed, but rather that men go unpunished at the hands of the Palestinian state and the flaws in its legal system. They also alluded to the rights discourse around the state's obligations to respect, protect and fulfil rights, in this case the state's duty to protect citizens from rights violations perpetrated by others within society. Violence against women is often viewed as a taboo topic and an issue to be confined to the realm of the private sphere in Muslim societies, meaning that it can be deemed beyond the remit of the state (Mahamid et al 2023). Since the work for this book was undertaken, the PA, along with international and local women's organisations, have sought to address issues such as violence against Palestinian women in the Family Protection Law (2020). However, research by Mahamid et al (2023) to assess the attitudes towards this law found that 61 per cent of participants disagreed with the general tenets of the law. Nevertheless, the refugee girls that I interviewed in 2015 were not afraid to contest this patriarchal practice and the state's complicity in it.

Whilst gender equality was a preoccupation for many participants, girls in the PS and UNGS schools seemed to contend for women's rights with different motivations in mind. For instance, whilst the right to freedom of movement is normally associated with the occupation, these girls related this right to the restrictions they face due to patriarchy, as Isra'a (student, UNGS) explained: 'Boys have more freedom to go out and freedom of movement'. Refugee girls wanted to enjoy the right to freedom of movement so that they could assemble with other demonstrators (as discussed below), whereas, in the PS, Nawja (student, PS) wanted to experience this right so that she could use taxis to travel around alone: 'Cabs are dangerous, not many girls here ride cabs'. In the West Bank, people often use taxis to travel short distances, but almost all taxi drivers are men (for notable exceptions, see Khalel 2015), leaving girls sometimes no choice than to be alone with a man in a society where men and women tend to socialise separately. What seemed to be most pressing for the PS students was that patriarchy posed a threat to their desire to live in more liberal ways. This was illustrated by Nadia (student, PS), who used the following example to explain how Palestinian women do not enjoy the same rights as men in public:

> It's as simple as walking in the street, if you're a man, nobody talks to you … you can wear whatever you want, you can go out shirtless for all anybody cares! But if you're a girl and you're wearing half a sleeve … you're going to hear a lot, just for being a

> girl ... but they don't notice what they're saying. They don't notice that it's sexist and that it's not supposed to be said.

Nadia viewed men in the public sphere as not only sexist, but also ignorant that their views are even discriminatory. She did not point to their ignorance as a way of pardoning them, but rather to imply that their patriarchal views were deeply entrenched. Whilst she did not think that she should have to afford her culture any role in legitimising the rights of women to dress as they choose, she knew the consequences women would face if they were to challenge cultural norms. Nonetheless, she connected her everyday experiences of gender inequality as a Palestinian girl to human rights.

Alternatively, refugee girls emphasised that patriarchal attitudes affect their ability to enjoy some of their civil and political rights. These girls discussed at length the way in which they longed to participate in demonstrations but that they faced multiple barriers including patriarchal practices.

> **Majd:** I would like to participate in a peaceful demonstration, but I know I can't because I know that the Palestinian Government will stop us.
>
> **Lina:** As a girl ... I cannot participate in peaceful demonstrations.
>
> **Nadiya:** In different situations, there are different challenges. Sometimes, it's the occupation, other times it's the Palestinian Authority or just because she's a girl and in our culture, it's not acceptable.
>
> **Nadine:** Also, some parents are afraid of people's 'talk'... So, they care more about gossip than our land (UNGS).

This exchange captures the multiple layers of marginalisation they face as Palestinian young people when it comes to enjoying their rights: the occupation, the PA's security forces and patriarchy. Nadiya (student, UNGS) went on to explain how the violence of the PA's security agents would also deter parents from allowing their daughters to attend protests: 'The Palestinian Authority will hit the girls and parents can't bear that'. The controversial role of the PA and the importance of the right to freedom of assembly has been explored more thoroughly in chapter five.

Nevertheless, the PA's violence towards demonstrators does not seem to bother parents when it comes to their sons to the same extent. As the girls clearly identify, patriarchal aspects of their culture are an additional hindrance when it comes to exercising their civil and political rights. These refugee girls seemed to channel their frustration about patriarchal attitudes primarily at their parents. They maintained that their parents prioritised the family honour above the resistance towards the occupation and defence of their 'land'. They also highlighted the role that the fear of gossip plays in maintaining the oppressive honour and shame system, as Nadine's (student, UNGS) comment illustrates:

> Some parents have a role in that they don't allow their daughters to go out, but they do care about what people gossip about each other ... they talk about what people

> say and they forgot that they have a homeland they need to defend so they just care about gossiping.

This was quite a damning evaluation of some parents' priorities, but it also reveals how some of these young people view the importance of contesting the occupation whilst also wanting to play a part. Intriguingly, participants juxtaposed the words 'gossip' and 'land', stating that their parents were more preoccupied with the former than the latter. It is likely that this word interplay was not coincidental, borrowing from the broader Palestinian master narrative. Land ownership has traditionally been a crucial part of the Arab honour code (Bisharat 1997). Therefore, it appears the girls were reminding their parents that there is a broader honour that is at stake because of the threat of the occupation. This seems to resonate with the wider literature which discusses how gossip and the fear of it is a mechanism which serves to perpetuate the honour code (Hamamra 2020; Cooney 2014; Chaban et al 2010; Hasan 2002; Rubenberg 2001).

Nonetheless, based on discussions with youths in the PS, the honour code does not seem to impact upon these girls' political participation. In fact, throughout their discussions both boys and girls often idealised girls who had recently been imprisoned for opposing the occupation at demonstrations. Nawja (student, PS) recollected: 'There was a teenager who was held captive a couple of months ago and she was sentenced to be put in jail for like no really good reason'. The city in which these young people lived was one of the lesser conservative areas of the West Bank and therefore the participation at demonstrations and the arrest of teenage girls may have been a more familiar concept. Also, their school facilitated the participation of male and female students in demonstrations, whereas pupils attending the UNGS school commented that they would face detention if they took part in protests (this will be explored in chapter seven). In the PS, there were no concerns voiced about family honour. This contrasted with the way girls from the refugee community in another city indicated they would be perceived if they were to attend a political protest. As Maryam (student, UNGS) explained: 'If a girl participates in a demonstration they look at her in a different way as if it's not normal to have a girl in a peaceful demonstration'. All the girls in the same room agreed with this sentiment.

From these discussions it was clear the girls believed they were hindered from this civil and political right, which is viewed as such a key form of resistance in the Palestinian struggle (as discussed in chapter five). According to Cooney (2014), honour violence is not only carried out as punishment for (or perceived) sexual or relational impropriety, but increasingly for acts of independent decision-making with regard to education, divorce (even in cases of abuse) and dress. Therefore, girls can potentially be subjected to violence if they refuse to obey their parents with regard to attending a demonstration. Sabina (student, UNGS) shed light on why a girl taking part in a protest could be perceived as a threat to the family honour:

> If a girl is taken by the soldiers, she will be a shame and a cause of a problem for her family that's why families do not agree to let their girls go out for demonstrations, it is a scandal for the family as well.

During our conversations, these girls explained how the individual actions of a girl, which could compromise her purity, have repercussions which not only affect her honour and reputation as an individual, but that of the whole *hamula* – extended family. As Haj (1992) explains, girls are taught that their sexuality is not their own to express or to withhold; instead, it belongs to the *hamula* since they are responsible for preserving the patrilineal line. Sabina's comment also suggests that the occupation adds another layer of complexity to the threats to their honour.

At this point it is helpful to return to the analysis of the YPAGs. When helping to analyse the data of their peers in relation to girls' participation in protests, a member of YPAG 1 explained that because girls are 'oversexualised' in Palestinian society, a family's primary concern if a girl is arrested is that she will bring shame upon the family: certain interrogation techniques might involve her having to remove clothing. According to this research advisor, a lot of adults base this fear of how females might bring shame upon them on the way in which male detainees are subjected to degrading treatment. Haj (1992) argues that Israeli forces are aware of the ideology of honour and utilise this as a strategy to instil fear into Palestinian society. However, this does not seem deter the refugee girls' pursuit of political agency and engagement in collective action against the occupation. Throughout their discussions, these girls criticised their parents for placing the honour code and a fear of gossip above the national struggle, as the following conversation highlighted:

> **Amal:** Sometimes because I'm a girl I cannot participate in a peaceful demonstration whereas boys can.
>
> **Sabina:** Boys can go out at night but girls, no.
>
> **Anwar:** We are citizens even if we are girls.
>
> **Sabina:** But no one hears us.
>
> **Girls together:** No one hears us (UNGS).

Once again, the motif of 'voice' was drawn upon to capture this additional layer of marginalisation that they face as girls in relation to their political rights. They pursue their rights as girls because they believe they have a unique role to play in the resistance movement, as Layla (student, UNGS) concluded after this discussion: 'I, as a Palestinian girl, need to defend my rights by facing the occupation'. What became apparent was that once the girls from the camp had been initiated into the discourse of rights (Emerson and Lundy 2013), they were also empowered to challenge the power inequalities that they face in Palestinian society as girls.

Despite the active role that women have played throughout the decades in contesting the injustices of the occupation (Shwaikh 2022; Kayali 2021;

Haj 1992), according to the youths I interviewed, girls still faced barriers when it came to challenging the occupation in their preferred ways. As can be seen from these conversations, because of the honour and shame culture, they are constantly under pressure to think about the implications their decisions will have on the extended family rather than themselves as individuals. According to Rubenberg (2001: 32–33), unlike most women in the West, 'Palestinians live and conceptualize their lives not as individuals but as members of a family group'. In a similar manner, young people were largely not encouraged to act out of their own interests, but the interests of the whole family. Even when refugee girls challenged the patriarchal system of their society, they did so with a collective goal in mind. They did not necessarily want freedom to go out at night or dress a certain way as individuals, but they want to participate in a collective nationalist struggle from which they considered their parents had disengaged.

On several occasions the young people situated themselves within their collective and intergenerational relationships (Mitchell and Elwood 2012), even looking to the generations that would follow after them. Within their narratives there was a preoccupation with the notion of legacy. For instance, when asked how they felt when their rights are respected, Rouan (student, UNGS) responded: 'Comfortable knowing that we will leave the community in safe hands. It will be safe for those who will come after us'. They seemed aware that they as young people pose a 'demographic threat' to the settler and its claims to the land both present and future (Shalhoub-Kevorkian 2015a: 224), and considered themselves (as girls) to be protagonists within the resistance to Israel's settler colonial project. Whilst dominant Eurocentric human rights discourse preferences individual rights, rights from the perspective of the colonised often privileges collective rights since they are engaged in struggles for self-determination (Barreto 2013c). Similarly, girls from the camp gave primacy to the rights of the Palestinian community rather than individual rights. In contrast, the girls in the PS largely contended for women's rights using a more Eurocentric framework in which individual rights were central.

Conversely, there were occasions when the youths also reproduced the patriarchal narratives inherent in their society. As explored above, while the boys in the BGS often contested patriarchal aspects of their culture, they were also the participants who were most likely to reiterate attitudes which deny women agency, as the following exchange demonstrates:

> **Abdullah:** If girls don't find a job they'll stay at home, but boys have more responsibilities and can't stay at home.
>
> **Laith:** Boys are the one who'll propose for marriage and be responsible for the family but what is the responsibility of the girl except herself, makeup and fashion? (BGS).

These boys were from communities which face high rates of unemployment and financial hardship, and the pressure to find work was a preoccupation across the discussions which took place among youths in this school. The way in which they expect to experience an overwhelming burden to find work and support a family could have led them to undermine the responsibilities of women. Laith (student, BGS) denied girls not only agency but intellectual ability by describing their duties as those which centres on physical appearance. This view reflects perspectives found among traditional Muslim scholars, who argue that men carry a greater economic burden than women and thereby endorse inheritance laws that allot women a smaller portion of their inheritance (Haque et al 2020). In contrast, non-traditional Muslim scholars refute these arguments, contending that *Qur'anic* texts on the topic of inheritance are not 'statements of obligation', but are 'declarations of rights' (Hattab and Abualrob 2023).

There were also times when girls reproduced stereotypes that they had encountered. However, when someone did this, they were often challenged by their peers, as the following exchange illustrates:

> **Majd:** But something else that I want to say is that maybe parents let boys go out to demonstrations because it's more cultural and that boys are stronger … So, it's a not a problem because the guy can defend himself not like the girl because she's weak that can't defend herself.
>
> **Nadiya:** [interrupts] No, it's not an excuse to differentiate between boys and girls, we girls are strong also.
>
> **Majd:** Girls are weak in their nature.
>
> **Randa:** Because human rights should be provided for everyone, also we can't live without it and there should be no discrimination between women and men (UNGS).

The stereotyping of women as 'weak' roused an impassioned response from the rest of the group. Randa (student, UNGS) challenged Majd (student, UNGS) by drawing on the universalist argument that women should enjoy the same rights as men regarding politics (Meyer 1999). Majd's comments echoed Islamist notions of justice, which are underpinned by a biological approach to equity (Roald 2013). According to this interpretation, demands for gender quality 'are regarded as leading to the oppression of women, as women would be forced to go beyond their "nature" if they were assigned tasks inappropriate to their biological constitution' (Roald 2013: 335).

The view that women are weak also emerged in a discussion in the GGS. When asked about gender inequality in Palestinian society, the following discussion ensued:

> **Jamila:** For example, we don't have a woman president.
>
> **Interviewer:** Why do you think there isn't a female president?
>
> **Farah:** Women are emotional and weaker than men.
>
> **Jamila:** No, there are women who are intellectual and not that emotional (GGS).

Unlike the discussion that took place among the girls attending the UNGS, these girls debated the emotional rather than physical strength of women in relation to men. There is a well-known proverb recited among Palestinians which reinforces the notions that emotion is a negative attribute and that women are inherently emotional in a way that men are not. It states: 'Women are emotional, they think from their hearts; that is why men should make all the decisions in the house' (Rubenberg 2002: 33). Yet again, Jamila (student, GGS) within the same group challenged her peer by making a counter-claim that 'there are women who are intellectual'. Arguably, she also reinforced the fact that men are not emotional and subsequently that emotion is a negative attribute which inhibits one from becoming a leader. However, more importantly she contested the view that a woman could not become president.

This discussion prompted me to ask a group of boys later interviewed at the BGS whether they thought there would ever be a female president in Palestine. They responded with the following discussion:

Omar: No way.

Interviewer: Why?

Thaer: She cannot, she's unable to do this.

Fawaz: There isn't a woman in such position in all over the world.

Khalid: No there is, and we have a woman who is in the position of a minister of education and also a woman who is a president of the Bethlehem municipality.

Thaer: But men are better as women are emotional (BGS).

In both the UNGS and GGS, there was one participant who reproduced the patriarchal narratives which prompted a reaction from the rest of the group, whereas the opposite was true in the BGS. This could be an indication of the presence of more patriarchal attitudes among the male participants. Not only did Thaer (student, BGS) once again draw upon the perception that women are 'emotional' and ill-suited to govern, but the other boys seemed genuinely shocked at the idea. The fact that Fawaz (student, BGS) could not conceive of the idea that there are women in political leadership elsewhere globally arguably suggests that the patriarchal political structure under which he lives makes it difficult to imagine anything different. These comments again, reflect gender roles endorsed by Islamist scholars and found in Islamic family legislation in which women are viewed as 'emotional and weak' and therefore in need of men's protection (Roald 2013: 335; Badawi 1995). Nonetheless, Khalid (student, BGS) challenged his peers by reminding them of women who do possess leadership roles in Palestinian politics. Alternatively, in their discussions, the boys from the BGS contested the more hierarchical aspects of patriarchy that deny young people a voice.

V. PATRIARCHAL ATTITUDES TOWARDS CHILDREN AND YOUNG PEOPLE

Hierarchies of age are often excluded in Western feminist definitions of patriarchy; however, in the Arab context, it is men as 'fathers' who seek to control women (Joseph 1996). Therefore, not only are the voices of men privileged over those of women, but the voices of those who are older over those who are younger.

The youths I interviewed articulated how they are marginalised as young people primarily through drawing on the rights discourse, especially their desire to have the right to a voice. Again, students from the PS approached this issue from a different angle than their peers at the non-private schools. They often depicted their homes and schools (schools will be discussed in the following chapter) as havens from patriarchal structures. Instead, they discussed the discrimination they encountered in the public sphere, as Nawja (student, PS) commented: 'Like as children, we're just not respected, like if you go to a restaurant and you're standing in line, if you're a kid, they will come in front of you, they won't care'.

It is in the context of a restaurant that she chose to illustrate her point that children are 'not respected' – a restaurant being a space where interactions take place between youths and adults who are strangers. Her choice of scenario also reveals something of the socio-economic privileges she may enjoy compared to other youths who were interviewed. This contrasts with young people from the non-private schools who discussed the private sphere of the home and centralised the right to freedom of expression and the right to participate in politics therein. Despite the lack of criticism of their school (as will be discussed in chapter eight), Marwan (student, PS) drew the following image (see Figure 6.1 below). This illustration displays the power dynamics which can exist between teachers and students (reading as in Arabic from right to left):

Figure 6.1 'Can I say my opinion?' (male student, PS)

Arguably, this cartoon-type image reflects the broader hierarchical structures which can exist between adults and young people. Many of the young people from the non-private schools highlighted how they encountered hierarchical structures in their own family lives: 'If we want to express our opinion at home no one listens to us because we are children' (Hadeel, student, UNGS). In the presence of these hierarchical structures, young people described their relationships with adults as 'vertical' (Barakat 2005). Basel (student, BGS) viewed his father in the same way as his teacher when it came to the vertical nature of relationships he had encountered with adults: 'The teacher or my father considers themselves as being in a higher level. You may know more than them, but they will not listen to you'. He claimed that these hierarchical relationships mean that youths' voices are disregarded irrespective of how knowledgeable they may be. By stating that youths may 'know more' than their elders he undermined these power relationships.

The family was also identified as a site in which many of the girls from the refugee camp felt excluded from sharing their political opinions. When discussing how they wished they could talk about political matters in school, Doha (student, UNGS) explained: 'Politics are not the problem because we can talk about it at home', to which her classmate Safa'a (student, UNGS) replied: 'But no one listens at home' (UNGS). These comments indicated that these girls may be willing to forgo the right to discuss political matters in one context such as school as long as there is an alternative space that would facilitate their right to express their views. Unfortunately, this space may not exist at home either. This was echoed by one of the younger educators Osama (teacher, PS), who was in his twenties. He also constructed the family as a sphere which does not enable the political participation of children and youths. In Arabic, the term 'youth' (*shabab*) can hold various meanings and encompass a range of ages, including those up to age 29, and so he could have included himself in the same category as his pupils. He described a scenario in which a family meeting takes place where children and adults are present:

> You are twelve or thirteen ... years old and you're a boy or a girl ... and you are sitting with your family and ... with your Dad, with your uncle, with your brothers ... you cannot talk about anything, you cannot give a political opinion ... because if you talk while [they're] talking they will say 'no ... you are younger ... than us, you cannot talk while [we're] here because you have to respect us'. It's about respect you know? And respect in [the] Arab world it's ... [a] thing ... you cannot get over it (Osama, teacher, PS).

It is interesting to consider who he includes in this hypothetical interaction and how he positions them. The young person whose voice is quashed could be a 'boy or a girl' and those who silence the younger member are male family figures such as the father, uncle and brother. He analyses this scene and concludes that the (unilateral) 'respect' that elders demand from the young trumps claims that young people should have freedom to engage in political discussions and ultimately have a voice in matters which concern them. This scenario also provides an illustration of how the generations communicate with one another, resonating with what Barakat (2005) describes as 'downward' and 'upward' communication. He explains that elders use *downward* forms of communication and speak to those who are younger through a set of commands, warnings and rebukes, while those who are younger will address their elders using *upward* forms of communication. This can take the form of silence, petitions and apologies. In this study, the young people alluded to these forms of communication and focused predominantly on the way in which adults sought to *silence* them.

According to the young people, one of the strategies which adults used to achieve this is through mockery and ridicule, as typified by Mohammad's (student, BGS) comment: 'Adults make fun of our opinion and ignore it because we are young'. This mockery of their views was frequently mentioned during the conversations with youths from non-elite backgrounds. Nonetheless, despite the way they may be silenced, ridiculed or ignored, they used the language of rights to challenge the discrimination they encountered as children and young people. They countered the notion that children have nothing valuable to contribute, and in doing so undermined the vertical relationships they experienced with adults.

When asked whether adults could learn from young people, this group of refugee girls responded:

> **Lina:** Yes, most young people are educated so they can educate their parents.
>
> **Nadiya:** Yes, maybe youths can see things that adults really miss, where adults can't see.
>
> **Majd:** Also, young people can correct some aspects of the past and correct that for the old people and to persuade them about those aspects (UNGS).

Their comments were subversive both in terms of how they addressed their elders using words such as 'educate' and 'correct', but also in their implication that they have made mistakes in the nation's struggle's past. This resonates with a perspective found within the Islamist movement in which the older generations are considered responsible for losing Palestine due to their lack of education and religious devotion (Hart 2004; Milton-Edwards 1996). Although these girls assumed the role of the educator, they did so out of a sense of national interest rather than in pursuit of individual power or personal gain. This sentiment was also voiced by girls in the government school, such as Farah (student, GGS), who maintained that adults 'should listen to us because we want to help them'.

Throughout the discussions, the young people urged adults to listen to their views and take them seriously. This was largely driven by their desire to participate politically. This contrasts with elements found within discussions among Western children's rights scholars who instead tend to emphasise Article 12 of the UNCRC, which stresses *consultation* without always exploring *political agency*. The young people's narratives problematised more depoliticalised conceptions inherent in Western notions of the child's voice. Furthermore, this also resonates with Hart (2008: 287), who interrogates the notion that children become politically 'conscious' since this assumes the 'political' exists as a 'distinct domain of thought and activity that children engage with or not'. Instead, he proposes that children who live in conflict-affected environments experience the 'political' in a more 'visceral' way. There was a sense that the youths I interviewed were engaging in a more visceral way with the political. Finally, they wanted to exercise agency, not so they could make decisions about their own lives as individuals, but rather to bring about societal transformation in a place where patriarchal attitudes prevail in an authoritarian state that is under a relentless occupation.

As with discussions around gender inequality, at times individuals reproduced the patriarchal narratives which deny young people a voice. Whilst most boys in the BGS claimed that they are denied a voice in the community, there was one boy, Laith (student, BGS), who reinforced the hierarchical power relations, as the following exchange captured:

> **Abdullah:** In our community opinions are said by old people but young people like us are ignored.
>
> **Yasser:** Maybe they can take our opinions through elections?
>
> **Laith:** We ask older people for opinions as they are more mature and have a wider experience in life but also young people have opinions. We have a special committee in the village that cares about youth opinions, ideas and listen to us. So, our voice is heard (BGS).

Yasser (student, BGS) questioned whether the more formal and individual political act of voting could facilitate their views sufficiently despite the fact that this would exclude him and his peers, who were below the voting age. This suggestion could have come to mind because voting is often traditionally considered one of the main ways in which a citizen can influence the political system (Ekman and Amna 2012). And yet, democratic elections have not been held in the OPT since 2006.

On the other hand, Laith (student, BGS) seemed content to reaffirm the hierarchical structure of society even if it meant diminishing the voices of young people. He did this through his construction of adults as those who are more informed. Whilst he did not completely deny that young people possess opinions, he seemed to sideline the significance of these perspectives. He concluded that the voices of young people were heard solely because there was a committee in the nearby village that listens to young people. He did not, however, consider the fact that some young people may not be able to participate in this committee. Furthermore, he confined the voices of youths to this one space and almost used the fact that this place exists as a justification for why young people's voices do not need to be heard in other spheres of life.

As when discussing women's rights, there were also instances when patriarchal attitudes were reproduced and then contested amongst peers:

> **Amjad:** Older people sometimes want to protect us by not letting us interfere in problems. That's why they ignore our opinion.
>
> **Basel:** It's not an excuse for not taking our opinion just to protect us. If I have children in the future, I'll let them express their opinion (BGS).

Although Basel (student, BGS) interpreted what Amjad (student, BGS) expressed as exempting adults from denying young people a voice, Amjad (student, BGS) may have been trying to make sense of the patriarchal system within which he finds himself. Narratives around protection versus participation are commonplace in children's rights discourse. Primacy is often given to a child's rights to protection rather than their right to participation despite the fact that young people and adults may understand risks and benefits differently (Canosa et al 2018; Lefevre et al 2018). Amjad's interpretation of why youths are denied a voice draws on this debate. As other youths in this study, Basel (student, BGS) looked ahead at securing the rights of future generations by talking about how he will allow his children to enjoy a right he currently cannot.

The youths not only countered the dominant narratives of adults, but they were not afraid to challenge their peers when they heard these views being reproduced. Therefore, despite being ignored, mocked or bullied, these young people were not deterred, and believed that they had something valuable to contribute to bringing about societal transformation – they just lacked the opportunities to have their opinions taken seriously and acted upon in their communities and homes.

VI. CONCLUSION

Religious and cultural perspectives influence to varying degrees how both adults and young people conceptualise human rights. Many youths and their educators highlighted the synergies between Islam and human rights, whereas some viewed patriarchy as an expression of Islam and thus at odds with certain human rights ideals. Even if the youths had encountered a rights narrative that was largely associated with resisting the occupation, they also appropriated this language to protest the oppression they faced at the hands of Palestinian adults in the form of patriarchy and to reclaim their agency. This resonates with an observation made by Kazziha (2010) that Palestinians are not an easily subjugated people, having been colonised by a string of different powers. In accordance with this, the youths resisted being subjugated by those in power, whether it was an Israeli soldier, the Palestinian police or the elders of their own families. Young people invoked human rights as a tool to challenge patriarchal attitudes that marginalise them.

Patriarchy was understood by the participants as needing to be challenged on two fronts: first, when it threatens the rights of girls and women; and second, when it denies a voice to children and youths. As the youth advisory group summarised, they are proud of their cultural identity and yet it is the patriarchal aspects of their culture which can facilitate gender inequality, and not prioritising the views of young people in matters that concern their lives. Unlike Western commentaries on the child voice, the young people conceptualised their right to a voice with political participation and agency rather than consultation in mind.

Girls contested patriarchy for different purposes, ranging from seeking freedom to wear what they wish, to wanting to participate in demonstrations alongside their male peers. Refugee girls struggled for their rights, not for personal enjoyment, but with the collective rights of the Palestinian people in mind. At times, the young people's conversations about inheritance laws and political participation indicated that attitudes across the generations might be increasingly diverging when it concerns their relations with their elders, and for girls their relations with their brothers, fathers, future husbands as well as Islamic family law and CEDAW.

A dissonance can emerge when the voices of suffering are juxtaposed against a rationalist, dry and sanitised human rights discourse (Baxi 2002). Chapters four, five and six have examined the former. However, inside school, Palestinian young people encounter the latter through their HRE programmes, which are mainly driven by the agendas of their Western funders. The next chapter invites the reader into the young people's schools to explore how they and their teachers respond to this discordance between their lived experiences of human rights outside school and the HRE they encounter inside school.

7

Human Rights Education in Palestinian Schools: Discordance between the Dominant Discourse of HRE in School and the Struggle for Rights Outside School

I. INTRODUCTION

IT WAS A particularly chilly Tuesday morning in February when I arrived at the refugee girls' school to interview Amina, the UNGS principal. Principal offices were not private spaces; staff and pupils entered regularly, sometimes interrupting participants mid-interview. This morning, I was poured a small cup of thick Arabic coffee releasing notes of cardamom throughout the office. Amina offered her apologies about the noise, pointing over at two men who were busy installing a heating unit in the corner. Moments later the principal's former English teacher stepped inside to say a quick hello and then two smartly dressed male colleagues from a different department of UNRWA and another jurisdiction entered the office and sat down. One had a head of white hair and was in his sixties and the other man was in his late thirties, both with a shy yet warm demeanour. Before sitting down, they greeted me by placing their hands on their hearts as a mark of respect, a sign of Muslim etiquette often used when interacting with women. As we sipped on the strong coffee, punctuated by drilling in the corner, I proceeded with the interview. When we reached the part of the interview where we were discussing levels of optimism towards human rights in the Palestinian context, Amina, a woman in her 40s, said that she believed youths were more hopeful than adults about the emancipatory potential of human rights for the Palestinian people. She then looked across at the older male colleague with white hair sitting to her right and said with an interjection of laughter, 'I think that sometimes he looks at us and says, "What can you do?"' He responded with a wry smile.

In this chapter, the reader is invited into the young people's schools, where I will examine how they and their educators respond to the discord between the dominant discourses of HRE in school and the struggle for rights outside school.

Many scholars and practitioners contend that HRE should include education *about*, *through*, and *for* human rights (Bajaj 2011a; Amnesty International 2009). This framework is often used to assess the effectiveness of HRE initiatives; however, this chapter will focus on how young people's constructions of human rights are influenced by these three components of HRE.

When it comes to education *about* human rights, this chapter explores how the young people defined human rights in a way that resisted and refashioned the dominant discourses they encounter at school due to their lived experiences. It considers the education *through* human rights component of HRE and how a school can act as a haven from, or a continuation of, rights denials experienced beyond the school gates, as well as the extent to which a school's rights climate can impact upon a young person's overall faith in human rights and their potential to contest injustices. The learning *for* human rights dimension of HRE is examined, and whether Palestinian young people are being presented with opportunities to engage in human rights praxis. The chapter concludes by exploring some of the challenges that educators encounter when teaching HRE in the OPT whose rights, like their pupils, are threatened by the occupation, the Palestinian pseudo-state or, for some, patriarchy.

II. EDUCATION *ABOUT* HUMAN RIGHTS: REPRODUCING, RESISTING AND REFASHIONING THE DOMINANT DISCOURSE

At the very start of focus group discussions, young people were asked to write or draw on post-it notes what they knew about human rights (see Figure 7.1). Analysis of these definitions and ensuing discussions indicated that to varying degrees they reproduced the dominant human rights discourse of rights as universal standards, but also resisted this, by refashioning rights as Islamic constructions, rights associated with the occupation, as promises juxtaposed with reality and rights as universal failures.

A. Reproducing the Dominant Human Rights Discourse: Rights as Universal Standards

The first category of definitions offered by the young people included rights defined as universal standards, as typified by this definition: 'Rights that should be given to everyone no matter what is the situation. Rights are universal' (female student, UNGS). This girl preceded 'given' with the word 'should', thus depicting how rights ought to function. The more universal and UN-centric definitions offered by the young people aligned with how the natural school constructs rights as 'given' universal entitlements (Dembour 2010: 11). For instance, refugee girls described human rights as that which cannot be bought, sold or inherited and referred to the indivisibility of rights or in their words 'rights can't be split'.

Figure 7.1 Human rights initial definitions (students, PS)

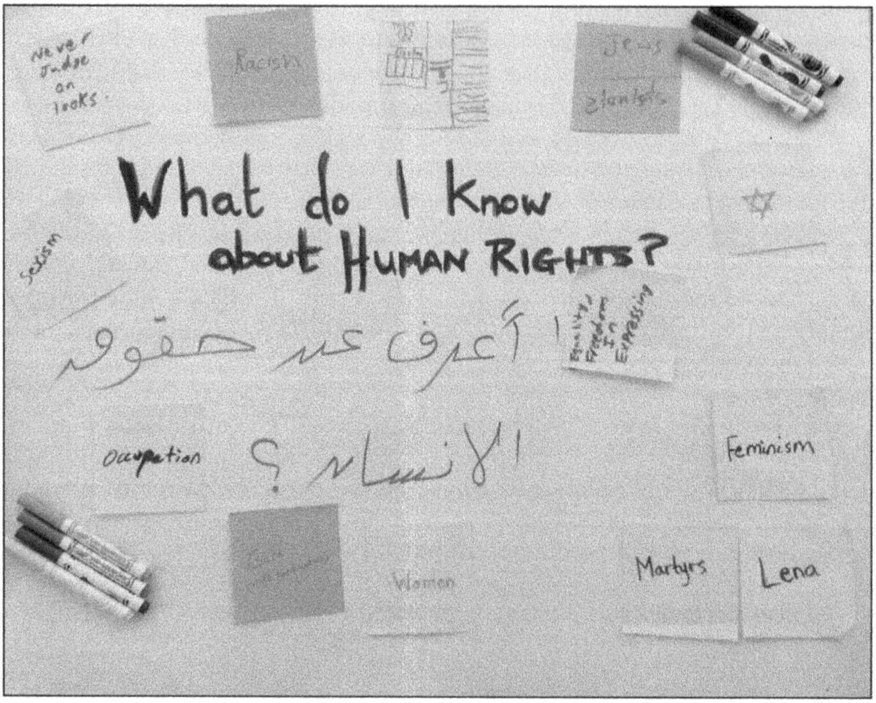

In accordance with this, youths who attended the UNGS, BGS and GGS occasionally wrote lists from memory of human rights as codified by international law.

Some of these iterations of rights reflected more 'restricted' or 'technical' conceptualisations of human rights (Coysh 2017; Goodale 2007), thus indicating the approach to HRE that their respective schools had adopted.

Analysis of extracts from the textbooks[1] also demonstrated that the content of the UNRWA HRE programme centralises and seeks to familiarise learners with UN statements and international covenants.[2] It is unsurprising that UNRWA-run schools prioritise a more 'declarationalist' (Keet 2007) approach to HRE when the UN has designed their programme (Albhaisi 2021). Similarly, contents from the Grade 9 MoEHE's *Civics Education* textbook refers to such

[1] Since the work for this research was conducted, the MoEHE's textbooks have been revised. The newer version was introduced in all government schools across the OPT at the start of the 2018/19 academic year. The older version that was in place for the government school pupils I interviewed in 2015 was informed by the Oslo process and 'mirrored the prevailing optimism that an independent Palestinian state living side by side with Israel could be created' (Alayan and Riley 2023: 25). This is helpful to bear in mind when I draw on analysis of extracts of MoEHE textbooks throughout this chapter.

[2] UDHR, ICCPR, ICESCR, CEDAW, CRC and CRPD (UNRWA 2012: 5).

instruments as 'legal, national and international guarantees to protect individuals and groups' (Qazzaz et al 2010: 28). The assumption that international human rights are universal pre-existing facts to be learned *about* also indicates how UNRWA and government-run schools take a largely *HRE for Global Citizenship* (Bajaj 2011a) approach to teaching about rights.

Another indicator that the young people encountered this dominant Eurocentric vision of HRE in school was that learners were presented with a largely decontextualised rights narrative in their curricula akin to the *HRE for Global Citizenship* model (Bajaj 2011a). Although differently articulated, all the schools' respective curricula positioned their learners as members of a global community. First, a desired outcome of the UNRWA's HRCRT programme is that students 'contribute positively to their society and the global community' (UNRWA 2012: 8). Second, to a lesser degree, the preface of the Grade 9 *Civics Education* textbook reminds learners that they are part of the 'family of mankind' and that this serves as the foundation for 'freedom, justice and peace in the world' (Qazzaz et al 2010: 3). Third, the curriculum followed by the PS encourages students to be internationally minded and to help build a world that is more peaceful. However, the young people that I interviewed in the PS rarely defined rights in a more UN-centric manner.

Constructing learners as members of a global community and presenting them with a decontextualised and depoliticised rights narrative suggests that UNRWA and the MoEHE did not want learners discussing human rights primarily in relation to the occupation. For instance, whilst the HRCRT material acknowledges that some of the activities may raise sensitive issues unique to the Palestinian refugee community, it discourages teachers from deviating from the vision of the HRCRT Programme, which is 'primarily about human rights education, not history' (UNRWA 2013: 27). The *Civics Education* textbook was largely silent about the occupation, although there are instances where it is alluded (ad hoc) such as the following example (see Figure 7.2) which appears without explanation other than the subheading, 'An image which represents the violation of the right to freedom of movement for the Palestinian people'.

For the most part, there was a notable reticence in this textbook when it came to discussing human rights issues in the context of occupation. Instead, it focused on the rights of 'vulnerable' groups in society such as women, children and the disabled, and even discussed sensitive topics such as domestic violence and child marriage. This resonates with Coysh's (2017) observations that HRE programmes tend to focus on disenfranchised groups within a population, assuming that these groups know nothing about human rights. However, the revised curricula are more explicit, depicting Israel as a settler colonial state, and a Grade 11 history textbook draws on international law to explain that it is an illegal occupation against which colonised people have the right to resist in order to exercise their right to self-determination (Alayan and Riley 2023).

Figure 7.2 Separation barrier (Grade 9 civics education textbook in Qazzaz et al 2010: 28)

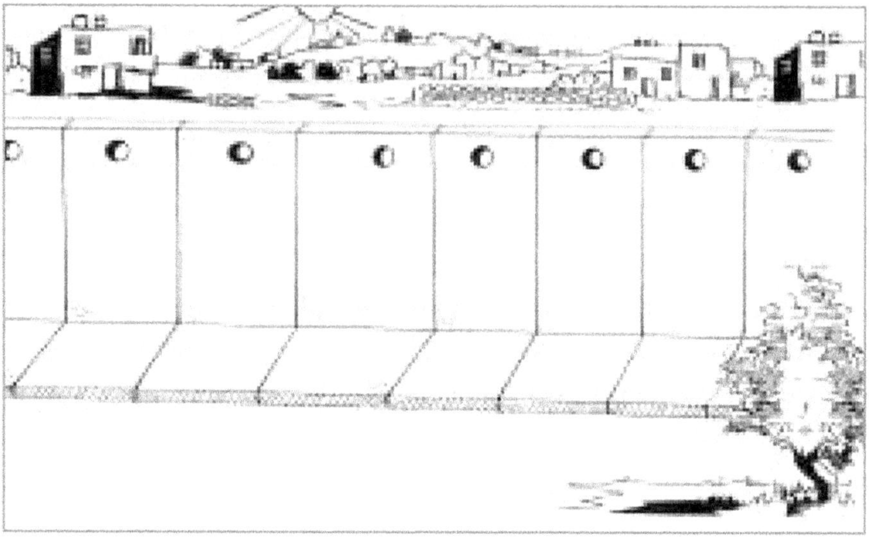

صورة تمثل إنتهاك حق التنقل للشعب الفلسطيني

Although young people from the UNGS, GGS and BGS could at times list from memory articles from human rights instruments, this was often at the very beginning of discussions. The rights that were written down most frequently were largely those that carried a particular significance for participants. For instance, girls who attended non-private schools often listed to the right to education, the right to play, and the right to freedom of assembly. As discussed in chapter six, taking part in demonstrations is a right that girls are often denied due to parental concerns around the shame–honour system. Girls from families who face economic hardship may also be at a greater risk of early or forced marriage, thus posing a threat to the completion of their education. Those attending non-private schools were from lower income families, some of whom lived in overcrowded refugee camps that are subjected to military raids. Therefore, this would help to explain why this group of youths frequently included the right to safety and the right to shelter and a standard of living in their initial definitions.

The right to work was also listed by this cohort, which reflected the boys' preoccupation about future unemployment during their discussions elsewhere. The most reoccurring rights that were listed across the school contexts included the right to freedom of movement, right to freedom of expression, and the right to life and freedom (or liberty). The right to self-determination and the right to return to one's country were included in the definitions provided by boys from the BGS. These frequently listed rights bore a particular significance to participants as Palestinians living in the occupied West Bank, as refugees, and as young people living in a society where patriarchal attitudes deny them a voice in matters that concern their lives. However, it was as conversations developed that they began to more often resist and refashion the global dominant discourse that they were encountering at school. The youths offered alternative readings of human rights often in response to how this top-down, abstract and decontextualised rights narrative was disconnected from their everyday lived experiences as those who are frequently victims of rights violations (as explored in chapters four, five and six).

B. Refashioning the Discourse: Rights as Islamic Constructions

One of the ways the youths resisted the Eurocentric HRE discourse was through offering Islamic constructions of human rights, as exemplified by the following definition: 'Human rights existed 1,500 years ago, and its origins are from the Islamic religion' (male student, BGS). This reflected the content that was privileged in the HRE lesson that I observed in this school. In the BGS, Nidal (teacher, BGS) taught his own religious conceptualisations about human rights during the lesson I observed, as opposed to more secular conceptualisations found in the MoEHE's civics education curriculum. Throughout the lesson he got students to read out some of the articles from the UDHR and then compared it to what is written in the *Qur'an*, claiming that: 'You see, it's the same as Islam. So, it was there before international law was written' (Nidal, teacher, BGS). By expanding HRE to include Islamic contributions to the development of human rights he was adopting the decolonial strategy of recontextualisation (Zembylas 2018).

Interestingly, whilst disputing the West as the sole author of human rights, he still used the UDHR as a reference point and did not critique its content. His criticism of the international human rights scheme was arguably due to the way it has come to be viewed as the moral arm of the West (Ignatieff 2001) rather than the values contained therein. Therefore, Nidal (teacher, BGS) contended: 'Most of the rights we have are from Islam but now they say they're from the West'. He also challenged the secular foundations of the international human rights system during one of the focus groups discussions with youths when he entered the room momentarily and interrupted the participants, as this exchange illustrates:

> **Interviewer:** So, you don't have human rights because international law gives you rights, but you have rights because you are human? Is that what you are saying?
>
> **Fadi:** Yeah, it's not about what international law says. Already, I have rights no matter what international law says. I do not wait for international law to tell me I have rights, as just because I am human, I have rights …

> **Nidal (teacher):** [interrupts] We take our rights from our Islamic religion. The Prophet Muhammad (PBUH) taught us about it … We learned about human rights from our Islamic religion 1400 years ago. The source and origins of human rights is the Islamic religion. International law is recent, and it didn't help us in terms of human rights.
>
> **Fadi:** But I'm not waiting for the international law to tell me I have rights because I'm a human who has rights.
>
> **Nidal (teacher):** Why are you human? This was told in the Islamic religion (BGS).

Both Fadi (student, BGS) and his teacher Nidal (BGS) did not view international law as the source of their rights; for Fadi it was his humanity. His words are reminiscent of those of Tunisian law professor Mohamed Charfi (2001: 24), who maintains that whilst the three monotheistic faiths did not conceive notions of human rights as such, their religious books 'contain messages of love, charity and liberty. It is said in the Qur'ān that humanity is God's vicar on earth'. Despite the direct challenge from his teacher, Fadi (student, BGS) was not necessarily persuaded by the entirely religious narrative. This interaction also demonstrated how young people did not necessarily accept the dominant narratives of those who deliver the curriculum. Further, during a HRE lesson, Nidal (teacher, BGS) constructed learners as members of the *Dar-al-Islam* (the household of Islam), meaning the Muslim regions of the world rather than of a global community. He used the phrase 'we as Muslims' numerous times and stated: 'For us, human rights were taken from the Islamic book … our Prophet Muhammad (PBUH) gave us human rights' (Nidal, teacher, BGS). By saying 'for us' he implied that human rights are constructed differently since their origins emanate from different foundations for Muslims than for non-Muslims; this could have risked excluding any Christian pupils in the class.

Most students from the UNGS and boys' and girls' government schools did not frame human rights 'in conceptions of history based exclusively on European milestones' such as 1948 and the Enlightenment (Barreto 2013a: 6). Instead, they referred to the arrival of Islam as a key milestone in the historical development of human rights and the *Qur'an* as an important text. The latter disrupted the textual form of the 'heaven–hell binary' that considers international human rights instruments as sacred and religious texts as the opposite (Okafor and Agbakwa 2001). For instance, a verse from the *Qur'an* was recited in unison during one of the HRE lessons that I observed in the UNGS. This was done as a way of consolidating the international human rights they had been learning about in that lesson.

Nonetheless, the majority of young people attending non-private schools attributed the source of rights to religion more generally, sometimes including other monotheistic religions (as discussed in chapter six) and as illustrated by Ghadeer's (student, GGS) comment: 'It's something from ancient times, the time of Christians and Muslims, so it's not something Western as all people know it'. Again, young people contested the West as the sole legitimate authors of human rights (as explored in chapter four). Alternatively, youths who attended the PS did not emphasise Islamic constructions of human rights in their definitions. However, Osama (teacher, PS) was the only educators interviewed who referred to the perspective of a Syrian human rights scholar and activist Radwan Ziadeh when discussing human rights. Thus, some of the young people (and their educators) rejected the West's hegemony over the rights discourse (see also chapter four), offering an Islamic vision of human rights and an alternative to the Eurocentric, secular discourse they encountered in their schools' HRE.

C. Refashioning the Discourse: Rights Associated with the Occupation

People's interpretations of human rights are informed by concrete experiences of human rights, or the absence of them, in their unique contexts (Perugini and Gordon 2015). Accordingly, the youths that I interviewed often associated rights with the occupation (as discussed in chapter four). This was also captured in the following initial definitions:

> Most of our rights are violated by the occupation (female student, GGS).
>
> In Palestine, we are not taking our rights completely (male student, BGS).

There was a more collective approach towards how rights were articulated; exemplified by the participants' choice of pronouns 'our' and 'we', which was also present throughout discussions. This was aligned with the protest school's tendency to adopt a more collective and social justice orientation towards rights (Dembour 2010) and Third World approaches that emphasise the collective nature of rights (Barreto 2013c).

The youths regularly emphasised the frailty of international law when discussing its relevance to the OPT. For instance, when asked if they viewed human rights as a powerful tool for Palestinian youths, these boys commented:

> **Mazin:** I don't think so because Israel can do whatever they want.
>
> **Elias:** There isn't anyone to stop them (PS).

When working alongside the YPAGs at the analysis phase, YPAG 2 used Dembour's (2010) schema and her prompts to explore how their peers' interpretations of human rights from the data compared with the four schools of thoughts (see Table 8.1 in chapter eight). When answering the prompt: 'Is human rights law important?' the YPAG members concluded that it was viewed by their peers who were interviewed as 'just ink on paper' and that 'it's not applicable here in Palestine most of the time, but if it was it would help'. Nonetheless, even after their critiques of the international human rights scheme, they maintained that learning about human rights was still particularly important for Palestinians, and some participants likened rights to life itself. Basel (student, BGS) who offered such rich and often poetic contributions, said that for him a 'life without rights is the same as being dead' and would mean 'a life of sadness'.

Others stressed the importance learning about rights had for their dignity, future and land.

As outlined above, the curricula followed at government and UNRWA schools presented a largely decontextualised rights narrative. However, what discussions with the young people and their teachers demonstrated was that in reality they discussed human rights very much in the context of occupation. Whilst textbooks can be presented as 'legitimised knowledge' (Apple 1992: 10), teachers and learners can also reject or accept aspects of this. This was demonstrated during a focus group at the UNGS school in which girls reflected on occasions when their teachers had deviated from the 'taught curriculum' to transmit their own values:

> **Majd:** Also, in our books the curriculum is written in a way that is against Palestine, like, you'll find Israel instead of Palestine written in our books so our teacher helps us always to remember that.
>
> **Randa:** Today we had a lesson with the title 'Palestinians in Israel', and our teacher changed it to 'Palestinians in occupied Palestine' – and we love that (UNGS).

The teacher's modification of the written content was applauded by the refugee girls. This can be viewed as a form of resistance to settler colonialism and how Palestinians have been fragmented from their land and one another (Jiménez 2023). Similarly, during the classroom observation, the right to safety was discussed in the context of soldiers invading their homes, and the right to freedom from torture, followed by a conversation about the practice of illegal medical testing on Palestinian prisoners by Israelis. Similarly, a decontextualised rights narrative was not being delivered in the BGS during a lesson I observed. Whilst it was clear that the teacher wanted to focus on the Islamic roots of human rights, his students kept changing the topic by stating rights they are denied as Palestinians, such as freedom of movement. In response, the teacher discussed Israel's disregard for the Fourth Geneva Convention, describing how 'Israelis target and shoot special cars for doctors – they're not applying human rights … Israelis can hit you with a bullet that can make you disabled' (Nidal, teacher, BGS). Then, he went on to compare this to Islamic teachings, which instruct combatants not to kill non-combatants such as the elderly and animals. When a pupil asked him if there was anyone who monitors the application of the Geneva Convention, he discussed the UN Security Council, and explained that the permanent members hold the unique ability to veto resolutions. He then added that the United States repeatedly vetoes resolutions that would hold Israel to account – as has been witnessed during Israel's most recent military campaign in Gaza (UN 2024).

Based on classroom observations and discussions with youths from the GGS and the BGS, teachers were mediating the textbook content in a way that did not always match the aims set out by the authors of their respective curricula. In the GGS, the lesson focused on harmful cultural practices such as honour killing and child brides rather than on human rights associated with the occupation.

There was only one brief reference to those who have become disabled due to the occupation. Bajaj (2011a: 492) argues that a *HRE for Global Citizenship* model (as promoted in the HRCRT) often leads to a 'de-territorialized' understanding of human rights. However, contrary to the apolitical approach to HRE in the MoEHE's curricula content (prior to its revision), the teachers and young people in the BGS discussed human rights from the perspective of the Palestinian experience by reintroducing their unique political context of living under military occupation. Palestinians have been denied not only their rights and land but their right to context and it is 'the totality of the Palestinian experience' that enables Palestinians to demand their rights in a meaningful way (Zreik 2004: 78).

D. Refashioning the Discourse: Juxtaposition of Human Rights Ideals and Reality

Another way the youths I interviewed sought to reintroduce their context and resist the dominant discourse was when they juxtaposed their concrete experiences of rights alongside the human rights ideals they learned about inside school, as typified by this example: 'No one can take away these rights from any human being, but in our reality, it's taken from our people' (female student, UNGS). The first half of this definition denotes rights according to the natural school of thought, but this universal claim is followed by the reality that Palestinians face. This two-part definition, among others, indicated how the promise-laden discourse conflicts with their experiences of suffering as Palestinians in the occupied West Bank.

Although the UNGS teachers were not afraid to relate human rights to the Palestinian context, they were less inclined to problematise the universality of human rights as presented in their HRE programmes. During one of the HRE lessons I observed, a young person in the UNGS brought up the right to freedom of movement, but then clarified: 'But we don't have it as Palestinians, but it's supposed to be for us like in Western countries' (female student, UNGS). The teacher responded to the pupil's comment by stating that the right to freedom of movement still remained a universal right regardless of whether they enjoyed it or not. This exchange highlighted the areas of dissonance that exist between the universalist claims that teachers are expected to teach versus the real-life experiences that their pupils (and they themselves) faced outside school.

A group of refugee girls interrogated the universality of human rights during their discussions because of Israel's settler colonial violence towards Palestinians (see chapter four for a more detailed discussion). This led these girls to debate among themselves whether or not all Israelis were deserving of human rights. There were diverse views among young people across the schools on the universality of human rights and it was apparent that they were critically engaging with the content that they were being taught in school, which promotes universalism.

In the PS, during a classroom observation of a lesson on human rights, the teacher also juxtaposed human rights as norms and standards alongside the reality of the Palestinian experience. At the start of the lesson, he seemed to adopt a neutral tone and began by systematically presenting human rights as listed in the UDHR. Whenever a student contextualised this, the teacher responded with a universalist claim, thereby avoiding discussing rights abuses particular to Palestinians, as this exchange captures:

> **Osama (teacher):** Governments shouldn't falsely imprison someone if they have not been given a fair trial and proven guilty.
>
> **Male student:** If this is the case, does this mean Israel is breaking the law because they have falsely imprisoned people and they arrest people without reason?
>
> **Osama (teacher):** Every human on earth should have the right to a fair trial (PS).

However, at the end of the lesson, Osama (teacher, PS) asked the class, having read all the rights contained in the UDHR, to discuss whether they enjoy these rights in their particular context. The class all laughed and said unanimously: 'None of them!' Thus, less restrictive notions of human rights began to emerge, different to those presented during the first part of the lesson. His pupils then expressed attitudes more aligned to the protest and discourse schools of thought in which the law is viewed with suspicion or as farcical (Dembour 2010). Although it was the students who critiqued the role of international law during this lesson, the teacher, by asking this question created space for them to do so. Notably, although Osama concentrated on the UDHR throughout his lesson, as aforementioned, young people from this school rarely defined rights in this normative way. Instead, they wrote single words that they associate with the enjoyment or threat of human rights (see Figure 7.1 above).

In HRE, human rights can be portrayed as 'a project which has been fully realised' (Osler and Starkey 2010: 17). However, for Palestinians, it is often perceived as a project which has been accomplished everywhere else apart from the OPT. Consequently, many of the young people I interviewed also assumed that rights were benignly bestowed upon individuals in the rest of the world, but that rights do not function this way for them, as typified by the following example:

> Human rights are for all human beings except Palestinians as human rights are delivered to people around the world in a peaceful way. However, in Palestine we cannot get our rights in a peaceful way or any other ways (Isra'a, student, UNGS).

Isra'a described rights as being 'delivered' to everyone apart from Palestinians as though rights are effortlessly enjoyed elsewhere without the need for struggle, be that non-violent or armed. This interpretation that human rights ought to, but do not, operate for Palestinians has the potential to lead them to experience a greater sense of marginalisation since, in their reality, rights require what they perceive to be an isolated and often futile struggle. Thus, even though the young people closely associated human rights with the occupation, they often held this in tension with the universalist narrative they were encountering at school, believing that this is the way rights *ought* to be realised. This illustrates how a universalist rights discourse can be problematic because those whose rights are threatened discover that 'if men – and women – are born equal, they do not remain equal the rest of their lives' (Mignolo 2013: 44). Not being given opportunities to critique the universalist claims of the dominant rights discourse can lead to cynicism towards human rights or rejection of it altogether. Disillusionment with the human rights system was most notable in the BGS.

E. Resisting the Discourse: Rights as Universal Failures

Some of the young people contested the dominant HRE discourse through their depictions of rights as failed concepts, or non-existent – interestingly, not only in the OPT, but also more broadly across the world, as typified by this definition: 'There are no rights' (male student, BGS).

These articulations of rights echoed that found within the discourse school, which views rights as unrealisable and their supposed universality a farce (see Dembour 2010). There were fewer examples of these definitions in the initial activity of defining human rights and, notably, they were mainly articulated by boys who attended the BGS. These young people doubted the applicability of rights locally and globally because of their lived experiences.

Analysis of the data provided by YPAG 1 offered insights into why cynicism had led these boys in particular to regard rights in such a bleak way. YPAG 1 coded these quotes as 'pessimistic'. They suggested that due to the gendering of roles, boys are more likely to participate in demonstrations and are therefore more likely to face arrest, torture or humiliation. Unlike children from elite backgrounds, these boys are not as shielded from settler colonial violence and are also more likely to experience economic hardship as a direct consequence of the occupation. The intersecting injustices they face due to the interplay between neoliberalism and settler colonialism undoubtedly impacted upon how they constructed their understandings of human rights (Jiménez 2023). It was the tension between the global HRE discourse that they had encountered at school and the reality of life on the ground which led to a sense of disillusionment with rights discourse, as this exchange captures:

> **Basel:** We learn and memorise things about human rights in school but it's not applicable.
>
> **Interviewer:** So, do you think there's a gap between what you get taught and real life?
>
> **Basel:** Yes, sure, we learn about human rights early in life until 9th grade. We know about human rights but there are no rights in reality. They [teachers] let us live in dreams that will not be fulfilled because there is no international voice to speak out our voice (BGS).

Basel (student, BGS) critiqued the more 'technical' approach to HRE (Coysh 2017) as well as the 'banking style' of education (Friere 1970) that this approach often assumes (see chapter three). He implied that acquiring knowledge about human rights that did not correlate to his material conditions was in some way cruel, and he apportioned blame to his educators for teaching this promise-laden narrative that will not be fulfilled. For him, the lack of third-party assistance and solidarity from the international community was a reason why rights cannot be experienced by Palestinians. Basel and his peers were not being presented with opportunities to explore more expansive conceptualisations of human rights theory at school to help them make sense of the more expansive conclusions that they were arriving at because of their personal experiences as non-elite Palestinians.

Life under occupation and the oppressive politics of the PA along with their own cultural, religious and political views influenced how the youths resisted and refashioned the dominant narratives they are taught *about* in their school's HRE programmes. Their definitions demonstrate that the authorship and agency of human rights belongs to and emerges from those engaged in resistance against oppressive forces (Barreto 2013c), such as colonialism, authoritarian governments and patriarchy.

HRE is often characterised as education *about*, *through* and *for* human rights. Learning *through* human rights will now be discussed and how the school's rights climate shaped the youths' attitudes towards human rights discourse.

III. EDUCATION *THROUGH* HUMAN RIGHTS: THE IMPACT OF A RIGHTS CLIMATE IN SCHOOLS

Learning *through* human rights relates to the *context* whereby learners experience the realisation of human rights or alternatively the denial of rights as explored in the previous three chapters. Education *through* human rights can also refer to a classroom and school culture as well as the pedagogical methods that are employed (Tibbitts 2017). Bearing in mind the particularities of the context within which the young people and their educators lived (discussed in chapters four, five, and six), I will now explore the extent to which HRE was being embodied at school level. It draws on lessons that were observed across the school contexts as well as discussions which took place with young people and their educators.

A. School as a Sanctuary from the Negative Experiences of Human Rights Outside School

Schools can offer an organic location in which a human rights culture can be encouraged (McEvoy and Lundy 2007). Based on conversations with the young people, it became apparent that schools played a largely constructive role in the lives of those who attended the PS, UNGS and GGS. These schools acted as a space of sanctuary for young people and were places where they experienced the enjoyment of rights that they might not have experienced at home (for some) or in society. Sabina's (student, UNGS) comment captured this sentiment: 'Out of school, in our community children have no rights'. The UNGS, PS and GGS seemed to prioritise nurturing a rights-respecting culture within their respective schools and this was confirmed by the young people.

Beginning with UNRWA-run schools, Bashar (senior educator, UNRWA), who had been involved in developing HRE, emphasised the importance of cultivating rights-respecting schools, stating: 'So, the idea is the school environment and culture becomes a human rights culture'. According to the young people at the UNGS, these aims seemed to be embodied in their school. For instance, some of the girls I interviewed described how their principal would consult them on the performance of teachers, as Lina (student, UNGS) explained: 'When there is a new teacher in school, later the principal will ask us our opinion, whether we find the teacher a good educator or not'. When asked what action the principal would take if they were to negatively evaluate the teacher in question, they claimed that the principal would meet with the teacher and ask them to change their approach. This example suggested that their views were not only being listened to, but also acted upon. It also indicated that the principal seemed to be comfortable with equalising power relations within the school between teachers and students.

In terms of the pedagogy employed, of all the lessons observed, the most participatory one was in the UNGS. This aligned with the aims of the HRCRT, which states, 'teaching practices are democratic and participatory' and 'all teachers and staff need to be able to both transmit and model human rights values' (UNRWA 2013: 9–10). This was observed during the lesson where some of the topics were driven by the students: students were invited to present their thoughts to the class and had brought in newspaper articles that discussed human rights issues. However, some of these efforts were undone at the end of the lesson when the teacher ended the class abruptly (whilst a girl was speaking). Thus, participatory efforts do not necessarily equate to a more critical approach to HRE; rather, they can act as a façade behind which a knowledge acquisition approach can hide (Coysh 2017). However, throughout the discussions, the young people in the UNGS school described their school as havens from rights violations they faced elsewhere.

Staff at the PS also seemed to be preoccupied with cultivating a rights-respecting culture. Osama (educator, PS) was particularly concerned with teaching HRE with authenticity, claiming that a teacher must: 'Let it go out with your attitude not with your words'. For him, HRE was not about teaching theory, but 'something bigger', saying: 'It's not a workshop or papers'. This emphasis on authenticity when teaching HRE appeared to stem from his own educational experiences in which corporal punishment had been used alongside receiving workshops about human rights. Reflecting on his own experience of HRE at school, he commented: 'You cannot bring a child to the maths class and kick him in the maths class because he didn't find the solution and after ... work with him in a workshop about human rights ... he will see the difference'. He viewed children as critical learners able to discern between knowledge *about* human rights and being given opportunities to enjoy rights. He discussed the rights-respecting culture that was fostered in the PS positively, describing his school as having: 'A different energy than other places in Palestine'.

Similarly, youths in this school were very positive about their school environment, often comparing it to their perception of other schools, as exemplified by Salim's (student, PS) comments: 'We have the freedom of expressing you know not like other schools' and 'teachers don't hit the students like they do in other schools'. In the PS, young people and teachers viewed their school as a haven buried within Palestinian society in which girls enjoyed equality with their male peers and where they had freedom to discuss political and religious matters freely unlike in other parts of Palestinian society.

Regarding pedagogy, the curriculum followed in the PS outlines that it differs from other educational programmes since it is learner-centred and fosters critical thinking. However, the lesson observed was largely non-participatory and more teacher-centred. Based upon comments made by both this teacher and students about his usual approach to teaching, this lesson was possibly uncharacteristically non-participatory. On the other hand, the teacher, in terms of classroom management style, appeared unconcerned with maintaining traditional power structures between teachers and students.

At the GGS, what was particularly notable was that teachers seemed to advocate for their students' rights in a way that some parents did not. For instance, educators in the GGS reported that they had played a role in trying to support their pupils not to marry early and to continue their education even when this went against their parents' wishes. They had intervened on behalf of their students by meeting with parents to convince them about the value of respecting their children's rights in this regard.

Thus, they took the role of what Bajaj (2011b: 216) terms 'legitimating agents', not only modelling human rights principles through their interactions with students, but also advocating for them when it came to their rights concerns. Another girl spoke about how the school would offer financial assistance to girls from families that needed economic support. During discussions, these teachers often choose to identify themselves with the young people. Doha (principal, GGS), when referring to the patriarchal aspects of the culture, argued that 'we need to rearrange a lot of things in Palestine' and went on to state: 'I think ... the woman should, all the young people ... we should make a rebellion'. She seemed willing to join forces with the young people since she viewed both women and the youths as those who needed to challenge patriarchal practices together.[3] The girls described their school as a place where teachers respected and listened to them, and treated them equally and without discrimination.

In terms of pedagogical practices, the preface to the MoEHE's *Civics Education* textbook encourages teachers to facilitate the participation of students, 'encouraging them to think, question things, negotiate ideas and to respect each other's opinions' (Qazzaz et al 2010: 5). Throughout the lesson in the GGS, girls shouted out their ideas, interrupting one another and the teacher. There was good rapport between the students and teacher including lots of laughter. The lesson was delivered in such a way that it did not seem textbook-driven despite the fact the teacher had used material from the textbook. Notably, Sally (teacher, GGS), whose lesson I observed, also criticised the traditional forms of teaching when I interviewed her:

> In general, education is like: 'Listen, don't talk, I'm the one who talks', but me and other teachers negotiate with students, give them a space to express their opinion or to disagree with things. We teach students that they can express themselves and their thoughts (Sally, teacher, GGS).

The girls in this school also affirmed this by reporting that their voices were not only listened to but acted upon, even when it concerned the way they were disciplined. Dania (student, GGS) explained: 'If the teacher said something wrong or screamed at one of the students we can negotiate with our principal and get a solution for it'.

Despite the fact that government schools for boys and girls followed the same curriculum, which outlines the same aims, there was a notable difference between their school environments. When the boys in the BGS tried to express themselves in the lesson observed, the teacher spoke louder, telling them he did not want to be sidetracked. Towards the end of the lesson, a boy said: 'I want to go home!' (male student, BGS). This was not only evident during the classroom observations, but also during the discussions with the young people attending these schools. In each of the focus group discussions, the boys argued fervently that they did not believe that their school environment was rights-respecting.

Therefore, young people who attended the UNGS, PS and GGS largely described their schools as spaces where their rights were enjoyed in a way that they were not necessarily respected in the community or at home (for some). Their teachers and the rights culture they fostered enabled the young people to feel their *humanity* compared to how they are dehumanised by the occupation (chapter four), to have a *voice* compared to how this is hindered by the state (chapter five), and exercise *agency* compared to how this is denied by the patriarchal aspects of their culture (chapter six). However, this was not the case for the boys who attended the BGS.

[3] As discussed in chs 2 and 6, patriarchy in Arab contexts can include hierarchies of age as well as gender.

B. School as an Extension of the Negative Experiences of Human Rights Outside School

School was depicted by boys who attended the BGS as an extension of the oppression they encountered at home (for some) and in society. They seemed to be the participants most likely to lack access to a space from which they could escape the marginalisation they faced outside school. Unlike their peers attending other school contexts, they did not differentiate between teachers and other adults, as this exchange illustrates:

> **Basel:** You talk but adults don't take your opinion seriously.
>
> **Fadi:** They ignore you.
>
> **Basel:** There are bullies in our school and society (BGS).

When asked to describe their school, Basel (student, BGS) switched to English and declared it: 'Rubbish, rubbish, rubbish!' His peer responded to Basel's comments by telling me that I was asking the wrong question: 'You should ask us "how does this school *disrespect* your rights?"' (Amjad, student, BGS). In a different group, Fawaz (student, BGS) remarked: 'Honestly, it's like a prison here'. Prior to Fawaz's comment, this group of boys had seemed initially hesitant to comment on their school. However, following Fawaz's comment, the rest of the boys erupted with descriptions of how it was an oppressive environment in which their rights were not upheld. When asked why their school felt like a prison, the following discussion ensued:

> **Milad:** Boring classes.
>
> **Thaer:** They are putting cameras all around the school.
>
> **Jamal:** Also, outside the bathroom. To find out those students who smoke secretly.
>
> **Omar:** But we are not scared.
>
> **Akram:** They hold sticks.
>
> **Jamal:** Not all teachers hit students.
>
> **Akram:** They want to practice power over us.
>
> **Omar:** But when the Ministry of Education visits our school, not one of the teachers dares to use the stick (BGS).

Although they did not explicitly use the language of rights, they alluded to a number of rights which they believed were being impinged upon, such as their right to privacy as a result of feeling under constant surveillance even when they were using the bathroom. They also highlighted how *vertical* relationships based on *unilateral* respect (Barakat 2005) occurred through the way they were exposed to physical forms of violence at the hands of their teachers. Therefore, they were aware that the rights they learnt about were not being embodied at school level. They not only exposed the oppression that they faced, but they also offered their analysis of why they thought teachers were using violent practices.

Akram (student, BGS) foregrounded the implement of violence – the sticks – and by describing his teachers as constantly armed he conveyed the asymmetrical power relations that existed between pupils and teachers. Furthermore, he focused not on the violence itself, but the constant presence of the threat of violence at school. The boys also clearly understood their teachers' use of physical punishment as a means of perpetuating the oppressive power inequalities, or in Akram's words: 'They want to practice power over us'. Notably, in response, Omar (student, BGS) then located his teachers within the broader hierarchical structures, constructing them as relatively powerless under the authority of the Ministry of Education, which moderates their use of corporal punishment.

When I visited another government school for boys (that I did not end up conducting interviews in), I happened to enter the playground during their lunch time. I saw a teacher herding the boys with a striped black-and-white baton that resembled those used by law enforcement officers. When I asked Yazan (counsellor, PS), who worked as a counsellor at the PS but had previously worked in the other school contexts, about the batons, he explained that the MoEHE turns a blind eye to teachers' use of these as long as the MoEHE did not witness it, and that it was often sympathetic to the challenges facing teachers in maintaining discipline. In the occupied West Bank, children are protected from violence according to Article 42 of the Child Law 2004, and under Article 39, the state is required to make decisions that prioritise 'the dignity of the child, particularly when adopting decisions or developing programs, which aim at prohibiting forms of violence in school' (End Corporal Punishment 2021: 2). However, corporal punishment is still legal in government-run schools in the occupied West Bank and Gaza, although the MoEHE advises against it (End Corporal Punishment 2021; DCI Palestine 2016).

Despite the oppressive school environment at the BGS, the students demonstrated resilience and that they were not scared to contest the power inequalities they encountered in school. They confronted the narratives of those with more power such as their principal and teachers. For instance, their principal described how the staff try their best 'to boost the students' confidence and self-esteem' (Naseef, principal, BGS). Conversely, the boys reported that their principal also used a stick to discipline them on occasions. Elsewhere, the views of teachers and students were contradictory; when describing the treatment of young people in Palestinian society, Wissam (teacher, BGS) stated:

> As a Muslim, in Palestine and as an Arab also … we sympathise strongly with young people. So, no abuse at all, no oppression and if you find some it's very rare … No oppression at all, no abuse at all never.

These opposing narratives demonstrate that had I not consulted the young people this layer of marginalisation that the boys encountered in school would not have been exposed. The boys also contradicted the perspectives of their teachers about the extent to which the rights of young people were being respected in school. When asked how his school respects human rights Wissam (teacher, BGS) responded:

> Discussion is a main point … the rules of this school are with the students, not against the students. For example, the students are allowed to go to the water closet, the first class, second and third class … Something else, if a student is for example tired some day and he says: 'Okay, I want to go home'. The school counsellor and headmaster calls his family and tells him: 'Your son is sick, what do you think?' 'Yes,' he will say 'Keep him there, I will come and take him' or 'Let him go home'. So, these rights are all covered and given to students.

Wissam (teacher, BGS) described the rights of his students as 'covered and given' by focusing on their dismissal when unwell and the number of toilet breaks they were allowed to take. This suggested that this teacher had a different understanding of what constituted the enjoyment of human rights than the young people attending this school. Even his example of allowing a student to go home early reflected how decision-making belonged to adults since it was the staff and the parents who negotiated the seriousness of a pupil's illness. Following this, he added another troubling example: 'If a student falls down and breaks his hand, breaks his leg, we take him to hospital and treat him and then send [him] to his home peaceful'. By selecting this scenario, the teacher did not seem to have any qualms about discussing the physical violence which takes place between students at the school and yet he did not mention the violence teachers were exercising towards students. However, he did not deny that conflict occurred between teachers and students. Elsewhere, he explained:

> Maybe some students are very nervous or upset because of something that happened with one of the teachers or … a difficult exam or a teacher is treating them badly. I give them the chance … to express themselves: 'Why do you think the teacher treated you like that?' (Wissam, teacher, BGS).

Whilst he did not expound upon how a teacher might be 'treating them badly', he seemed comfortable acknowledging this. Nonetheless, by constructing himself as a mediator between staff and students, and thereby distinguishing himself from his colleagues, he claimed that he enabled the students' right to express their views.

A similar scenario was also described by a student, but they portrayed the role of the teacher quite differently:

> If there is a problem between two students, they respect them in the way that they take both of them. On the other hand, they disrespect them by not letting them to express their opinion. They will tell them to 'shut up' if they tried to express their opinions (Ahmad, student, BGS).

Similar to Wissam (teacher, BGS), Ahmad (student, BGS) acknowledged that conflicts arose between pupils and that teachers may hold them equally responsible; nonetheless, he painted a different picture when it concerned the role teachers play in enabling the voices of pupils. Unlike his teacher, he claimed that they are even told to 'shut up'. In response to this comment, his peer Amjad (student, BGS) added: 'In general, teachers do not really care about listening to us, but they show they care in front of people in high positions'. In doing so, Amjad scrutinised the human rights performances of his teachers. Once more, young people from this school situated their teachers within the broader hierarchical structures under which they are positioned. Situating their teachers as subordinates to the MoEHE or, in this example, 'people in high positions' suggests that the boys were critical of the hierarchical nature of their society, but also the way in which their teachers wanted to be seen to be upholding children's rights though that was not necessarily the case in reality. These narratives mirrored how they scrutinised the human rights performances of the PA as explored in chapter five.

Youths in the BGS were able to discern staged human rights acts from sincere embodiments of rights, which indicated that they are engaging critically with rights concepts even if they are sadly more familiar with their limitations rather than their emancipatory potential. Nevertheless, these boys were not afraid to use their voices to counter the narratives of the powerful – in this case, their teachers. They refused to accept this behaviour and it was apparent that the boys were able to deploy the language of rights to question the conduct of their educators when it did not line up with human rights values.

They gave examples of how they attempted to do this in their daily lives at school. For instance, one group of boys from this school explained that they were not wearing their uniform as a deliberate act of protest against their teachers. They explained that teachers were designing a new uniform and had asked for their opinion, but had disregarded their input. Majdi (student, BGS) explained that 'they imposed it on us as we wanted a grey T-shirt, but they ignored our opinion' and Abdullah (student, BGS) added that the teachers had only asked them about the colour of the tie. Even though they were consulted to a point about the school uniform, they did not feel this consultation was adequate and as a result had decided to wear their own clothes. Whilst these boys did want to be consulted by adults in decision-making about certain matters, such as their school uniform, there were instances where they were critical of being afforded *only* this kind of voice. Sometimes, the boys criticised their teachers' attempts at involving them in decision-making at school level; Majdi (student, BGS) explained that their opinion was only sought on 'the simplest issue. For example, if we want to postpone the test'.

In contrast, the principal listed involving students in this way as an example of how his school respects students' rights: 'If I want to put the exam schedule up for students, I'll bring a group of students in to discuss with them how to put the schedule in a way that is psychologically appropriate for the students' (Naseef, principal, BGS). It is possible that he genuinely thought that in doing this he was helping his students to realise their rights. However, there was a gap between the views of teachers and students regarding meaningful consultation. The boys in this school seemed to long for their teachers to authentically model the human rights values they learned about.

Whilst at times their faith in human rights wavered (as their definitions of rights as failures indicated), their faith in human rights principles was not entirely lost; instead, the greatest impact was seen in their faith in adults and their ability to embody these rights with sincerity.

It is helpful to remember that these boys would have had more opportunities to exercise some of their civil and political rights, such as attending demonstrations, compared to their female peers, and yet this cohort of the young people seemed to lack a 'space' where they could enjoy rights and relationships based on mutual respect. Nonetheless, even when their rights were threatened, these boys contested this through subtle acts of protest. Their narratives and acts of resistance mirror a defiance that they displayed towards the occupation (chapter four), the PA (chapter five) and adults' patriarchal attitudes (chapter six), all of which sought to quash their agency.

Whilst they encountered largely asymmetrical power relations with their teachers, they identified one person who seemed to listen to their views: the school counsellor. In fact, school counsellors were repeatedly praised by students across the school contexts. Many boys distinguished their school counsellor from their teachers; for example: 'He's the only one who listens to us and helps us' (Fadi, student, BGS). It seemed that the school counsellors were the few adults in the lives of these boys who facilitated their voices in matters which concerned them. Time spent with the counsellor may have been one of the few spaces in which they could enjoy mutual respect and escape the oppressive power structures that they encountered elsewhere in society and school. Therefore, the school climate and the way learning was taking place *through* human rights at school contributed towards young people's overall faith in or cynicism towards human rights.

IV. EDUCATION *FOR* HUMAN RIGHTS: LIMITED OPPORTUNITIES

Education *for* human rights emphasises that learners should be empowered to uphold their own rights and the rights of others, and is aligned to a transformative approach to HRE (see chapter three). The young people that I interviewed had limited opportunities when it came to the action-oriented dimension to human rights. As previously outlined, the MoEHE is functioning with limited autonomy, is reliant upon foreign aid, and is accountable to the US, Israel and the PA (see chapter three). Similarly, the UNRWA is dependent upon outside donors and emphasises political neutrality. Therefore, it was unsurprising that transformative approaches to HRE were not adopted in these schools since mobilising learners to engage in human rights praxis would risk disrupting the way in which international donors, Palestinian elites and their occupier seek to socialise them (Tarrow 1992). Nonetheless, during interviews, teachers in the UNGS and government schools highlighted the opportunities their students had *for* human rights action. School parliaments exist in all UNRWA schools and students vote for their representatives. Hala (teacher, UNGS) shared about different weekly activities including keeping a calendar for human rights, visiting community organisations and cleaning the school yard. However, young people suggested that these activities *for* human rights were not necessarily the forms of participation they would choose.

Whilst the government schools' *Civics Education* textbook did not follow an explicitly *HRE for Coexistence* approach (Bajaj 2011a), what became apparent from the educator interviews was that the principal of the BGS did personally view human rights as playing a healing role between Christians and Muslims within Palestinian society. He commented:

> I'm living in a city where I have Muslim and Christian neighbours. I would love to teach the students how to understand each other and to spread the culture of forgiveness between each other since we are living under occupation and we need to be united (Naseef, principal, BGS).

His personal circumstances had impacted the way in which he viewed othered groups within Palestinian society. This divided aspect of Palestinian society is often overlooked because of the broader military occupation, depicted as a conflict that is solely between Muslims and Jews (Karam 2010) rather than an anticolonial struggle. Christians form a minority in Palestinian society and, due to their tradition of taking a largely non-violent stance against the occupation, can be marginalised within their own struggle (Karam 2010). However, Naseef's (principal, BGS) motivation for building peace between Christians and Muslims was so that they could resist the occupation together. This belief in seeking reconciliation between the two groups had also influenced action he had taken as a principal in a school with a Christian minority. He explained:

> I went to Nablus a week ago with 15 of our students with a project that is called 'Co-living between Christians and Muslims'. We visited religious Muslim and Christian places and it was the first time to be in such places. I feel afraid to take students to such places because I'm afraid that they'll be arrested by the occupation (Naseef, principal, BGS).

This example illustrated how educators play a key role in what approaches are privileged in HRE. Nonetheless, as explored, the principal's approach contrasted with that of his colleague, Nidal (teacher, BGS), who taught about human rights as from an exclusively Islamic perspective even though not all his pupils were necessarily Muslims. Furthermore, Naseef's comment also demonstrates how the occupation casts a shadow on educational initiatives like this.

As explored at the start of this chapter, the textbooks used in UNRWA and government schools adopt a predominantly depoliticised tone, arguably in keeping with the MoEHE's instructions that forbid political discussion and UNRWA's commitment to observe political neutrality (see also chapter five). This policy of not discussing political matters limits the potential of education *for* human rights. This was notable particularly in the UNGS where the girls articulated numerous times that they had a strong desire to talk about political matters and participate in peaceful demonstrations. They explained that their teachers would prevent them from engaging in protests against the occupation: 'The principal will tell us that she'll give us detention if we want to participate in the demonstrations' (Anwar, student, UNGS). This was reiterated by a teacher who explained that they discouraged students from attending demonstrations. By contrast, the PS permitted certain grades and pupils who were part of the school's student parliament, to attend demonstrations. Nonetheless, some of the young people that I spoke to who attended the PS reported that their school's policy was unfair, as this exchange illustrates:

> **Nawja:** Our school is different because we are allowed to join protests ... this is the negative part ... only some grades are allowed to do it even though, like age shouldn't be a concern.
>
> **Jiries:** Yeah ... they don't choose everyone ... they choose like five, six because they're more ...
>
> **Salim:** They're more concerned with politics.
>
> **Jiries:** Yeah and I don't understand how they can know this, you know? (PS).

The contrast between the children attending the UNGS and the PS, when it came to having their political participation facilitated by their schools, was illustrated when YPAG 2 (made up of refugee girls) analysed this piece of data. After reading the extract above, they scoffed: 'Do they feel oppressed by this?'

Regardless of the lack of opportunities to take action *for* human rights, the youths introduced notions around agency when discussing human rights issues. For instance, in a human rights lesson in the GGS, a story was read about a child who was forced to marry an old man. In the story, the girl goes on to have a daughter whom she wishes could attend school. However, the older husband refuses his wife's wish because their child is a girl. When the teacher asked the students to identify the rights that had been denied as found in the UNCRC, a girl asked: 'But why didn't the girl defend herself and her rights in the story?' (female student, GGS). By questioning the passivity of the victims of the story she reintroduced the notion of struggle and individual agency. However, the teacher denied the girl in the story agency; her response to the pupil's question was that the girl was 'young and innocent and was unaware of the full extent of what was going on – just think she was calling her husband "Uncle"' (Sally, teacher, GGS).

The teacher's response also reflected a trend within the textbooks whereby vulnerable groups were portrayed as 'passive victims' (Meyers 2011) in need of others to defend their rights for them. This echoes Coysh (2017), who contends that the dominant HRE discourse depicts victims of rights abuses as those who lack knowledge about their rights. Children were represented in this way elsewhere in the *Civics Education* textbook, for example, where learners were asked to discuss how the need for specific provisions for children arises from:

- the weakness of children – as they lack the ability to defend their rights
- parents' ability to defend children's rights (Qazzaz et al 2010: 35).

In this extract, children are constructed as those who lack agency to defend their own rights and parents are portrayed as those who can do so on their behalf. This emphasis on solidarity over agency could be part of the hidden curriculum in which the PA seek loyal and obedient subjects (Hajjar 2001). It also highlights the tension that young people experience as those who are expected to struggle for rights without being granted the agency to do so (this will be explored in chapter eight). According to Alayan and Riley (2023), the revised textbooks used in government-run schools in the OPT emphasise gender equality compared with the previous materials. However, analysis of whether there have been any changes with regard to how children are portrayed would be useful since hierarchies of age are a part of patriarchy in Arab contexts (as discussed in chapters two and six). Throughout my discussions, it was apparent that young people wanted to engage in human rights praxis, but those who attended non-private schools were presented with very limited opportunities to do so.

Having reflected on HRE from the point of view of the young people, it is only fair to explore the educators' experiences and views of teaching about human rights in a context where these values are continually threatened.

V. CHALLENGES OF TEACHING HRE IN PALESTINIAN SCHOOLS

Non-private-school teachers discussed how their faith in the human rights system had been impacted by their own negative experiences of human rights. When asked why Palestinian teachers may be reluctant to teach about human rights, Naseef (principal, BGS) explained: 'Teachers are depressed about our social reality and their hard lives'. Educators at the UNGS answered the same question with an air of vulnerability and shared the discomfort they experienced at times when teaching about human rights:

> What we teach sometimes conflicts with their real situation. Here we find it difficult, we are talking about the human rights. 'Ok you have the right to sleep safely' but in [*sic*] midnight, the soldiers are coming and they took your brother or father in the middle of the night. So, here's the conflict – between real life and what we are teaching (Amina, principal, UNGS).

Amina (principal, UNGS) juxtaposed the right to safety alongside the reality faced by those living in refugee camps who are often subjected to military raids and arbitrary arrests. This mirrored the way in which some of the young people constructed their definitions of human rights by referring to a right alongside how Palestinians are denied this right. The educators in this school also offered reflections on how these inconsistencies gave rise to different emotions, ranging from guilt to embarrassment. Amina described how she personally felt:

> You will be punished from … even the kids say: 'Teacher, why are you talking like that but we are living something else?' So, you feel that you … don't say the truth, no? So, you are blaming yourself that I teach something but I couldn't give them that thing.

As she reflected, she seemed uneasy about some of the more UN-based narratives and notions of universality taught through HRE at her school since she believed she and her colleagues were presenting a false narrative. Her comments implied that she assumed responsibility for securing the rights of her students and her inability to deliver the ideals she was expected to promote made her question the integrity of what she was teaching. On another occasion, she described feeling 'embarrassed' when her pupils asked her questions about the applicability of human rights. Her colleague, Hala (teacher, UNGS), also discussed the unique challenges facing her students as a result of the location of the camp:

> Protection of children inside and outside. For example, tear gas. How do you protect children from gas? Some of them have asthma and other breathing difficulties. Teaching about human rights in class when they face this. For instance, when the soldiers are so close, how do you protect them if the soldiers want to talk to them?

She constructed herself as a type of disempowered protector due to the proximity of Israeli soldiers who have the power to immediately undo the rights principles that she is trying to teach. Therefore, whilst these educators taught about human rights, they possessed an underlying cynicism towards the content they were delivering.

For Bashar (senior education, UNRWA), rights violations caused by the occupation was not a reason for Palestinian educators to abandon the pursuit of human rights at a more local level. Bashar reflected on the time when he and his colleagues were first tasked with encouraging teachers to promote a human rights culture in schools:

> One of the challenges that faced us in the past was that people were associating human rights with the occupation. And it was difficult for them to see … how they can practice human rights … irrelevant of if there is a checkpoint or settlement opposite to your school or to your camp. Yes, your rights are being violated but this should not be a reason why all other rights among the community living within the camp should not be observed (Bashar, senior education, UNRWA).

He portrayed the Palestinian refugee community as active participants who could uphold rights in the local sphere rather than viewing themselves as merely powerless victims of Israeli rights abuses. Nevertheless, he did not diminish the hardship of life under occupation and also acknowledged that this continued to have a negative effect upon the HRE programme when he went on to explain:

> It's not only children … Teachers – they arrive at the school and they feel that they are frustrated. The overall frustration of … finding [a] peaceful political solution and

> ending … this conflict continues to cast a shadow upon the programme despite the fact that people are convinced now (Bashar, senior education, UNRWA).

He acknowledged how political violence hinders the aims of the HRE programme. However, he argued that the teachers no longer lacked faith in human rights values and the delivery of HRE since they were 'convinced now'.

In contrast, according to educators that I interviewed at the UNGS, faith in human rights seemed to fluctuate. Hala (teacher, UNGS) shared how she personally had wrestled with the dissonance between the aspirational and internationalised framework of human rights norms and the facts on the ground. She reflected:

> As Palestinians, teaching them about human rights when Israeli soldiers are abusing and neglecting rights for example, the [Palestinian] boy in East Jerusalem who was burnt alive. It's contradictory- it feels like nothing will be done in reality. No one is doing anything (Hala, teacher, UNGS).

Here, she referred to 16-year-old Mohammed Abu Khdeir, who was kidnapped and burnt alive as a revenge killing for the murder of three Israeli teenagers in the West Bank around six months prior to the interview. His death, along with other forms of settler colonial violence, caused her to reflect on the supposed universality of human rights that she was expected to promote through HRE. She went a step further than her colleague by describing teaching about human rights as 'contradictory' as opposed to conflictive. At this point in the interview, she articulated a lack of belief in human rights and her hopeless pronouncements that 'nothing will be done in reality' reflected attitudes found within the discourse school – the 'nihilists' of human rights (Dembour 2010: 10).

Nevertheless, there were other occasions during the interview where she expressed more hope in the potential of human rights: 'Human rights make the world realise they [Palestinian young people] exist, our situation is on the map' (Hala, teacher, UNGS). Whilst viewing human rights as a discourse that internationalises the injustices that Palestinians face, at other times her optimism in human rights waned. On another occasion, she referred back to the lesson which she had taught (and I had observed), and reflected:

> You saw one of the students expressing her opinion about if a man is forced to leave his job, that he is entitled to certain rights to challenge this action taken against him? However, you feel like you are frustrating the students by saying the reality is that the man will have to wait a long time for his case to be heard and then nothing will probably change for him in the end anyway (Hala, teacher, UNGS).

She not only questioned the applicability of rights as a result of the occupation, but also because of inequalities found within Palestinian society itself. She was concerned that exposing the discrepancy between the rights she is teaching her pupils about and that they are incorporating into their own discourse would result in her feeling as though she is goading the students. Consequently, she chose not to reveal the potential limitations of human rights in certain scenarios. This may have resulted in her providing her students with a more 'superficial engagement with rights concepts' (Osler and Starkey 2010: 17). However, she did this out of a sense of care towards her pupils.

What emerged from the honest reflections of these UNGS educators was that they were exploring the strengths and limitations of rights concepts they were expected to teach, but that they were weary of exploring these with their pupils. This stemmed from a desire not to frustrate the young people, and not to hinder the young people's faith in human rights. The latter they would not do if they too did not have a degree of confidence in the usefulness of the human rights discourse (for the next generation) in the Palestinian struggle. Thus, educators were the ones who were often left to manage the discordance which arose between the HRE dominant narrative that they were expected to teach inside school and the threat of rights violations they and their students faced outside school.

VI. CONCLUSION

Decolonial theory is interested in notions of agency and how the colonised interrupt or resist the dominant narratives that perpetuate their marginalisation (Subedi and Daza 2008). The young people did this by authoring Islamic constructions of human rights, associating rights with the occupation, juxtaposing rights ideals along with the reality they face as Palestinians, and by conceiving rights as universal failures. These were grassroots definitions shaped by their everyday lived experiences and their cultural, political and religious views.

Learning *through* human rights at school played an important role in the lives of young people. This was because, for some, school offered sanctuary from the negative experiences of rights they encountered in other spheres of life outside school. This was unfortunately not the case for boys who attended the BGS, who depicted their school as an extension of the negative experiences of human rights they faced elsewhere. Consequently, this component to HRE also influenced young people's constructions of human rights and their levels of optimism in the discourse as a potential tool to challenge injustice.

Despite the fact their schools did not adopt transformative approaches to HRE and thus had limited opportunities to learn *for* human rights, the youths sought to engage in human rights praxis. This illuminates that there is a need for a critical, transformative and decolonised HRE in the OPT (and elsewhere), which I will unpack in the final chapter.

Out of care for their pupils, educators attempted to conceal their own cynicism towards human rights. However, the young people interrogated notions of universalism, rationalism and secularism as they critically engaged with the broader human rights discourse. Moreover, young people frequently referred to how adults more generally had lost hope in the potential for human rights to deliver liberation for the Palestinian people. This left them with the sense that they were isolated in their struggle for rights.

8

Conclusions

I. YOUTHS ISOLATED IN THEIR STRUGGLE FOR RIGHTS

In June 2023, female classmates carried the dead body of Sadeel Naghniyeh, a 15-year-old refugee girl killed by Israeli gunfire while standing in her driveway in the PA-controlled West Bank city of Jenin (Humaid 2023). At her funeral, friends draped her body in her striped school uniform – a pinafore that most of the female participants I interviewed had worn. Sadeel's death, alongside around 9,000 Palestinian children killed in 2023 alone, demonstrates that Palestinian young people are often targets of settler colonial violence (Jiménez 2023). This is because they are viewed as a 'demographic threat' to the settler's control over land both present and future (Shalhoub-Kevorkian 2015a: 224).

Four months on, Razan Nasrallah, a 12-year-old schoolgirl, was also shot dead in Jenin by Palestinian security forces while demonstrating against an attack on al-Ahli Arab Hospital in Gaza City (Tahhan 2023). Palestinians in the West Bank joined demonstrations in response to Israel's bombing of Gaza. Alongside this, they criticised the PA for its inaction. The PA's security forces responded by cracking down on demonstrations and firing at protestors. Both the shootings of Sadeel and Razan happened in an area that is supposed to be off-bounds for Israelis and is meant to be under PA control. And yet, neither girl was safe, and nor were their rights upheld. Similarly, a group of refugee girls that I interviewed told me they expected to encounter multiple barriers if they attempted to take part in demonstrations: 'In different situations, there are different challenges. Sometimes, it's the occupation, other times it's the Palestinian Authority or just because she's a girl and in our culture, it's not acceptable' (Nadiya, student, UNGS). This captures how their rights can be threatened by different factors.

This book has identified that Palestinian youths faced at least three layers of marginalisation when it came to their human rights: the Israeli occupation that denies them their *humanity*; the Palestinian pseudo-state that hinders their *voice*; and the patriarchal aspects of their culture that prevent youths generally, and girls specifically, exercising their *agency*. Consequently, Palestinian young people often constructed themselves as isolated in their struggle for rights.

II. RESPONSIBILITY WITHOUT RIGHTS AND AGENCY

Many of the youths I interviewed were aware of cynicism among adults towards human rights, often referring to how their elders had 'lost hope'. The institutionalisation of human rights, along with failed peace talks and the PA's capitalist politics and security arrangement with Israel, has resulted in adults' disengagement with politics and disillusionment with the human rights system (Allen 2013). None of this has led to the end to the occupation or brought about the political transformation many had hoped for. Youths believed they had a significant role to play in resisting the occupation, but sometimes questioned whether one day they would end up just as pessimistic. Overall, whilst situated within their collective and intergenerational relationships, young people were not easily deterred by adults' anti-political attitudes, whether those of their elders or those representing the Palestinian pseudo-state, instead seeing their acceptance of the occupation as all the more reason to take on the role of protagonists within the Palestinian struggle for rights. Some cited examples of youths in jail and those who had been martyred to illustrate how they were already on the frontline of the resistance.

Reflecting on his research over the years in Palestine, Marshall (2019: 153) found that adults sometimes place hope upon younger generations and can also speak disparagingly about them, even referring to them as the '*Jeel al-KitKat* (the easily broken "Kit Kat" generation)'. Whilst this latter sentiment was reiterated by one educator in my research, most adult participants saw their pupils as the generation that could achieve what they had failed to do within the Palestinian struggle. Educators noted that, unlike them, young people had energy and hope, and were not afraid to confront soldiers when mistreated. However, during my conversations with the youths, it seemed they were caught in the predicament of being expected to take a lead in the national struggle for rights (as Palestinians), spurred on by older generations, without simultaneously being given the rights and agency to achieve this (as young people, or as girls) due to patriarchal structures and the PA's elite gerontocratic politics and oppressive practices.

This book has foregrounded the multiple theorisations, interpretations and struggles for human rights of Palestinian youths living in the occupied West Bank and has discussed the various factors that influence these understandings and agentic acts. Chapter two examined the dominant discourse of human rights punctuated with decolonial critiques demonstrating that the international human rights scheme is not neutral or apolitical, but rather has been an accomplice to colonial endeavours. Discussion of Islamic contributions and critiques of the human rights scheme dispelled assumptions that Islam and human rights are ideologically opposed and highlighted that where caution towards the international human rights system exists in Arab and Muslim contexts, this has arisen out of concerns of Western moral imperialism, the hypocrisy of the West in the realm of human rights, and its harmful policies past and present. Drawing on Dembour's (2010) four schools of thought (natural, deliberative, protest and discourse), chapter three considered how these mainstream conceptualisations of human rights, which are Eurocentric, declarationalist and decontextualised (in keeping with the natural school), also underpin HRE approaches more generally and in the OPT. The thematic analysis (guided by the YPAGs' analysis) emphasised that Palestinian youths encounter three layers of marginalisation: the occupation (chapter four), the Palestinian quasi-state (chapter five), and patriarchy (chapter six).

Discussion of these barriers raised questions about how young people (and their educators) engage with the dissonance between the mainstream representations of human rights they learn about through HRE inside school and the struggles for rights they experience outside school.

III. THE NEED FOR A CRITICAL, TRANSFORMATIVE AND DECOLONISED HRE

The diverse and complex ways that Palestinian youths understood and deployed human rights highlights the need for a critical, transformative and decolonised HRE in the OPT (and more generally). HRE needs to be appraised not only by academics and practitioners, but by young people themselves. Palestinian youths learned about human rights through HRE whether they attended private, government or UNRWA-run schools. Issues arose for young people and their educators where in school they were having to engage with a more 'restrictive' or 'technical' discourse around rights – more akin to the natural school of thought in school (explored in chapter seven), when the reality they faced outside school (examined in chapters four, five, and six) was leading them to conceptualise rights in more 'expansive' ways (Coysh 2017; Dembour 2010; Goodale 2007).

Educators were often tasked with navigating this discordance. Whilst aware of the limitations of the discourse they were required to teach, educators were hesitant to discuss the more problematic aspects of human rights with their pupils for fear of frustrating or confusing them. This meant their pupils were being exposed to a more 'superficial engagement' with rights concepts in the classroom (Osler and Starkey 2010: 17). What educators failed to fully comprehend was that their pupils were already scrutinising the dominant discourse they encountered in HRE. This highlighted a significant issue. In school, both educators and learners were struggling to reconcile the mainstream narrative presented in HRE with life outside school, and yet they were not engaging critically with rights discourse *together*. Irrespective of the lack of opportunities for critical engagement in school, the youths resisted the dominant narrative in light of their unique lived experiences, as seen in their Islamic constructions of rights or depictions of rights as universal failures (explored in chapters four and seven).

Alternatively, when it came to the supposed universality of human rights, some young people sought to reconcile this aspect of the hegemonic discourse learnt at school with their lives outside it. This came to the fore when they juxtaposed rights ideals with their reality as Palestinians living under occupation (see chapter seven). Some believed that rights in their 'true' form were what their schools' HRE curricula was promoting – universalist and declarationalist. They also assumed that human rights functioned this way for most people across the globe and consequently, they are cruelly an exception to this rule, thus increasing their sense of dehumanisation. Understanding human rights in this way potentially leads to cynicism towards the discourse or eventual abandonment of it altogether. It also unearthed another significant issue.

As appealing as the notion of universalism is, learners need to be presented with opportunities to interrogate this aspect of rights discourse, even more so in contexts where oppression abounds and rights are under constant threat. Learners need to be allowed to critique human rights discourse and realise that the discourse endorsed by the UN (and adopted in most HRE models and programmes globally, as discussed in chapters two and three) is only one vision of human rights and not the only option available to them when it comes to conceptualising and mobilising human rights. Encountering alternative human rights theories, histories and struggles could enable young people to engage critically with rights discourse and assist them to make sense of the intersecting inequalities they face outside school, and to explore the options available when it comes to deploying rights to challenge the injustices they face. This builds on arguments made by Zembylas (2018) that recontextualisation of human rights and HRE can enable HRE pedagogy and curriculum to be both decolonised and decolonising.

This book has revealed that there is also a need for a transformative HRE grounded in notions of agency and solidarity. Chapter seven revealed the key role teachers played in cultivating a space within which young people could escape the layers of marginalisation they faced. Apart from the BGS, schools often acted as spaces of sanctuary for the enjoyment of rights. However, teachers in the GGS went a step beyond this by taking the role of 'legitimating agents' (Bajaj 2011b: 216). Both young people and their educators shared examples of how teachers had convinced parents to respect the rights of their children, such as preventing early marriage and supporting girls' ongoing engagement with education. School counsellors were also depicted in this positive way across the school contexts, being described by Fadi (student, BGS) as 'the only one who listens to us and helps us'. This suggests that schools, whilst providing a necessary space for the embodiment of rights, could not only be havens but powerhouses where learners and educators alike are empowered to challenge the injustices which take place outside school. Bajaj (2011a) contends that opportunities like this emerge when transformative approaches to HRE are adopted because they are grounded in community notions of agency and solidarity.

However, becoming legitimising and 'coalitional agents' are not roles confined to pupil–teacher relationships, but can also be applied to pupil–pupil relations. Bajaj (2011a: 495) defines coalitional agents as those who show a 'willingness to act with or on behalf of victims and is guided by the belief that injustice faced by any target group represents a threat to the society as a whole'. Throughout my discussions, young people displayed this sense of solidarity with the Palestinian community, such as those under siege in Gaza. In fact, they were often far more focused on looking for opportunities to take action for the rights of others within the Palestinian community above and beyond themselves as individuals. This was seen in chapter six when refugee girls talked about how they wished to exercise their right to freedom of assembly so as to participate in the collective struggle despite their parents' concerns about the impact this could have on their honour. Therefore, if Palestinian schools adopted more transformative approaches to HRE, this could facilitate the mobilisation of intergenerational struggles for rights that would counter how Palestinians have been dislocated from one another and their lands.

Reforming HRE in the OPT may feel out of the hands of many Palestinians due to reasons outlined in chapter three, but schools have the potential to create very necessary spaces where young people can experience rights they may not enjoy elsewhere, as demonstrated in chapter seven. This also has the potential to deepen their understandings of rights discourse and explore how this language can be used as a vehicle in the struggle for justice. As argued, the young people illustrated that human rights can offer young people a tool by which they can understand, engage and challenge conflict and oppression (Ignatieff 2001). Thus, they displayed how young people more generally need to not only learn *about* human rights, but also *through* human rights. To put it another way, learners need to see authentic embodiments of human rights so that they may be 'initiated into this discourse' (Emerson and Lundy 2013: 10), which can in turn enable them to play a transformative role in their society and to dismantle the injustices they face. However, HRE also needs to undergo decolonisation both in the OPT and more generally.

The imposition of this Eurocentric and rationalistic HRE is not necessarily an issue unique to the OPT, but is apparent in global HRE initiatives adopted and endorsed by governments, NGOs and the UN, as outlined in chapter three. In particular, youths who attended non-private schools were not only exposed to more restricted constructions of human rights via their schools' HRE, but also Eurocentric ones. Nonetheless, young people and their educators sought to decolonise human rights and by extension HRE. They offered alternative interpretations of human rights and in doing this presented other discourses that exist at grassroots level. Young people's desanitised versions of human rights challenged the more legalistic, abstract and rationalist Eurocentric rights language. This was exemplified when the youths described their everyday encounters between Israelis and Palestinians in the West Bank and shared stories of suffering under occupation (chapter four).

In accordance with decolonial arguments they also interrogated the individual versus collective features of rights and theories of secularism and liberalism underpinning the mainstream narrative. By engaging in decolonial strategies, adults and youths exposed the prevalence of specifically Orientalist attitudes that prevail within the international rights system. It is this Orientalist narrative that has vilified and dehumanised Palestinians. This arose when they interrogated and reclaimed the 'human' in 'human rights' and concluded that this is not a universal entity as it often excludes *Muslims* and *Palestinians* (see chapter four). This echoes decolonial critiques that point out that although human rights declarations state that all humans are equal, often swathes of humanity are excluded (Mignolo 2013).

Participants emphasised that the West needs to recognise that its discourse around rights is steeped in Orientalism and is therefore not a neutral discourse since it discriminates against those who are not White, Euro-American, (Christian) and male. This is even more pertinent in the War on Terror era in which Muslims have become increasingly vilified due to the re-emergence of neo-Orientalist attitudes (Maira 2013; Anghie 2005). The need to dismantle the West's ownership of human rights is also necessary for other countries where governments have used human rights as a justification for military intervention in the Middle East (Perugini and Gordon 2015). Learners need to be allowed to scrutinise how the West has invoked human rights discourse both as a tool of emancipation and also a tool of domination, and how the latter has been used by powers in the Global North to justify its neo-Orientalist foreign policies (Beitz 2009). This once more highlights the need to develop approaches to HRE that attend to the perspectives of the colonised and oppressed, and that space needs to be cultivated for the counter-narratives of the colonised within human rights discourse, such as Palestinian youths.

Including non-Eurocentric constructions of human rights in HRE does not mean that these conceptualisations become free from scrutiny. Rather, as decolonial scholars contend, Eurocentric constructions of human rights should not be completely abandoned, but their discourse on rights needs to 'escape its soliloquy' and engage with other conceptualisations of human rights (Barreto 2013c: 32), enabling space for epistemic diversity. Teachers and young people need to be presented with opportunities to engage in 'epistemic disobedience' (Mignolo 2009) by which they can dismantle and reframe the dominant narratives that they are required to teach or learn at school. They also need to be able to supplement the conventional discourses to allow for epistemic diversity, cultivating ground for discussion between different constructions of human rights that arise from different spaces. This should include the space for grassroots schools of thought to emerge.

IV. TOWARDS A PALESTINIAN SCHOOL OF THOUGHT

At different points in this book, I have drawn upon Dembour's (2010) schema to analyse how the different schools of thought may conflict with or align with interpretations found within the Palestinian rights discourse. As part of the final session with YPAG 2, they offered conclusions related to how their peers viewed human rights using a number of Dembour's questions as prompts (see Table 8.1). In accordance with the transformative paradigm, it is fitting that conclusions based on their analysis of the data are included here.

Table 8.1 Towards a Palestinian school of thought (YPAG 2)

Child-friendly adaptation of prompts found in Dembour (2010)	YPAG 2 responses after analysis of extracts of focus group data
Who are human rights for?	Human rights are for all people from different levels of society, but especially for those who are ignored or forgotten about.
Is human rights law important?	It's just ink on paper; it's not applicable here in Palestine most of the time, but if it was, it would help.
How do young people receive their rights?	We struggle – demonstrate, claim our rights and through education as well as from our parents.
Why do human rights exist?	To live with dignity, equality and justice. There is no community without rights – it would have corruption. Rights support the community.
Are human rights universal?	As Palestinians, we believe that everyone should have rights apart from those who don't respect rights, eg the occupation. But not everyone receives their rights here.
Where do human rights come from?	From people or the community, religion, those appreciate humanity – even the weakest person. They are not from anywhere [ie, specific civilisation]. I get my rights when I do my duties.

These conclusions suggest that Palestinian youths generally lean towards a protest school of thought whilst borrowing from other schools. This is indicated by their distrust of the law, the way they centralised struggle, and viewed human rights as primarily for the disenfranchised – all of which echo the protest school. Alternatively, in keeping with the discourse school, many did not necessarily view human rights as universal since they were cognisant of how universality of rights simply does not apply in the OPT. They also placed contingencies upon the rights of their occupier and even themselves, as indicated when they stated that their rights are secured by fulfilling their duties. There are also threads of the natural school's narrative interwoven through their constructions, such as when they alluded to the transcendental nature of rights when describing it as devoid of a distinct origin.

Nonetheless, using these indicators to identify how individuals conceive human rights can be problematic since there is an assumption as to what it means to be 'unorthodox'. In the case of the Palestinian youths interviewed, conceiving rights in this way was largely influenced by their lived experiences which is *their* orthodoxy. Dembour's (2010) model is used to assess scholars and therefore risks excluding other conceptualisations that may exist within indigenous or oppressed groups who are not necessarily represented in academia. And so, there is a need for a grassroots model to emerge: one that is guided by human rights praxis and which allows for epistemic diversity. A question arising from this is how those theoretical spaces would be created for children and young people.

V. CARVING SPACE CONCEPTUALLY AND METHODOLOGICALLY FOR INDIGENOUS YOUTHS

Children and young people's theorisations and voices are often deemed unimportant within society. This was demonstrated in chapter six, where, due to patriarchal attitudes, the youths reported being ignored, mocked or bullied by adults when they expressed their views. Similarly, chapter five explored how the PA hindered the civil and political rights of non-elites in school and politics by oppressive bureaucratic means and violent acts. As underscored in chapter one, assumptions are often made that children are only able to offer 'incomplete statements of their societies' values' (Hart 2004: 174). However, the young people's narratives in this book contest this since they did not simply replicate the views of their parents, teachers or politicians, but often offered counter-narratives that exposed and dismantled what these very people claimed.

Whilst the notion that children can only offer deficit views is contested by a number of childhood and children's rights scholars, these attitudes broadly prevail in academia. Chapters four, five, six and seven have intentionally amplified the voices of young people in an attempt to challenge power imbalances, not only within Palestinian society itself, but also within research. For instance, had the views of young people not been sought, certain layers of marginalisation would not have been exposed. This became apparent when young people used human rights as a vehicle to critique the state (chapter five), something which educators, for understandable reasons, such as fear of losing their jobs or being arrested, chose not to do. Furthermore, power structures were also revealed when young people employed human rights as a vehicle to challenge patriarchy (chapter six).

Poignantly, boys from the BGS also gave perspectives which came into direct conflict with those of their teachers when describing their school climate (chapter seven). This also points to another related issue when it comes to conducting research in the OPT or in other oppressed communities. Due to the scale of the rights violations committed by the Israeli occupation, some of the oppressive practices that take place *within* Palestinian society are diminished or can be used by certain individuals as a smoke screen for minimising other important issues. I do not believe that I would have gained this level of insight into the barriers facing the youths had I only asked adults about what young people think.

When asked what they would like to say to adults if they knew they would listen to their views, many young people stated that they were rarely given space to discuss with adults how the occupation is affecting them (see chapter four). I want to emphasise that they wished to talk about the political situation not from the position of victims but as equals and agents within Palestinian society (as explored in chapter six). This is significant because Western notions of childhood are often imposed upon non-Western young people, especially in societies affected by violence. According to Eurocentric ideas about childhood(s), children should be shielded from the adversity adults experience and when they are not, their childhoods are deemed deficit. Consequently, these children can be viewed as victims of conflict, not agents within it (Hart and Tyrer 2006). Alternatively, many of the youths I interviewed viewed themselves as protagonists very much with agency. As Darweish and Rigby (2015: 176) recommend, Palestinians need to adopt a strategy of resistance that 'envisions a role for all' irrespective of their political conviction, gender or age.

One of the aims of this study was to demonstrate that young people can and should also have agency within the research process. The YPAGs' own analysis has guided and been interwoven into my own since they provided a more nuanced picture when it came to the occupation (chapter four), internal political matters (chapter five), and cultural and religious complexities within the OPT (chapter six). Children's rights-based approaches to research emphasise the notion that children are 'experts in their own lives' (Lundy and McEvoy 2009: 4). However, I suggest that working in consultation with local (child) research advisors in cross-cultural research also has potential as a decolonising strategy since the community under investigation is able to form theories about their own experiences (Jiménez 2021). Working in consultation with YPAGs helped disrupt the dichotomy that often exists in studies between the so-called 'theoretical north' and the 'empirical south' (Balagopalan 2019). This dimension of adopting a children's rights-based approach ought to be explored further when researching the lives of children in the Global South. As I have argued elsewhere, this will then allow their own theorisations to shape scholarly debates on matters impacting their lives (Jiménez 2021).

Overall, this book has attempted to elevate the youths' diverse and complex stories of suffering and agency. In doing so, it has sought to broaden perspectives on human rights discourse and, by extension, HRE, creating space for the inclusion of these young people's theorisations of human rights within the discourse.

So far in this final chapter, I have offered some of the conceptual and methodological contributions of this work. Now I want to look at some implications that this research has for a Western audience; this was important for the youths I interviewed and seems more fitting since, in the OPT, educators are delivering HRE under occupation, caught between the agendas of foreign donors and the authoritarian PA who have chosen not to mobilise the people against the occupation. The youths wanted the attention of a global audience, to enable them to become acquainted with the dimension of pain that is so often missing from the conventional Eurocentric rights discourse.

VI. FORGING INTERNATIONAL NETWORKS OF SOLIDARITY

The youths described being isolated in their struggle for rights, not only because of patriarchy and the oppressive practices of the PA and their occupier, but also because of the inaction of those in the international arena. This was captured in the words of Basel (student, BGS), who contended: 'There is no international voice to speak out our voice' and surmised that 'this is our pain as Palestinians. Even if we struggle, no one hears us or listens to our voice'. His words echo the observations of Shalhoub-Kevorkian (2015b, 238), who explains that Palestinian children 'occupy a liminal space in which their suffering is visible to the world, but they remain uncounted'. Never has this been more apparent than in the scenes that have emerged from Gaza at the time of writing, which have been met by the indifference of Western political powers. This sense of being uncounted was certainly articulated by the youths I interviewed back in 2015.

Over the years, Palestinians have sought the additional leverage of international solidarity activists and the participation of their respective governments in order to contest the occupation (Darweish and Rigby 2015). Similarly, the participants and YPAGs I met also attempted to forge international networks of solidarity through this research, using it as a vehicle to have their voices heard beyond Palestine. For instance, after his interview, Naseef (principal, BGS) told me that he saw individuals like me as 'peacemakers' who could 'convey the Palestinian cause abroad'. Sometimes the youths switched from writing in Arabic to English during focus group activities to address those to whom they lacked access to as Palestinians (see Figures 8.1 and 8.2).

Figure 8.1 'Don't kill all our children' (female student, GGS)

International solidarity can take on different forms: attending demonstrations; writing to political representatives; engaging in BDS; wearing a *keffiyeh*; sports, cultural and academic boycotts; strike action; walkouts; and solidarity visits to the OPT, to name a few. What is significant about acts such as these is that they can reassure Palestinians that they are not alone in their struggle for rights (Darweish and Rigby 2015). I suggest that international solidarity may carry even more significance for youths whose isolation is more pronounced than that of their elders.

Returning to HRE, what might this mean on a practical level for human rights educators and learners elsewhere who, from a distance, encounter narratives of human rights violations such as those belonging to the youths I interviewed? How can human rights educators encourage privileged learners, who might be inadvertently entangled in the systems that perpetuate these global inequalities (Bajaj 2015), go beyond merely feeling sorry for people like Palestinians? I agree with Zembylas (2018; 2017d), who suggests that human rights educators need to consider the role of sentimentality in HRE. He suggests that pedagogical spaces can be cultivated so that learners can explore the role of emotions and the asymmetries of suffering in the processes whereby human rights are demanded. This can alert learners to the pitfalls of 'cheap sentimentality' and instead enable 'self-empowerment, solidarity and action-orientated empathy with others' (Zembylas 2017d: 18). Activism does not always have to be large-scale or iconic (Zembylas 2013). In fact, small everyday acts of solidarity can gradually and collectively advance change and contribute to social justice. Therefore, empathetic solidarity can take on different forms and can be enacted by learners themselves. As Gordon (2024) remarked at a teach-in on Gaza, these acts of protest make up part of a story and 'one day all these stories will come together somehow connect together and the ruling elites will have to listen'.

Ultimately the youths who spoke to me wanted to see an end to the occupation and their rights enjoyed. But they knew that in order to end the occupation, its brutality must be exposed. And in order to campaign for the human rights of Palestinians, Palestinians needs to be recognised as humans. And for these aims to be achieved, space needs to be carved out for Palestinian voices and experiences because they are often eclipsed, silenced or erased.

After sharing in Arabic how his uncle had been killed whilst planting olive trees, Yusef (student, PS) wrote on a post-it note in English (see Figure 8.2).

Figure 8.2 'Please help us and stand with us' (male student, PS)

The youths, like Yusef, appealed to the potential readers of this book, not in pursuit of an 'outside saviour' (Mignolo 2013), but rather to extend an invitation for those who encountered their perspectives to recognise their humanity, listen to their narratives of pain, and out of that place become 'coalitional agents' in the struggle for the human rights of the Palestinian people. I will end with the words of Fadi (student, BGS), who upon hearing Basel's less than hopeful commentary above, urged him and his peers to persevere: 'But it's important to keep struggling as maybe we will be heard one day or someone will feel for us'.

VII. TIME TO LISTEN TO THE LISTENERS

Israel's disregard for international humanitarian and human rights law in its latest military campaign against Palestinians, alongside the complicity of Western powers in an unfolding genocide, has once more undermined the legitimacy of the West as the champions of human rights and the UN as its trustworthy guardian. This has implications not only for Palestinians, but also other minoritised groups who look towards international law and human rights discourse as a tool to achieve their struggles for rights. In his Christmas address broadcast live from Bethlehem, the Rev Dr Munther Isaac offered the following rebuke: 'To our European friends: I never ever want to hear you lecture us on human rights or international law again. We are not white – it does not apply to us according to your own logic' (Isaac 2023). His argument can be traced in the youths' analyses in this book and bring us back to Lina's (student, UNGS) challenge posed at the start of this book: 'Yeah, so what do you expect from us? We learn about rights because of what is happening to us daily'.

On 8 November 2023, a group of Palestinian children staged a press conference in front of a Gaza hospital, one month into the war. They explicitly addressed adults in power; speaking in English, a boy read: 'We come now to shout and invite you to protect us' (Al Jazeera English 2023). His words could not have been clearer and yet, despite his plea for children's rights to be upheld, as I write this in January 2024, the siege has not been lifted, more hospitals have been bombed, the death toll continues to rise and Western powers continue to support Israel's offensive. The voices of children impacted by war are largely missing in decision-making processes and commentaries. And adults do not necessarily listen or act when they do speak out. But as Marwan (student, PS) explained to me: '[adults] don't understand that we are mature enough to understand our world'. As Gaza is dubbed a 'graveyard for children' (UN 2023) and the fragility of international law is once more laid bare, never before has it been so pertinent to 'listen to the "listeners" – all those who must endure the theories, policies and practices concocted by governments and non-governmental agencies alike' (Woessner 2013: 99). This includes marginalised groups like Palestinian youths when it comes to their human rights concerns.

As I travelled around the West Bank, I was often drawn in by the graffiti on the separation wall. One phrase has continued to be relayed in my mind: 'Now that I have seen, I am responsible'. I have written this book with a sense of responsibility towards the young people I met. Weeks after my last visit to one of the schools, I was told that a pupil had been killed at an Israeli checkpoint. His death, along with the thousands of children that have since been killed in the West Bank and Gaza, makes it even more clear that there is an urgency when it comes to carving out spaces within the fractured context of the OPT for young people to have their voices heard, agency exercised and their humanity recognised.

Appendix: A Timeline of Key Historical and Political Events in Relation to the Palestinian–Israeli Conflict

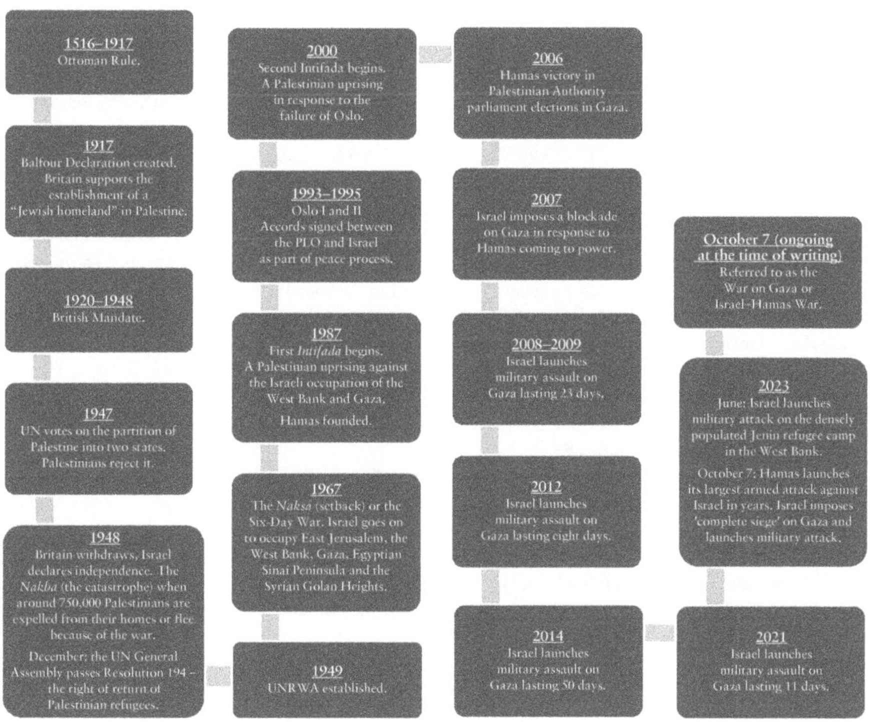

Bibliography

Abdelnour, S (2010) 'A New Model for Palestinian Development' Policy Brief (Washington, DC, Al Shabaka) www.al-shabaka.org/briefs/new-model-palestinian-development.

Abou El Fadl, K (2003) 'The Human Rights Commitment in Modern Islam' in S Runzo, NM Martin and A Sharma (eds), *Human Rights and Responsibilities in the World Religions* (Oxford, Oneworld Publications) 301–64.

Abu-Lughod, L (2002) 'Do Muslim Women Really Need Saving? Anthropological Reflections on Cultural Relativism and its Others' 104 *American Anthropologist* 783.

Abu Lughod, IA (2000) 'Palestinian Higher Education: National Identity, Liberation and Globalization' 27 *Boundary* 75.

Abu Moghli, M (2020) 'Re-conceptualising Human Rights Education: from the Global to the Occupied' 4 *International Journal of Human Rights Education* 5.

—— (2017) 'The Struggle to Reclaim Human Rights Education in Palestinian Authority Schools in the Occupied West Bank' (PhD thesis, University College London).

Abu-Saad, I and Champagne, D (2006) 'Introduction: A Historical Context of Palestinian Arab Education' 49 *The American Behavioral Scientist* 1035.

Ahmed, AK (2021) 'Human Rights Education' *Oxford Research Encyclopedia of Education*.

—— (2018) 'Bridging the "Values Gap": Human Rights Education, Ideology, and The Global-Local Nexus' in M Zembylas and A Keet (eds), *Critical Human Rights, Citizenship, and Democracy Education: Entanglements and Regenerations* (London, Bloomsbury Academic) 173–89.

Ahmed, AK, Martin, JP and Uddin, S (2020) 'Human Rights Education 1995–2017: Wrestling with Ideology, Universality, And Agency' 42 *Human Rights Quarterly* 195.

Ahmed, L (1992) *Women and Gender in Islam: Historical Roots of a Modern Debate* (New Haven, Yale University Press).

Ahmed-Ghosh, H (2008) 'Dilemmas of Islamic and Secular Feminists and Feminisms' 9 *Journal of International Women's Studies* 99.

Alayan, S (2012) 'History Curricula and Textbooks in Palestine: Between Nation Building and Quality Education' in A Rohde and S Dhouib (eds), *The Politics of Education Reform in the Middle East: Self and Other in Textbooks and Curricula* (New York, Bergham Books) 209–36.

Alayan, S and Riley, C (2023) 'The New Palestinian Textbooks: A Strategy for National Identity and Self-Determination' *Nations and Nationalism* 1.

Albhaisi, N (2022) 'Towards a Decolonial Curriculum of Human Rights Education in Palestine' 78 *Journal of Social Issues* 146.

Al-Daraweesh, F and Snauwaert, DT (2012) 'Towards a Hermeneutical Theory of International Human Rights Education' 63 *Educational Theory* 389.

Al-Hibri, A (1997) 'Islam, Law and Custom: Redefining Muslim Women's Rights' 12 *American University Journal of International Law and Policy* 1.

—— (1982) 'A Study of Islamic Herstory: Or How Did We Ever Get Into This Mess?: To the Memory of My Mother, Yusra Mīdanī, Who was an Active, Independent, and Capable Muslim Woman' 5 *Women's Studies International Forum* 207.

Ali, K (2006) *Sexual Ethics and Islam: Feminist Reflections on Qur'an, Hadith and Jurisprudence* (Oxford, Oneworld).

Ali, SS (2006) *Conceptualising Islamic law, CEDAW, and Women's Human Rights in Plural Legal Settings: A Comparative Analysis of Application of CEDAW in Bangladesh, India, and Pakistan* (New Dehli, UNIFEM-South Asia Regional Office) www.ngdp-ncsw.org.pk/storage/5feb0668e51f7.pdf.

Al-Jubeh, M, Hayya, AA, and Hmeidat, H (2014) 'Palestinian Women and Inheritance' (Women's Centre for Legal Aid and Counselling (WCLAC)) www.wclac.org/english/userfiles/Summary%20 Inheritance%20Study%20English.pdf.

Al Jazeera (2023) 'Palestinian Leader Abbas Visits Jenin Camp After Israeli Raid' (12 July) www.aljazeera/news/2023/7/12/palestinian-leader-abbas-visits-jenin-camp-after-israeli-raid.

—— (2015) 'Israeli Soldiers Kill Palestinian During West Bank Raid' (24 February) www.aljazeera.com/news/2015/2/24/israeli-soldiers-kill-palestinian-during-west-bank-raid.

Al Jazeera and News Agencies (2023) '"Islamophobic Policy": French High School Goes on Strike Over Abaya Ban' (7 September) www.aljazeera.com/news/2023/9/7/islamophobic-policy-french-high-school-goes-on-strike-over-abaya-ban.

Al Jazeera English (2023) 'Palestinian Children Plead for Protection in Gaza Press Conference' (7 November) www.youtube.com/watch?v=zLxHBRPLzow.

Al Tahhan, Z (2023) 'Palestinian Authority Cracks Down on Protests Over Israel Gaza Attacks' *Al Jazeera* (18 October) www.aljazeera.com/news/2023/10/18/palestinian-authority-cracks-down-on-protests-over-israel-gaza-attacks.

Al Zaanin, F (2021) 'Feminist Protests in Palestine, Mapping the Fight for Women's Liberation in Gaza and the West Bank' *Rosa Luxemburg Stiftung* (8 March) www.rosalux.de/en/news/id/44203/feminist-protests-in-palestine.

Allen, L (2013) *The Rise and Fall of Human Rights: Cynicism and Politics in Occupied Palestine* (California, Stanford University Press).

—— (2009) 'Martyr Bodies in the Media: Human Rights, Aesthetics, and the Politics of Immediation in the Palestinian Intifada' 36 *American Ethnologist* 161.

Alston, P (2013) 'Does the Past Matter? On the Origins of Human Rights: An Analysis of Competing Histories of the Origins of International Human Rights Law' 126 *Harvard Law* Review 2043.

Alzaroo, S and Hunt, GL (2003) 'Education in the Context of Conflict and Instability: The Palestinian Case' 37 *Social Policy & Administration* 165.

Amnesty International (2017a) 'Evidence Shows Palestinian Security Forces Violently Suppressed Peaceful Protest in Ramallah' Press Release (13 March) www.amnesty.org/en/latest/press-release/2017/03/evidence-shows-palestinian-security-forces-violently-suppressed-peaceful-protest-in-ramallah/.

—— (2017b) 'Human Rights Activist Arrested by Palestinian Security Forces over Facebook Posts' Press Release (4 September) www.amnesty.org/en/latest/press-release/2017/09/human-rights-activist-arrested-by-palestinian-security-forces-over-facebook-posts/.

—— (2017c) 'Human Rights Friendly Schools Toolkit' (London, Amnesty International Ltd) www.amnesty.org/en/documents/pol32/6609/2017/en/.

—— (2015) 'Egypt: Generation of Young Activists Imprisoned in Ruthless Bid to Crush Dissent' (30 June 2015) www.amnesty.org/en/latest/news/2015/06/egypt-generation-of-young-activists-imprisoned-in-ruthless-bid-to-crush-dissent/.

—— (2010) 'Our World Our Rights: Learning about Human Rights in Primary and Middle Schools' (London, Amnesty International UK) www.amnesty.org.uk/files/2017-10/Our%20World%2C%20Our%20Rights.pdf?VersionId=zEeg9AtPenZxhRySN4JnnnN2zysVp.Lo.

Anderson, P (2013) 'The Politics of Scorn in Syria and the Agency of Narrated Involvement' 19 *Journal of the Royal Anthropological Institute*, 463.

Anghie, A (2013) 'Whose Utopia? Human Rights, Development, and the Third World' 22 *Qui Parle* 63.

—— (2005) 37 *Imperialism, Sovereignty and the Making of International Law* (Cambridge, Cambridge University Press).

An-Naim, AA (2021) *Decolonizing Human Rights* (Cambridge, Cambridge University Press).

—— (2011a) 'Islam and Human Rights' in J Witte and MC Green (eds), *Religion and Human Rights: An Introduction* (Oxford, Oxford University Press) 56–70.

—— (2011b) *Muslims and Global Justice* (Philadelphia, University of Pennsylvania Press).

Arat, ZFK (2020) 'Economic Rights and Justice in the Qur'an' 42 *Human Rights Quarterly* 85.

Apple, MW (1993) 'The Politics of Knowledge: Does a National Curriculum Make Sense?' (1993) 14 *Discourse* 1.

Badawi, J (1995) *Gender Equity in Islam: Basic Principles* (Plainfield, Indianapolis, American Trust Publication).

Baderin, M (2022) 'Engaging with Abdullahi An-Na'im's Philosophy on Islam and Engaging with Abdullahi An-Na'im's Philosophy on Islam and Human Rights Human Rights' 36 *Emory International Law Review* 605.

BADIL Resource Center for Palestinian Residency and Refugee Rights (2015) 8 *Survey of Palestinian Refugees and Internally Displaced Persons 2013–2015* 1728–679 (Ramallah, Al-Ayyam Printing, Press, Publishing and Distribution Company) www.badil.org/phocadownloadpap/badil-new/publications/survay/Survey2013-2015-en.pdf.

Bajaj, M (2017) 'Between Rights and Realities: Human Rights Education for Immigrant and Refugee Youth in an Urban Public High School' 48 *Anthropology and Education Quarterly* 124.

—— (2012) *Schooling for Social Change: The Rise and Impact of Human Rights Education in India* (New York, Bloomsbury).

—— (2011a) 'Human Rights Education: Ideology, Location, and Approaches' 33 *Human Rights Quarterly* 481.

—— (2011b) 'Teaching to Transform, Transforming to Teach: Exploring the Role of Teachers in Human Rights Education in India' 53 *Educational Research* 207.

Balagopalan, S (2019) 'Childhood, Culture, History: Redeploying "Multiple Childhoods"' in S Spyrou, R Rosen and DT Cook DT (eds), *Reimagining Childhood Studies* (London, Bloomsbury Academic) 23–39.

Banchoff, T and Wuthnow, R (2011) *Religion and The Global Politics of Human Rights* (New York, Oxford University Press).

Barakat, H (2005) 'The Arab Family and the Challenge of Social Transformation' in H Moghissi (ed), *Women and Islam: Social Conditions, Obstacles and Prospects* (London, Routledge) ch 2.

Barakat, R (2018) 'Writing/Righting Palestine Studies: Settler Colonialism, Indigenous Sovereignty and Resisting the Ghost(s) of History' 8 *Settler Colonial Studies* 349.

Barghouti, O (2011) *BDS: Boycott, Divestment, Sanctions: The Global Struggle for Palestinian Rights* (Chicago, IL, Haymarket Books).

Barlas, A (2009) *Believing Women in Islam: Unreading Patriarchal Interpretations of the Qur'an* (Austin, University of Texas Press).

Barreto, J-M (2015) 'Six Books: International Law, Human Rights and the Politics of the Turn to History' *Critical Legal Thinking* (27 March) www.criticallegalthinking.com/2015/03/27/six-books-international-law-human-rights-politics-turn-history/#:~:text=This%20book%20offers%20a%20history,Terror%20of%20the%2021st%20century.

—— (2013a) 'Introduction: Decolonial Strategies and Dialogue in the Human Rights Field' in J-M Barreto (ed), *Human Rights from a Third World Perspective: Critique, History and International Law* (Newcastle Upon Tyne, Cambridge Scholars Publishing) 1–42.

—— (2013b) 'Human Rights and Emotions from The Perspective of The Colonized: Anthropofagi, Legal Surrealism and Subaltern Studies' 5 *Revista de Estudos Constitucionais, Hermenêutica e Teoria Direito* 106.

—— (2013c) 'Imperialism and Decolonization as Scenarios of Human Rights History' in J-M Barreto (ed), *Human Rights from a Third World Perspective: Critique, History and International Law* (Newcastle Upon Tyne, Cambridge Scholars Publishing) 140–71.

Bar-Tal, D (1990) 'Causes and Consequences of Delegitimization: Models of Conflict and Ethnocentrism' 46 *Journal of Social Issues* 65.

Bar-Tal, D and Salomon, G (2006) 'Israeli–Jewish Narratives of the Israeli–Palestinian Conflict: Evolution, Contents, Functions, and Consequences' in RI Rotberg (ed), *Israeli and Palestinian Narratives of Conflict: History's Double Helix* (Bloomington, Indiana University Press) 19–46.

Baxi, U (2007) *Human Rights in a Posthuman World* (New Delhi, Oxford University Press).

—— (2002) *The Future of Human Rights* (New Delhi, Oxford University Press).

—— (2000) 'Suffering Between Movements and Markets' in R Cohen and SM Rai (eds), *Global Social Movements* (London, Continuum) 33–45.

BBC News (2022) '"Women, Life, Freedom": The Rallying Cry of Iran's Protests' (BBC Newsnight, 6 October) www.youtube.com/watch?v=mp2fLcx0fk4.

Beaumont, P (2014) 'Palestinian Boy Mohammed Abu Khdeir was Burned Alive, Says Official' *The Guardian* (5 July) www.theguardian.com/world/2014/jul/05/palestinian-boy-mohammed-abu-khdeir-burned-alive.

Beaumont, P, and Orlando, C (2014) 'Bodies of Three Missing Israeli Teenagers Found in the West Bank' *The Guardian* (30 June) www.theguardian.com/world/2014/jun/30/bodies-missing-israeli-teenagers-found-west-bank.

Begum, R (2019) 'When it mattered Palestinian Law Failed Israa Ghrayeb. It's High Time That Changed' *The New Arab* (18 September) www.newarab.com/opinion/lethal-cost-being-woman-palestine.

Beitz, CR (2009) *The Idea of Human Rights* (Oxford, Oxford University Press).

Bernard, J and Maître, J (2006) 'Studies on the Palestinian Curriculum and Textbooks: Consolidated Report' (Ramallah, UNESCO) www.unesdoc.unesco.org/ark:/48223/pf0000151551.

Bisharat, GE (1997) 'Exile to Compatriot: Transformations in the Social Identity of Palestinian Refugees in the West Bank' in A Gupta and J Fergusson (eds), *Culture, Power, Place: Explorations in Critical Anthropology* (Durham, Duke University Press) 203–33.

Black, I (2015) 'Isis claim of Beheading Egyptian Copts in Libya Shows Group's Spread' *The Guardian* (15 February) www.theguardian.com/world/2015/feb/15/isis-21-egyptian-coptic-christians-beheading-libya.

Bogues, A (2013) 'The Dual Haitian Revolution and The Making of Freedom in Modernity' in J-M Barreto (ed), *Human Rights from a Third World Perspective: Critique, History and International Law* (Newcastle Upon Tyne, Cambridge Scholars Publishing) 208–36.

Bohlander, M (2014) 'Sisters in Law – Using Maqāsid al-Shari'ah to Advance the Conversation between Islamic and Secular Legal Thinking' 28 *Arab Law Quarterly* 257.

Bouachrine, I (2014) *Women and Islam: Myths, Apologies, and the Limits of Feminist Critique* (Lanham, Lexington Books).

Bowring, B (2012) 'Human Rights and Public Education' 42 *Cambridge Journal of Education* 53.

Boyden, J and de Berry, J (2004) *Children and Youth on the Front Line: Ethnography, Armed Conflict and Displacement* (New York, Berghahn).

Brichs, FI and Lampridi-Kemou, A (2013) 'Sociology of Power in Today's Arab World' in FI Brichs (ed), *Political Regimes in the Arab world: Society and the Exercise of Power* (New York, Routledge) 6–37.

Bricmont, J (2006) *Humanitarian Imperialism: Using Human Rights to Sell War* (New York, New York University Press).

Broeck, S (2013) 'The Legacy of Slavery: White Humanities and Its Subject' in J-M Barreto (ed), *Human Rights from a Third World Perspective: Critique, History and International Law* (Newcastle Upon Tyne, Cambridge Scholars Publishing) 102–16.

Brohi, AK (1978) 'Islam and Human Rights' in A Gauhar (ed), *The Challenge of Islam* (London, Islamic Council Europe) 179–81.

Brown, W (2004) '"The Most We Can Hope for …": Human Rights and the Politics of Fatalism' 103 *South Atlantic Quarterly* 451.

Brown, NJ (2018) 'Palestine: The Unseen Conflict Over the Hidden Curriculum' in E Podeh and S Alayan (eds), *Multiple Alterities: Views of Others in Textbooks of the Middle East* (London, Palgrave Macmillan) 55–75.

—— (2012) *Gaza Five Years On: Hamas Settles in* (Washington DC, Carnegie Endowment for International Peace)

—— (2006) 'Contesting National Identity in Palestine' in RI Rotberg (ed), *Israeli and Palestinian Narratives of Conflict: History's Double Helix* (Bloomington, Indiana University Press) 225–43.

Browne, BC and Bradley, B (2021) 'Promoting Northern Ireland's Peacebuilding Experience in Palestine–Israel: Normalising the Status Quo' (2021) 42 *Third World Quarterly* 1625.
Brunstetter, DR and Zartner, D (2011) 'Just War Against Barbarians: Revisiting the Valladolid Debates Between Sepúlveda and Las Casas' 59 *Political Studies* 733.
Bryman, D (2011) 'Israeli's Pessimistic View of the Arab Spring' 34 *Washington Quarterly* 123.
B'Tselem (2019a) 'Settlements' (16 November) www.btselem.org/settlements.
—— (2019b) 'Hebron City Center' (26 May) www.btselem.org/topic/hebron.
Canosa, A, Graham, A and Wilson, E (2018) 'Reflexivity and Ethical Mindfulness in Participatory Research with Children: What Does it Really Look Like?' 25 *Childhood* 400.
Carbajosa, A (2011) 'Gazan Youth Issue Manifesto to Vent Their Anger with All Sides in The Conflict' *The Guardian* (2 January) www.theguardian.com/world/2011/jan/02/free-gaza-youth-manifesto-palestinian.
Cardenas, S (2005) 'Constructing rights? Human Rights Education and the State' 24 *International Political Science Review* 363.
Césaire, A (2000) *Discourse on Colonialsim* (New York, Monthly Review Press) translated by J Pinkham.
Chaban, S, Daraghmeh, R and Stettler, G (2010) 'Palestinian Women and Security: Why Palestinian Women and Girls Do Not Feel Secure' (Geneva Centre for the Democratic Control of Armed Forces (DCAF)) www.dcaf.ch/sites/default/files/publications/documents/Palest_Women_Security_ENG.pdf.
Chagankerian, A (2013) 'The Delegitimizing Power of the "Terrorism" Label' *e-International Relations.*
Challand, B (2009) *Palestinian Civil Society: Foreign Donors and the Power to Promote and Exclude* (Abingdon, Routledge).
Charfi, M (2001) 'Religion, Droits de l'Homme et Education' 27 *Islamochristiana* 23.
Chilisa, B (2005) 'Educational Research Within Postcolonial Africa: A Critique of HIV/AIDS Research in Botswana' 18 *International Journal of Qualitative Studies in Education* 659.
Christensen, P and Prout, A (2002) 'Working with Ethical Symmetry in Social Research with Children' 9 *Childhood* 477.
Clarke, E and McCreanor, T (2006) 'He Wahine Tangi Tikapa … Statutory Investigative Processes and the Grieving of Maori Families Who Have Lost a Baby to SIDS' 1 *Kotuitu: New Zealand Journal of Social Sciences Online* 25.
Clarno, A (2018) 'Neoliberal Colonization in the West Bank' 65 *Social Problems* 323.
Cohen, L, Manion, L and Morrison, K (2007) *Research Methods in Education* (Oxon, Routledge).
Cole, WM (2013) 'Does Respect for Human Rights Vary Across "Civilizations"? A Statistical Reexamination' 54 *International Journal of Comparative Sociology* 345.
Cooney, M (2014) 'Death by Family: Honor Violence as Punishment' 16 *Punishment and Society* 406.
Coysh, J (2017) *Human Rights Education and the Politics of Knowledge* (London, Routledge).
—— (2014) 'The Dominant Discourse of Human Rights Education: A Critique' 6 *Journal of Human Rights Practice* 89.
Cranston, M (1973) *What are Human Rights?* (London, Bodley Head).
Cunningham, RB, Sarayrah, YK and Sarayrah, YE (1994) 'Taming "Wasta" to Achieve Development' 16 *Arab Studies Quarterly* 29.
Dana, T (2015) 'The Structural Transformation of Palestinian Civil Society: Key Paradigm Shifts' 24 *Middle East Critique* 191.
—— (2014) 'Disconnecting Civil Society from its Historical Extension: NGOS and Neoliberalism in Palestine' in S Takahashi (ed), *Human Rights, Human Security, and State Security: The Intersection* (Bloomsbury Publishing) 117–38.
Darweish, M (2017) 'Israeli Peace and Solidarity Organizations' in A Özerdem, C Thiessen and M Qassoum (eds), *Conflict Transformation and the Palestinians: The Dynamics of Peace and Justice Under Occupation* (London, Routledge) 229–46.

Darweish, M and Rigby, A (2015) *Popular Protest in Palestine: The Uncertain Future of Unarmed Resistance* (London, Pluto Press).

De Coninck, D (2022) 'The Refugee Paradox During Wartime in Europe: How Ukrainian and Afghan Refugees are (not) Alike' 57 *International Migration Review* 578.

Defense for Children International (DCI) Palestine (2024) 'Palestine Distribution of Palestinian Child Fatalities by Month' (9 February) www.dci-palestine.org/child_fatalities_by_month.

—— (2016) 'Ramallah Students Say, "I'm Here to Learn, Not to Be Hit!"' (9 December) www.dci-palestine.org/ramallah_students_say_i_m_here_to_learn_not_to_be_hit.

Dembour, M (2010) 'What are Human Rights? Four Schools of Thought' (2010) 32 *Human Rights Quarterly* 1.

—— (2001) 'The Movement of a Pendulum: Between Universalism and Relativism' in JK Cowan, M Dembour and RA Wilson (eds), *Culture and Rights: Anthropological Perspectives* (Cambridge, Cambridge University Press) 56–79.

Desai, C (2021) 'Disrupting Settler-Colonial Capitalism: Indigenous Intifadas and Resurgent Solidarity from Turtle Island to Palestine' 50 *Journal of Palestine Studies* 43.

De Vitoria, F (1992) *Political Writings* (Cambridge, Cambridge University Press).

Donnelly, J (2013) *International Human Rights* (Boulder, Westview Press).

—— (1989) *Universal Human Rights: in Theory and Practice* (New York, Cornell University Press).

Douzinas, C (2003) 'Humanity, Military Humanism and the New Moral Order' 32 *Economy and Society* 159.

—— (2000) *The End of Human Rights: Critical Legal Thought at the Turn of the Century* (Oxford, Hart Publishing).

Dussel, E (2013) 'Las Casas, Vitoria and Suárez, 1514-1617' in J-M Barreto (ed), *Human Rights from a Third World Perspective: Critique, History and International Law* (Newcastle Upon Tyne, Cambridge Scholars Publishing) 172–207.

Ekman, J and Amna, E (2012) 'Political Participation and Civic Engagement: Towards a New Typology' 22 *Human Affairs* 283.

Elboubekri, A (2015) 'Is Patriarchy an Islamic Legacy? A Reflection on Fatima Mernissi's Dreams of Trespass and Najat El Hachmi's The Last Patriarch' 10 *Journal of Multicultural Discourses* 25.

Embrick, DG and Williams, JE (2023) 'Alienation, Racial Capitalism, and the Racialization of Palestinians' 49 *Critical Sociology* 939.

Emerson, L and Lloyd, K (2017) 'Measuring Children's Experience of Their Right to Participate in School and Community: A Rights-Based Approach' 31 *Children and Society* 120.

Emerson, L and Lundy, L (2013) 'Education Rights in a Society Emerging from Conflict: Curriculum and Student Participation as a Pathway to the Realization of Rights' in BB Swadener, L Lundy, J Habashi and N Blanchet-Cohen (eds), *Children's Rights and Education: International Perspectives* (Oxford, Peter Lang) 1–20.

End Corporal Punishment (2021) 'Country Report for the State of Palestine' (January) www.endcorporalpunishment.org/wp-content/uploads/country-reports/StateOfPalestine.pdf.

Erakat, N (2015) 'Palestine Becomes a State Party to the ICC: An Occasion to Return to The Register of Israel's Racialized Violence' *Jadaliyya* (1 April) www.jadaliyya.com/Details/31944.

Eyber, C and Ager, A (2004) 'Researching Young People's Experiences of War: Participatory Methods and the Trauma Discourse in Angola' in J Boyden and J de Berry (eds), *Children and Youth on the Front Line: Ethnography, Armed Conflict and Displacement* (New York, Berghahn) 189–208.

Falah, G-W (2004) 'Truth at War and Naming the Intolerable in Palestine' 26 *Antipode* 596.

Farsakh, L (2005) *Palestinian Labour Migration to Israel: Labour, Land and Occupation* (London, Routledge).

Fasheh, MJ (1995) 'The Reading Campaign Experience within Palestinian Society: Innovative Strategies for Learning and Building Community' 65 *Harvard Educational Review* 66.

Fathzadeh, F (2021) 'The Veil: An Embodied Ethical Practice in Iran' 30 *Journal of Gender Studies* 150.

Feldman, I (2009) 'Gaza's Humanitarianism Problem' 38 *Journal of Palestine Studies* 22.

Fields, AB (2003) *Rethinking Human Rights for the New Millennium* (Basingstoke, Palgrave Macmillan).

Firer, R and Adwan, S (2004) *The Israeli–Palestinian conflict in history and civics textbooks of both nations* (Hannover, Verlag Hahhnsche Buchhandlung).

Flowers, N (2003) 'What is Human Rights Education?' *A Survey of Human Rights Education* (Gütersloh, Bertelsmann Verlag) 107–18.

Freeman, H (2023) 'Next Time Sisters Uncut Protest About Gaza, Perhaps They Could Take a Look at Hamas's Record on Women's Rights' *The Jewish Chronicle* (1 November) www.thejc.com/lets-talk/next-time-sisters-uncut-protest-about-gaza-perhaps-they-could-take-a-look-at-hamass-record-on-womens-rights-igxi4i5e#:~:text=In%20Gaza%2C%20there%20are%20no,requiring%20male%20permission%20to%20travel.

Freeman, M (2017) *Human Rights*, 3rd edn (Cambridge, Polity Press).

—— (2002) *Human Rights: An Interdisciplinary Approach* (Cambridge, Polity Press).

—— (1994) 'The Philosophical Foundations of Human Rights' 16 *Human Rights Quarterly* 491.

Friere, P (1990) *Pedagogy of the Oppressed*, reprint (London, Penguin).

Froman, N (2015) 'Human Rights Education and the International Baccalaureate Diploma Programme' 17 *Current Issues in Comparative Education* 36.

Ganor, B (2010) 'Defining Terrorism: Is One Man's Terrorist Another Man's Freedom Fighter? 3 *Police Practice and Research,* 287.

Gathii, JT (2011) 'TWAIL: A Brief History of Its Origins, Its Decentralized Network, and a Tentative Bibliography' 3 *Trade Law and Development* 26.

Geertz, C (1973) *The Interpretation of Cultures: Selected Essays* (New York, Basic Books).

George, E, Schmidt, C, Vella, G and McDonagh, I (2017) 'Promoting the Rights and Responsibilities of Children: A South Australian Example' 24 *Global Health Promotion* 53.

Gerber, P (2004) 'Black Rights/White Curriculum: Human Rights Education for Indigenous People' 9 *Deakin Law Review* 61.

Gerner de Garcia, B (2004) 'Literacy for Latino Deaf Students: A Socio-Cultural Approach' *Research at Gaullaudet Newsletter* 7.

Ghai, Y (2018) 'Universalism and Relativism: Human Rights as a Framework for Negotiating Interethnic Claims' 21 *Cardozo Law Review* 1095.

Gilroy, P (2010) *Darker than Blue: On the Moral Economies of Black Atlantic Culture* (Cambridge, MA, Harvard University Press).

Goddard, V (1987) 'Honour and Shame: The Control of Women's Sexuality and Group Identity in Naples' in P Caplan (ed), *The Cultural Construction of Sexuality* (London, Tavistock) 166–93.

Golley, NA (2004) 'Is feminism Relevant to Arab Women?' 25 *Third World Quarterly* 521.

Goodale, M (2007) 'Introduction: Locating Rights, Envisioning Law Between the Global and the Local' in M Goodale and SE Merry (eds), *The Practice of Human Rights: Tracking Between the Global and the Local* (Cambridge, Cambridge University Press) 1–38.

Gordon, N (2024) 'Zionism in Crisis after October 7? What Crisis?' *Polity Magazine* www.ssalanka.org/polity/zionism-in-crisis-after-october-by-neve-gordon.

—— (2008) 'From Colonization to Separation: Exploring the Structure of Israel's Occupation' 29 *Third World Quarterly* 25.

Gordon, N and Berkovitch, N (2007) 'Human Rights Discourse in Domestic Settings: How Does It Emerge?' 55 *Political Studies* 243.

Grewal, I (2001) 7 'On the New Global Feminism and the Family of Nations: Dilemmas of Transnational Feminist Practice' in E Shohat (ed), *Talking Visions: Multicultural Feminism in a Transnational Age* (Cambridge, MA, MIT Press) 501–30.

Habashi, J (2011) 'Children's Agency and Islam: Unexpected Paths to Solidarity' 9 *Children's Geographies* 129.

—— (2008) 'Language of Political Socialization: Language of Resistance' (2008) 6 *Children's Geographies* 269.

Haj, S (1992) 'Palestinian Women and Patriarchal Relations' 17 *Signs* 761.

Hajjar, L (2006) 'Religion, State Power, and Domestic Violence in Muslim Societies: A Framework for Comparative Analysis' 29 *Law and Social Enquiry* 1.
—— (2001) 'Human Rights in Israel/Palestine: The History and Politics of a Movement' 30 *Journal of Palestine Studies* 21.
Halliday, F (1993) 'Orientalism and its Critics' 20 *British Journal of Middle Eastern Studies* 145.
Hamamra, BT (2020) 'The Misogynist Representation of Women in Palestinian Oral Tradition: A Socio-Political Study' 29 *Journal of Gender Studies* 214.
Hanafi, S (2012) 'The Arab Revolutions; the Emergence of a New Political Subjectivity' 5 *Contemporary Arab Affairs* 198.
Hantzopoulos, M (2016) *Restoring Dignity in Public Schools: Human Rights Education in Action* (New York, Teachers College Press).
—— (2012) 'Considering Human Rights Education as U.S. Public School Reform' 24 *Peace Review* 36.
Haque, MF, Solihin, SM, Ahmad, N and Jani, MS (2020) 'Women Rights to Inheritance in Muslim Family Law: An Analytical Study' 4 *International Journal Islamic Business & Management* 15.
Hart, J (2012) 'The Spatialisation of Child Protection: Notes from The Occupied Palestinian Territory' 22 *Development in Practice* 473.
—— (2008) 'Displaced Children's Participation in Political Violence: Towards Greater Understanding of Mobilisation' 8 *Conflict, Security & Development* 277.
—— (2004) 'Beyond Struggle and Aid: Children's Identities in a Palestinian Refugee Camp in Jordan' in J Boyden and J de Berry (eds), *Children and Youth on the Front Line: Ethnography, Armed Conflict and Displacement* (New York, Berghahn) 167–86.
Hasan, M (2002) 'The Politics of Honour: Patriarchy, the State and the Murder of Women in the Name of Family Honor' 21 *Journal of Israeli History* 1.
Hatem, MF (2003) 'Discourses on the "War on Terrorism" in the U.S. and its Views of the Arab, Muslim, and Gendered "Other"' 11/12 *The Arab Studies Journal* 77.
Hattab, M and Abualrob, M (2023) 'Under the Veil: Women's Economic and Marriage Rights in Palestine' 10 *Humanity Social Science Community* 110.
Hille, R (2006) 'Human Rights and Islam: Is The "Clash of Civilizations" Already Pre-Programmed?' 30 *Evangelical Review of Theology* 352.
Hirsch, A (2008) 'Sharia Law Incompatible with Human Rights Legislation, Lords Say' *The Guardian* (23 October) www.theguardian.com/world/2008/oct/23/religion-islam.
Høigilt, J (2016) 'Fatah from Below: The Clash of Generations in Palestine' 43 *British Journal of Middle Eastern Studies* 56.
Hovsepian, N (2008) *Palestinian State Formation: Education and the Construction of National Identity* (Newcastle, Cambridge Scholars Publishing).
Hunter, S, and Hunter, ST (2008) *Reformist Voices of Islam: Mediating Islam and Modernity* (Oxon, Routledge).
Ignatieff, M (2001) *Human Rights as Politics and Idolatry* (Princeton, NJ, Princeton University Press).
Imseis, A (2023) *The United Nations and the Question of Palestine: Rule by Law and the Structure of International Legal Subalternity* (Cambridge, Cambridge University Press).
Isaac, M (2023) 'Christ in the Rubble: A Liturgy of Lament (2023 Message by Rev. Dr. Munther Isaac)' (23 December) www.youtube.com/watch?v=qbHzqU3ZdTs.
Jad, I (2007) 'NGOs: Between Buzzwords and Social Movements' 17 *Development in Practice* 622.
Jaffal, Z, Shawabkeh, F and Al Obeidi, AH (2022) 'Toward Constructive Harmonisation of Islamic Family Law And CEDAW: A Study on The UAE's Reservation to CEDAW Article 16 And Equal Rights to Marriage and Family Relations' 28 *Australian Journal of Human Rights* 139.
Jenness, V, Smith, DA and Stepan-Norris, J (2006) 'Editor's Note: Israeli–Palestinian Conflict: A Challenge for Scholarship' 35 *Contemporary Sociology* vii.
Jiménez, E (2023) 'The Occupation Wants to Delete Us': Palestinian Youth's Interpretations of and Resistance to Settler Colonialism' 44 *Third World Quarterly* 2351.

—— (2021) 'Decolonising Concepts of Participation and Protection in Sensitive Research with Young People: Local Perspectives and Decolonial Strategies of Palestinian Research Advisors' 28 *Childhood* 346.

Johnson, MG and Symonides, J (1998) *The Universal Declaration of Human Rights: A History of its Creation and Implementation, 1948–1998* (Paris, UNESCO).

Johnston, DL (2015) 'Islam and Human Rights: A Growing Rapprochement' 74 *American Journal of Economics and Sociology* 113.

Joseph, S (1996) 'Patriarchy and Development in the Arab world' 4 *Gender and Development* 14–19.

Kamali, MH (2003) *Principles of Islamic Jurisprudence*, 3rd edn (Cambridge, The Islamic Texts Society).

Karam, A (2010) 'Democracy and Faith: The Continuum of Political Islam' in NJ Brown and EE Shahin (eds), *The Struggle Over Democracy in the Middle East: Regional Politics and External Policies* (London, Routledge) 60–81.

Kayali, L (2021) *Palestinian Women and Popular Resistance: Perceptions, Attitudes, and Strategies* (London, Routledge).

Kayaoğlu, T (2012) 'It's Time to Revise the Cairo Declaration of Human Rights in Islam' *Brookings Institute* (23 April) www.brookings.edu/articles/its-time-to-revise-the-cairo-declaration-of-human-rights-in-islam/.

Kazziha, W (2010) 'The Fantasy of Arab Democracy without a Constituency' in NJ Brown and EE Shahin (eds), *The Struggle over Democracy in the Middle East: Regional Politics and External Policies* (London, Routledge) 42–59.

Keet, A (2015) 'It is Time: Critical Human Rights Education in an Age of Counter-Hegemonic Distrust' 19 *Education as Change* 46.

—— (2012) 'Discourse, Betrayal, Critique: The Renewal of Human Rights Education' in C Roux (ed), *Safe Spaces, Human Rights Education in Diverse Contexts* (Rotterdam, Sense Publishers) 7–27.

—— (2010) *Human Rights Education: A Conceptual Analysis* (Saar bracken, Lambert Academic Publishers).

—— (2007) 'Human Rights Education or Human Rights in Education: A Conceptual Analysis' (PhD thesis, University of Pretoria).

Khalel, S (2015) 'Palestine's Only Female Taxi Driver Has Big Plans' *Al Jazeera* (5 September) www.aljazeera.com/economy/2015/9/5/palestines-only-female-taxi-driver-has-big-plans.

Khalidi, R (2009) *Sowing Crisis: The Cold War and American Dominance in the Middle East* (Boston, Beacon Press).

Khalidi, R and Samour, S, 'Neoliberalism as Liberation: The Statehood Program and The Remaking of The Palestinian National Movement' (2011) 40 *Journal of Palestine Studies* 6.

Khalidi, W (2009) 'The Hebrew *Reconquista* of Palestine: *From* the 1947 United Nations Partition Resolution to the First Zionist Congress of 1897' 39 *Journal of Palestine Studies* 24.

—— (1997) 'Revisiting the UNGA Partition Resolution' (1997) 27 *Journal of Palestine Studies* 5.

Khan, Z, (2014) 'Words Matter in "ISIS" War, So Use "Daesh"' *The Boston Globe* (9 October) www3.bostonglobe.com/opinion/2014/10/09/words-matter-isis-war-use-daesh/V85GYEuasEEJgrUun0dMUP/story.html?arc404=true.

Khatib, H (2015) 'Political Instrumentalization of Islam in a Violent State Crisis: The Case of Syria' 10 *Journal of Applied Security Research* 341.

Kimmerling, B and Migdal, JS (2003) *The Palestinian People: A History* (London, Harvard University Press).

Kiwan, D (2015) 'Contesting Citizenship in the Arab Revolutions: Youth, Women, and Refugees' 11 *Democracy and Security* 129.

Koraytem, T (2001) 'Arab Islamic Developments on Human Rights' 16 *Arab Law Quarterly* 255.

Landy, D (2013) 'Talking Human Rights: How Social Movement Activists are Constructed and Constrained by Human Rights Discourse' 28 *International Sociology* 409.

Las Casas, B (1999) *In Defense of the Indians* (translated and edited by CM Stafford Poole) (DeKalb, Northern Illinois University Press).
—— (1992) *A Short Account of the Destruction of the Indies* (London, Penguin Books).
Lefevre, M, Hickle, K and Luckock, B (2018) '"Both/And" Not "Either/Or": Reconciling Rights to Protection and Participation in Working with Child Sexual Exploitation' 49 *The British Journal of Social Work* 1837.
Lewis, B (1998) *Islam and the West* (Oxford, Oxford University Press).
Lloyd, D (2012) 'Settler Colonialism and the State of Exception: The Example of Palestine/Israel' 2 *Settler Colonial Studies* 59.
Lohrenscheit, C (2002) 'International Approaches in Human Rights Education' 48 *International Review of Education* 173.
Lucas, MH (2019) 'Women's Rights, Secularism, and the Colonial Legacy' 33 *Canadian Woman Studies/les cahiers de la femme* 1.
Lundy, L and McEvoy, L (2012a) 'Children's Rights and Research Processes: Assisting Children to (In)Formed Views' 19 *Childhood* 129.
—— (2012b) 14 'Childhood, the United Nations Convention on the Rights of the Child, and Research: What Constitutes a "Rights-Based" Approach?' in M Freeman (ed), *Law and Childhood Studies: Current Legal Issues* (Oxford, Oxford University Press) 75–91.
—— (2009) 'Developing Outcomes for Education Services: A Children's Rights-Based Approach' 1 *Effective Education* 43.
—— (2007) 'E-consultation with Pupils: A Rights-Based Approach to the Integration of Citizenship Education and ICT' 16 *Technology, Pedagogy and Education* 305.
Lundy, L, McEvoy, L and Byrne, B (2011) 'Working with Young Children as Co-Researchers: An Approach Informed by the United Nations Convention on the Rights of the Child' 22 *Early Education and Development* 714.
Lybarger, LD (2007) 'For Church or Nation?: Islamism, Secular-Nationalism, and the Transformation of Christian Identities in Palestine' 75 *Journal of the American Academy of Religion* 777.
Mahamid, F, Hattab, M and Berte, D (2023) 'Palestinian Law to Protect Family and Prevent Violence: Challenges with Public Opinion' 23 *BMC Public Health* 412.
Maira, S (2009) '"Good" and "Bad" Muslim Citizens: Feminists, Terrorists, and U.S. Orientalisms' 35 *Feminist Studies* 631.
Majid, A (1998) 'The Politics of Feminism in Islam' 23 *Signs* 321.
Maldonado-Torres, N (2021) 'On the Coloniality of Human Rights' in B De Sousa Santos and B Martins (eds), *The Pluriverse of Human Rights: The Diversity of Struggles for Dignity* (New York, Routledge) 62–81.
Marshall, DJ (2013) '"All the Beautiful Things"' Trauma, Aesthetics and the Politics of Palestinian Childhood' 17 *Space and Polity* 53.
Marx, K (1975) *Collected Works* (New York, International Publishers).
Marzouk, ZHS (2022) 'Zwaju Alqasrat Wthdyd Abtda' Sn Alzwaj Drash Fqhyh Mqarnh [Marriage of Underage Girls and Determining the Beginning of the Marriage Age 'A Comparative Jurisprudence Study'] 34 *Journal of the Faculty of Sharia and Law in Assiut* 234.
Maududi, AA (1976) *Human Rights in Islam* (Leicester, The Islamic Foundation).
Mazawi, AE (2011) '"Which Palestine should we teach?" Signatures, palimpsests, and struggles over school textbooks' 30 *Studies in Philosophy and Education* 169.
—— (2000) 'The Reconstruction of Palestinian Education: Between History, Policy Politics and Policy Making' 15 *Educational Policy* 371.
McEvoy, L and Lundy, L (2007) 'In the Small Places: Education and Human Rights Culture in Conflict-Affected Societies' in G Anthony, J Morison and K McEvoy (eds), *Judges, Transition and Human Rights* (Oxford, Oxford University Press) 495–514.
McKernan, B (2023) 'Thousands of Palestinians Flee Jenin Reufgee Camp After Major Israeli Raid' *The Guardian* (4 July) www.the guardian.com/world/2023/jul/04/jenin-refugee-camp-west-bank-israel-military-operation.

Mejias, S (2013) 'NGOs and Human Rights Education in The Neoliberal Age: A Case Study of an NGO-Secondary School Partnership in London' (PhD thesis, University of London).
Melhem, A (2019) 'Hebron Tribes Oppose UN Pact, "Suspicious" Feminists' *Al-Monitor* (31 December) www.al-monitor.com/originals/2019/12/cedaw-palestinian-clans-tribes-hebron-feminist-abbas-decree.html.
Mernissi, F (1975) *Beyond the Veil* (New York, John Wiley and Sons).
Merry, SE (2006) *Human Rights and Gender Violence: Translating International Law into Local Justice* (Chicago, University of Chicago Press).
Mertens, D (2010) 'Transformative Mixed Methods Research' 469–474 *Qualitative Inquiry*, 1.
—— (2007) 'Transformative Paradigm: Mixed Methods and Social Justice' 1 *Journal of Mixed Methods* 212.
Merry, SE (2006) *Human Rights and Gender Violence: Translating International Law into Local Justice* (Chicago, University of Chicago Press).
Merz, F (2014) 'Adversarial Framing: President Bashar Al-Assad's Depiction of the Armed Syrian Opposition' 5 *Journal of Terrorism Research* 30.
Meyer, EA (1999) *Islam and Human Rights: Tradition and* Politics, 3rd edn (Boulder, Westview Press).
Meyer, J, Bromley-Martin, P and Ramirez, F (2010) 'Human Rights in Social Science Textbooks: Cross-National Analyses, 1970–2008' 83 *Sociology of Education* 111.
Meyers, DT (2011) 'Two Victim Paradigms and the Problem Of "Impure" Victims' 2 *Humanity: An International Journal of Human Rights, Humanitarianism, and Development* 255.
Mignolo, W (2013) 'Who Speaks for the "Human" In Human Rights?' in J-M Barreto (ed), *Human Rights from a Third World Perspective: Critique, History and International Law* (Newcastle Upon Tyne, Cambridge Scholars Publishing) 44–64.
—— (2011) *The Darker Side of Western Modernity: Global Futures, Decolonial Options* (Durham, NC, Duke University Press).
—— (2009) 'Epistemic Disobedience, Independent Thought and Decolonial Freedom' 26 *Theory, Culture & Society* 159.
—— (2006) 'Citizenship, Knowledges, and the Limits of Humanity' 18 *American Literary History* 312.
—— (2002) 'The Geopolitics of Knowledge and the Colonial Difference' 101 *South Atlantic Quarterly* 57.
Ministry of Education and Higher Education (MoEHE) (2014) *Education Development Strategic Plan EDSP 2014–2019: A Learning Nation* (March).
Milton-Edwards, B (2011) *Contemporary Politics in the Middle East* (Cambridge, Polity Press, 2011).
—— (2008) 'The ascendance of political Islam: Hamas and consolidation in the Gaza Strip' 29 *Third World Quarterly* 1585.
—— (1996) *Islamic Politics in Palestine* (London, Tauris Academic Studies).
Mir-Hosseini, Z, 'The Construction of Gender in Islamic Legal Thought and Strategies for Reform' (2003) 1 *Hawwa* 1.
—— (1999) *Islam and Gender: The Religious Debate in Contemporary Iran* (Princeton, NJ, Princeton University Press).
Mitchell, K and Elwood, S (2013) 'Intergenerational Mapping and the Cultural Politics of Memory' 17 *Space and Polity* 33.
Moghissi, H (2011) 'Islamic Feminism Revisited' 31 *Comparative Studies of South Asia, Africa and the Middle East* 76.
Monforte, T (2018) 'Broad Strokes and Bright Lines: A Reconsideration of Shari'a Based Reservations' 35 *Columbia Journal of Gender and Law* 28–29.
Moosa, E (2000) 'The Dilemma of Islamic Rights Schemes' 15 *Journal of Law and Religion* 185.
Morris, P (1983) 'Teachers' Perceptions of their Pupils: a Hong Kong Case Study' 29 *Research in Education* 81.
Morsink, J (1999) *The Universal Declaration of Human Rights: Origins, Drafting, And Intent* (Philadelphia, University of Pennsylvania Press).

Moughrabi, F (2001) 'The Politics of Palestinian Textbooks' 31 *Journal of Palestine Studies* 5.
Moyn, S (2018) *Not Enough: Human Rights in an Unequal World* (Cambridge, Mass, Harvard University Press).
—— (2010) *The Last Utopia: Human Rights in History* (Cambridge, MA, Harvard University Press).
—— (2012) 'Human Rights, Not So Pure Anymore' *New York Times* (12 May) www.nytimes.com/2012/05/13/opinion/sunday/human-rights-not-so-pure-anymore.html.
Mutua, M (2009) *Human Rights NGOs in East Africa: Political and Normative Tensions* (Philadelphia, University of Pennsylvania Press).
—— (2002) *Human Rights: A Political and Cultural Critique* (Philadelphia, University of Pennsylvania Press).
—— (2001) 'Savages, Victims, and Saviours: The Metaphors of Human Rights' 42 *Harvard Law Journal* 201.
Naik, T (2021) 'Women's Succession Rights under Muslim Law' 5 *International Journal of Legal Science and Innovation* 247.
Nash, JC (2001) *Mayan visions: The Quest for Autonomy in an Age of Globalization* (London, Routledge).
Nasr, SVR (1996) *Mawdudi and the Making of Islamic Revivalism* (New York, Oxford University Press, Incorporated).
Nasr, SH (1981) *Islamic Life and Thought* (London, Allen and Unwin).
Navaro-Yashin, Y (2002) *Faces of the State: Secularism and Public Life in Turkey* (Princeton, Princeton University Press).
Nayak, M (2006) 'Orientalism and "Saving" US State Identity After 9/11' 8 *International Feminist Journal of Politics* 42.
Nazeer, T (2023) '"I am fearful": Muslim Women in France Speak Out Against the Abaya Ban' *The New Arab* (8 September) www.newarab.com/features/muslim-women-france-speak-out-against-abaya-ban.
Nguyen-Gillham, V, Giacaman, R, Naser, G and Boyce, W (2008) 'Normalising the Abnormal: Palestinian Youth and The Contradictions of Resilience in Protracted Conflict' 16 *Health and Social Care in the Community* 291.
Nicolai, S (2007) *Fragmented Foundations: Education and Chronic Crisis in The Occupied Palestinian Territory* (Paris, International Institute for Educational Planning and Save the Children UK) www.unesdoc.unesco.org/ark:/48223/pf0000150260.
Okafor, O and Agbakwa, S (2001) 'Re-imagining International Human Rights Education in Our Time: Beyond Three Constitutive Orthodoxies' 14 *Leiden Journal of International Law* 563.
Osler, A (2015) 'Human Rights Education, Postcolonial Scholarship, and Action for Social Justice' 43 *Theory & Research in Social Education* 244.
Osler, A and Starkey, H (2010) *Teachers and Human Rights Education* (Stoke on Trent, Trentham Books Ltd).
Paine, T (1792) *Common sense; addressed to the inhabitants of America* (London, Paternoster-Row).
Palestinian Central Bureau of Statistics (PCBS) (2020) 'Dr. Awad, Highlights the Situation of the Palestinian Women on the International Women's Day' (8 March) www.pcbs.gov.ps/site/512/default.aspx?lang=en&ItemID=4458#:~:text=About%2010%25%20of%20currently%20or,parties%20through%20calls%20or%20messages).
Panepinto, A (2022) *Truth and Transitional Justice: Localising the International Legal Framework in Muslim Majority Legal Systems* (Oxford, Hart Publishing).
Pateman, C (1988) *The Sexual Contract* (Stanford University Press, Stanford).
Patierno, N (2015) 'Palestinian Liberation Theology: Creative Resistance to Occupation' 26 *Islam and Christian-Muslim Relations* 443.
Perugini, N and Gordon, N (2015) *The Human Right to Dominate* (Oxford, Oxford University Press).

Petras, J and Veltmeyer, H (2001) *Globalisation Unmasked: Imperialism in the 21st Century* (London, Zed Books).

Pinto, G (2014) '"A Cultural Occupation?" UNRWA's Human Rights, Conflict Resolution and Tolerance Programme: Perspectives from Balata Camp' 14 *Educate* 57.

Pitner, J (2000) 'NGOs' dilemmas' 30 *Middle East Report*, 34 www.merip.org/2000/03/ngos-dilemmas/.

Polinsky, S (2022) 'Dogs in the Islamic Tradition: A Revisionist Examination' 1 *Society and Animals* 1.

Pollis, A and Schwab, P (1979) 'Human Rights: A Western Construct with Limited Applicability' in A Pollis and P Schwab (eds), *Human Rights: Cultural and Ideological Perspectives* (Michigan, Praeger) 1–18.

Powell, KA (2011) 'Framing Islam: An Analysis of U.S. Media Coverage of Terrorism Since 9/11' 62 *Communication Studies* 90.

Qazzaz, H, Zamel, M, Al Bishawi, S, Al Moughrabi, A, and Abu Al Homos, A (2010) *Civics Education*, 3rd edn [Al Tarbiya Al Madaniya] 9th Grade (Ramallah, Al-Ayyam).

Qutteneh, S, Yousef, D, Toma, R, Rabah, S, Dweikat, A, Odeh, H, Al-Rashayda, R and Hammoudeh, G (2013) 'Eight Palestinian Youth Speak to President Obama' 18 *Palestine-Israel Journal of Politics, Economics & Culture* 78.

Rajagopal, B (2003) *International Law from Below: Development, Social Movements, And Third World Resistance* (Cambridge, Cambridge University Press).

Randall, V (2004) 'Using and Abusing the Concept of The Third World: Geopolitics and the Comparative Political Study of Development and Underdevelopment' 25 *Third World Quarterly* 41.

Rehman, J (2011) 'Religion, Human Rights Law and The Rights of the Child: Complexities in Applying the Sharia in Modern State Practices' 62 *Northern Ireland Legal Quarterly* 153.

—— (2010) *International Human Rights Law*, 2nd edn (Harlow, Longman).

Rishmawi, M (2005) 'The Revised Arab Charter on Human Rights: A Step Forward?' 5 *Human Rights Law Review* 361.

Roald, AS (2013) '"Benevolent Patriarchy": Palestinian Women between "Ideal" and "Reality"' 24 *Islam and Christian–Muslim Relations* 333.

Roberts, CN (2014) *The Contentious History of the International Bill of Human Rights* (New York, Cambridge University Press).

Rohde, A (2012) 'Bridging Conflicts Through History Education? A Case from Israel/Palestine' in A Rohde and S Dhouib (eds), *The Politics of Education Reform in the Middle East: Self and Other in Textbooks and Curricula* (New York, Bergham Books) 237–60.

Roth, K (2009) 'Article 26: A Principled Statement on Education' 8 *Journal of Human Rights* 139.

Roy, S (2012) 'Reconceptualizing the Israeli–Palestinian Conflict: Key Paradigm Shifts' 41 *Journal of Palestine Studies* 71.

Rubenberg, C (2002) *Palestinian Women: Patriarchy and Resistance in the West Bank* (Boulder and London, Lynne Rienner Publishers).

Rubiés, J-P (2005) 'Oriental Despotism and European Orientalism: Botero to Montesquieu' 9 *Journal of Early Modern History* 109.

Russell, SG, Sirota, S and Ahmed, AK (2019) 'Human rights education in South Africa: Ideological shifts and curricular reforms' 63 *Comparative Education Review* 1.

Sachedina, A (2009) *Islam and the Challenge of Human Rights* (Oxford, Oxford University Press).

—— (2007) 'The Clash of Universalisms: Religious and Secular in Human Rights' 9 *Hedgehog Review* 49.

—— (1993) 'Review of Abdullahi Ahmed An-Naʿim Review of Toward an Islamic Reformation: Civil Liberties, Human Rights, and International Law' 25 *International Journal of Middle East Studies* 155.

Saeed, A (2018) *Human Rights and Islam: An Introduction to Key Debates Between Islamic Law and International Human Rights Law* (Cheltenham, Edward Elgar Publishing).

Safi, LM (2001) 'Towards an Islamic tradition of human rights' 18 *American Journal of Islam and Society* 16.

Said, E (1985) 'Orientalism Reconsidered' 1 *Cultural Critique* 89.

—— (1984) 'Permission to Narrate' 13 *Journal of Palestine Studies* 27.

—— (1978) *Orientalism: Western Conceptions of the Orient*, reprint (London, Penguin Books).

Salameh, BW (2010) 'The Mirror of a City's Culture is its Residents: A Comparative Study of Heron and Bethlehem' 12 *Idafat Journal* [Arab Journal of Sociology] 95.

Save the Children (2024) 'Gaza: 10,000 Children Killed in Nearly 100 Days Of War' (11 January) www.savethechildren.net/news/gaza-10000-children-killed-nearly-100-days-war#:~:text=Jason%20Lee%2C%20Save%20the%20Children's,blight%20on%20our%20common%20humanity.

Schacht, J (1967) *The Origins of Muhammadan Jurisprudence* (Oxford, Clarendon Press).

Schiocchet, L (2013) 'Palestinian Sumud: Steadfastness, Ritual and Time Among Palestinian Refugees' in A Khalil (ed), *Palestinian Refugees: Different Generations, But One Identity* (Ibrahim Abu-Lughod Institute of International Studies) 67–90.

Schulz, HL (1999) *The Reconstruction of Palestinian Nationalism: Between Revolution and Statehood* (Manchester, Manchester University Press).

Shaheed, F and Shaheed, AL (2011) *Great Ancestors: Women Claiming Rights in Muslim Contexts* (Karachi, Oxford University Press).

Shalhoub-Kevorkian, N (2019) *Incarcerated Childhood and the Politics of Unchilding* (Cambridge, Cambridge University Press).

—— (2015a) 'Childhood: A Universalist Perspective for How Israel is Using Child Arrest and Detention to Further Its Colonial Settler Project' 12 *International Journal of Applied Psychoanalytic Studies* 223.

—— (2015b) 'Necropolitical Debris: The Dichotomy of Life and Death' 4 *State Crime Journal* 34.

—— (2014) 'Human Suffering in Colonial Contexts: Reflections from Palestine' 4 *Settler Colonial Studies* 277.

Sharabi, H (1992) *Neopatriarchy: A Theory of Distorted Change in Arab Society* (Oxford, Oxford University Press).

Sharma, A and Gupta, A (2006) *The Anthropology of the State: A Reader* (Oxford, Blackwell).

Shlaim, A (2005) 'The Balfour Declaration and its Consequences' in WR Louis, (ed), *Yet More Adventures with Britannia: Personalities, Politics and Culture in Britain* (London, IB Tauris), 251–70.

Shor, E (2019) 'Counterterrorist Legislation Effects on Human Rights and Civil Liberties: A Global Perspective' in E Short and S Hoadley (eds), *International Human Rights and Counter-Terrorism* (Singapore, Springer Nature) 203–18.

Shwaikh, M (2022) 'Engendering Hunger Strikes: Palestinian Women in Israeli Prisons' 49 (2022) *British Journal of Middle Eastern Studies* 507.

—— (@MalakaShwaikh) (2023) 'Palestinian Youths from Gaza Just Publish This Statement' (22 October) www.twitter.com/MalakaShwaikh/status/1716164427307758003.

Sidani, Y (2005) 'Women, Work, and Islam in Arab Societies' 20 *Women Management Review* 498.

Sinclair, R (2004) 'Participation in Practice: Making it Meaningful, Effective and Sustainable' 18 *Children & Society* 106.

Singer, J (2021) 'West Bank Areas A, B and C–How Did They Come into Being?' 26 *International Negotiation* 391.

Sirota, S (2017) 'The inconsistent Past and Uncertain Future of Human Rights Education In the United States' 47 *Prospects* 101.

Sliwinski, S (2005) 'Thinking Without Banisters: Toward a Compassionate Inquiry into Human Rights Education' 55 *Educational Theory* 219.

Spierings, N (2014) 'Islamic Attitudes and the Support for Gender Equality and Democracy in Seven Arab Countries, and the Role of Anti-Western Feelings' 3 *Multidisciplinary Journal of Gender Studies* 423.

Spivak, C (1988) 'Can the Subaltern Speak?' in R Morris (ed), Can the Subaltern Speak?: Reflections on the History of an Idea (New York, Columbia University Press) 21–78.

Spyrou, S (2011) 'The Limits of Children's Voices: From Authenticity to Critical, Reflexive Representation' 18 *Childhood* 151.

Stammers, N (2009) *Human Rights and Social Movements* (London, Pluto).

Stenner, P (2011) 'Subjective Dimensions of Human Rights: What Do Ordinary People Understand By "Human Rights?"' 15 *The International Journal of Human Rights* 1215.

Suarez, D and Ramirez, F (2004) *Human Rights and Citizenship: The Emergence of Human Rights Education* (Stanford, CA, Center on Democracy, Development and the Rule of Law).

Suárez, DF (2007) 'Human Rights and Curricular Policy in Latin America and the Caribbean. Comparative' 51 *Education Review* 329.

Subedi, B (2013) 'Decolonising the Curriculum from Global Perspectives' 63 *Educational Theory* 621.

Subedi, B and Daza, SL (2008) 'The Possibilities of Postcolonial Praxis in Education' *Race Ethnicity and Education* 1.

Subramanian, A (2009) *Shorelines: Space and Rights in South India* (Stanford, CA, Stanford University Press).

Taha, MM, (1987) *The Second Message of Islam* (Syracuse NY, Syracuse University Press).

Tarrow, N (1992) 'Human Rights Education: Alternative Conceptions' in J Lynch, C Modgil and S Modgil (eds), *Human Rights, Education and Global Responsibilities* (London, Falmer Press) 21–50.

Tatir, A (2023) 'Palestine: How Western Aid Enables Israel's Colonialism' *Middle East Eye* (21 July) www.middleeasteye.net/opinion/palestine-israel-western-aid-colonialism-enabled-how#:~:text=That%20aid%20was%20key%20to,in%20peace%20next%20to%20Israel.

Tawil-Souri, H (2012) 'Uneven Borders, Coloured (Im)Mobilities: ID Cards in Palestine/Israel' 17 *Geopolitics* 153.

The New Arab (2019) 'Palestinian Authority Outlaws Child Marriage in Occupied West Bank' (7 November) www.newarab.com/news/palestinian-authority-outlaws-child-marriage-occupied-west-bank.

The New Arab Staff (2023) 'Teenage Girl Patient Killed in Shelling of Gaza's Nasser Hospital as Israel Takes Aim at Health Facilities' *The New Arab* (18 December) www.newarab.com/news/teenage-girl-killed-shelling-gazas-nasser-hospital#:~:text=Israeli%20forces%20shelled%20the%20Nasser,her%20parents%20and%20two%20siblings.

Tibbitts, F (2017a) 'Evolution of Human Rights Education Models' in M Bajaj (ed), *Human Rights Education: Theory, Research, and Praxis* (Philadelphia, University of Pennsylvania Press) 69–95.

—— (2017b) 'Revisiting "Emerging Models of Human Rights Education"' 1 *International Journal of Human Rights Education* 1.

—— (2002) 'Understanding What We Do: Emerging Models for Human Rights Education' 48 *International Review of Education* 159.

Tierny, B (2004) 'The Idea of Natural Rights-Origins and Persistence' 2 *Northwestern University Journal of International Human Rights* 2.

Triandis, HC (2001) 'Individualism-Collectivism and Personality' 69 *Journal of Personality* 907.

Tuastad, D (2017) 'The Violent Rise of Palestine's Lost Generation' 26 *Middle East Critique* 159.

Tuck, E and Yang, KW (2012) 'Decolonisation is Not a Metaphor. Decolonisation: Indigeneity' 1 *Education & Society* 1.

Twining, W (2013) 'Human Rights, Southern Voices: Yash Ghai and Upendra Baxi' in J-M Barreto (ed), *Human Rights from a Third World Perspective: Critique, History and International Law* (Newcastle Upon Tyne, Cambridge Scholars Publishing) 256–309.

Twum-Danso Imoh, A (2016) 'From the singular to the plural: Exploring diversities in contemporary childhoods in sub-Saharan Africa' 23 *Childhood* 455.

UN (2023) 'Gaza "Becoming a Graveyard for Children", Warns UN Secretary-General, Calling for Humanitarian Ceasefire- Press Release' SM/SM/22021 (6 November) www.un.org/unispal/document/gaza-becoming-a-graveyard-for-children-warns-un-secretary-general-calling-for-humanitarian-ceasefire-press-release/#:~:text=Gaza%20is%20becoming%20a%20graveyard,in%20at%20least%20three%20decades.

—— (2014) 'UN Confirms Receipt of Palestinian Applications to Join Global Conventions, Treaties' UN News Item (2 April) www.un.org/unispal/document/auto-insert-200148/.

UN Economic and Social Commission for Western Asia (2014) 'Palestine, the Occupation and the Fourth Geneva Convention Facts and Figures' www.unescwa.org/sites/default/files/pubs/pdf/palestine-occupation-fourth-geneva-convention-facts-figures-english.pdf.

UN General Assembly (UNGA) (2011) United Nations Declaration on Human Rights Education and Training (Resolution A/RES/66/137).

—— (1993) Vienna Declaration and Programme of Action (A/CONF.157/23) www.ohchr.org/en/instruments-mechanisms/instruments/vienna-declaration-and-programme-action.

—— (1947) Resolution 181: The Palestine Partition Plan (29 November) A/RES/181.

UNICEF (2024) 'US Vetoes Algerian Resolution Demanding Immediate Ceasefire in Gaza' United Nations News Global Perspective Human Stories (20 February) www.news.un.org/en/story/2024/02/1146697.

—— (2022) 'Palestine Education Fact Sheets 2022: Analyses for Learning and Equity Using MICS Data' State of Palestine (Survey Year 2019–2020) https://data.unicef.org/resources/mics-education-analysis-for-global-learning-and-equity/.

United Nations Office for the Coordination of Humanitarian Affairs for the occupied Palestinian territories (UN OCHA oPt) (2024) 'Hostilities in the Gaza Strip and Israel – reported impact | Day 145' (29 February) www.ochaopt.org/content/hostilities-gaza-strip-and-israel-reported-impact-day-145.

—— (2023) 'West Bank Access Restrictions' (May) www.ochaopt.org/content/west-bank-access-restrictions-may-2023.

—— (2019) 'In the Spotlight: The Humanitarian Situation in the H2 Area of Hebron City Finding of Needs Assessment' (April) www.ochaopt.org/sites/default/files/h2_spotlight_april_2019.pdf.

United Nations Relief Works and Agency (UNRWA) (2022) Pledges to UNRWA's Programmes (Cash and IN-Kind)- Overall Donor RANKING AS 31 Dec 2022 in USD' www.unrwa.org/our-partners/government-partners.

—— (2016) 'Education Reform Final Report 2015' (5 August) www.unrwa.org/resources/reports/education-reform-final-report-2015.

—— (2014) '2014 Gaza Conflict' www.unrwa.org/2014-gaza-conflict.

—— (2013) 'Human Rights, Conflict Resolution, and Tolerance Education Teacher Toolkit' (Amman, Education Department, June) www.unrwa.org/resources/strategy-policy/human-rights-conflict-resolution-and-tolerance-education-teacher-toolkit.

—— (2012) 'UNRWA Policy on Education for Human Rights, Conflict Resolution and Tolerance (HRCRT)' (Amman, Education Department) www.unrwa.org/resources/strategy-policy/unrwa-policy-education-human-rights-conflict-resolution-and-tolerance.

Vašák, K (1977) 'Human Rights: A Thirty-Year Struggle: The Sustained Efforts to give Force of Law to the Universal Declaration of Human Rights' 30 *UNESCO Courier: A Window Open on the World* 29.

Ventura, L (2017) 'The "Arab Spring" and Orientalist Stereotypes: The Role of Orientalism in the Narration of the Revolts in the Arab World' 19 *Interventions* 282.

Verdirame, G (2011) *The UN and Human Rights: Who Guards the Guardians?* (Cambridge, Cambridge University Press).

Vincent, A (2010) *The Politics of Human Rights* (New York, Oxford University Press).

Velloso de Santisteban, A (2002) 'Palestinian Education: A National Curriculum Against the Odds' 22 *International Journal of Educational Development* 145.

Wadud, A (2006) *Inside the Gender Jihad: Women's Reform in Islam* (Oxford, Oneworld Publications).

—— (1999) *Quran and Women: Rereading the Sacred Text from a Woman's Perspective* (New York, Oxford University Press).

Wahl, R (2013) 'Policing, Values and Violence: Human Rights Education with Law Enforcers in India' 5 *Journal of Human Rights Practice* 220.

Waltz, S (2004) 'Universal Human Rights: The Contribution of Muslim States' 26 *Human Rights Quarterly* 799.
Warren, CS (2008) 'Lifting the Veil: Women and Islamic Law' 15 *Cardozo Journal of Law & Gender* 33.
Wellman, C (2000) 'Solidarity, the Individual and Human Rights' 22 *Human Rights Quarterly* 639.
—— (1999) *The Proliferation of Rights: Moral Progress or Empty Rhetoric?* (London, Westview Press).
Wessells, MG (2018) 'Supporting Resilience in War-Affected Children: How Differential Impact Theory Is Useful in Humanitarian Practice' 78 *Child Abuse & Neglect* 13.
Wilson, N (2016) 'West Bank Teachers' Strike Goes on Despite PA Crackdown' *Al Jazeera* (9 March) www.aljazeera.com/news/2016/3/9/west-bank-teachers-strike-goes-on-despite-pa-crackdown.
Woessner, M (2013) 'Provincializing Human Rights? The Heideggerian Legacy from Charles Malik to Dipesh Chakrabarty' in J-M Barreto (ed), *Human Rights from a Third World Perspective: Critique, History and International Law* (Newcastle Upon Tyne, Cambridge Scholars Publishing) 65–101.
Wolfe, P (2006) 'Settler Colonialism and the Elimination of the Native' 8 *Journal of Genocide Research* 387.
Women's Centre for Legal Aid and Counselling (WCLAC) (2018) 'WCLAC Annual Report 2018' www.wclac.org/files/annual_reports/2018/o8w1xrico0azfytkhklpv1.pdf.
Yamani, M (1996) *Feminism and Islam: Legal and Literary Perspectives* (New York, New York Press).
Yang, KW (2015) 'Afterword: Will Human Rights Education Be Decolonising?' in SR Katz and A McEvoy Spero (eds), *Bringing Human Rights Education to US Classrooms: Exemplary Models from Elementary Grades to University* (New York, Palgrave Macmillan) 225–35.
Zakaria, F (2003) *The Future of Freedom: Illiberal Democracy at Home and Abroad* (New York, WW Norton & Co).
Zavala, M (2013) 'What Do We Mean by Decolonizing Research Strategies? Lessons from Decolonizing, Indigenous Research Projects in New Zealand and Latin America' 2 *Decolonization: Indigeneity, Education and Society* 55.
Zeid, M, and Thawaba, S (2018) 'Planning Under a Colonial Regime in Palestine: Counter Planning/Decolonizing the West Bank' 71 *Land Use Policy* 11.
Zembylas, M (2018) 'Towards a Decolonizing Approach in Human Rights Education: Pedagogical Openings and Curricular Possibilities' in M Zembylas and A Keet (eds), *Critical Human Rights, Citizenship, and Democracy Education: Entanglements and Regenerations* (London, Bloomsbury Academic) 35–50.
—— (2017a) 'The Quest for Cognitive Justice: Towards a Pluriversal Human Rights Education' 15 *Globalisation, Societies and Education* 397.
—— (2017b) 'Re-contextualising Human Rights Education: Some Decolonial Strategies and Pedagogical/Curricular Possibilities' 25 *Pedagogy, Culture and Society* 487.
—— (2017c) 'Emotions, Critical Pedagogy, and Human Rights Education' in M Bajaj (ed), *Human Rights Education: Theory, Research, Praxis* (Philadelphia, University of Pennsylvania Press) 47–68.
—— (2015) 'Foucault and Human Rights: Seeking the Renewal of Human Rights Education' 50 *Journal of Philosophy of Education* 384.
—— (2013) 'Critical Pedagogy and Emotion: Working Through Troubled Knowledge in Posttraumatic Societies' 54 *Critical Studies in Education* 176.
Zembylas, M and Keet, A (2018) *Critical Human Rights, Citizenship, and Democracy Education: Entanglements and Regenerations* (London, Bloomsbury Academic).
Žižek, S (1989) *The Sublime Object of Ideology* (London, Verso).
Zreik, R (2004) 'Palestine, Apartheid, and the Rights Discourse' 34 *Journal of Palestine Studies* 68.

Index

www.ingramcontent.com/pod-product-compliance
Ingram Content Group UK Ltd.
Pitfield, Milton Keynes, MK11 3LW, UK
UKHW020259051026
15470UKWH00021B/1542

9 781509 954827